Manisha Agarwal

The Visionary Director

Other Redleaf Press Books by Margie Carter and Deb Curtis

The Art of Awareness: How Observation Can Transform Your Teaching, second edition

Designs for Living and Learning: Transforming Early Childhood Environments

Learning Together with Young Children: A Curriculum Framework for Reflective Teachers

Reflecting Children's Lives: A Handbook for Planning Child-Centered Curriculum, second edition

Spreading the News: Sharing the Stories of Early Childhood Education

Training Teachers: A Harvest of Theory and Practice

The Visionary Director

A Handbook for Dreaming, Organizing, and Improvising in Your Center

Second Edition

MARGIE CARTER — DEB CURTIS

www.redleafpress.org
800-423-8309

Published by Redleaf Press
10 Yorkton Court
St. Paul, MN 55117
www.redleafpress.org

First edition published 1998. Second edition 2010.
Cover design by Erin Kirk New
Interior design by Erin Kirk New
Typeset in Adobe Garamond Pro and Syntax
Interior illustrations by Claire Schipke, except those found on pages ii, v, 32, 51, 61, 110, 121, 218, 247, and 255, which are by Janice Porter
Developmental editing by Beth Wallace
Printed in the United States of America

Library of Congress Cataloging-in-Publication Data
Carter, Margie.
The visionary director : a handbook for dreaming, organizing, and improvising in your center / Margie Carter and Deb Curtis. — 2nd ed.
p. cm.
Previous edition cataloged under Curtis, Debbie.
Includes bibliographical references.
ISBN 978-1-60554-020-7
1. Day care centers—United States—Administration. 2. Early childhood education—United States. I. Curtis, Debbie. II. Title.
HQ778.63.C87 2010
362.71'2068—dc22

2009020826

Printed on 30 percent postconsumer waste paper

U16-02

To Maryann Ready, who offered me my first experience of working in a program with a visionary leader who put the ideas throughout this book into practice.

—DC

To Denise Benitez, who has taught me to find my breath and let it guide me through challenges; Denise has served as an extraordinary role model for teaching.

—MC

To Paula Jorde Bloom, who has worked with tireless imagination and diligence to offer directors foundations and structures to build and support their visions.

—MC and DC

We cannot neglect our interior fire without damaging ourselves in the process. A certain vitality smolders inside us irrespective of whether it has an outlet or not. *When it remains unlit, the body fills with dense smoke.* I think we all live with the hope that we can put off our creative imperatives until a later time and not be any the worse for it. But refusing to give room to the fire, our bodies fill with an acrid smoke, as if we had covered the flame and starved it of oxygen. The interior of the body becomes numbed and choked with particulate matter. The toxic components of the smoke are resentment, blame, complaint, self-justification, and martyrdom.

The longer we neglect the fire, the more we are overcome by the smoke.

—**David Whyte,** *The Heart Aroused*

I say—

Where is your fire?

You got to find it and pass it on
You got to find it and pass it on
from you to me from me to her from her
to him from the son to the father from the
brother to the sister from the daughter to
the mother from the mother to the child.

Where is your fire? I say where is your fire?

—**Sonia Sanchez,** "Catch the Fire"

The Visionary Director

Chapter 2

A Framework for Your Work 45

Chapter 3

Your Role in Building and Supporting Community 71

Chapter 5

Your Role of Managing and Overseeing 171

Foreword to the Second Edition

In the world of publishing, booksellers often use the term "shelf life" to capture the window of opportunity for marketing a new book. Shelf life is both an indicator of the timeliness of the content of a book and a realistic projection for book distributors to gauge sales. Most books have a pretty short shelf life, one to two years. A few, like the Holy Bible or Qur'an, have a timeless message that ensures an audience forever. A few others, like Oprah's Book Club selections, ride a wave of healthy sales and multiple reprints over several years.

In the early childhood education arena, there are a handful of classics that embrace a timely message and merit regular updates and reprints. I believe *The Visionary Director* has earned a rightful place in that esteemed category of professional essentials. For this reason, I was pleased to learn that Margie and Deb had decided to write a new edition of their book to ensure it would remain available for directors across the country.

In my work supporting early childhood administrators at the McCormick Tribune Center for Early Childhood Leadership, I have seen firsthand the power of *The Visionary Director* in the hands of directors. One of the initiatives we sponsor at the center is a year-long leadership training program called Taking Charge of Change. The goal of the program is to help directors see themselves as change agents and empower them to create care and education environments that are active learning communities both for children and adults. *The Visionary Director* has been a required book in Taking Charge of Change since it was first published a decade ago. More than any other professional resource available for directors, I have felt this book has the transformational power to help our participant directors visualize what excellence means in the context of their programs and turn their dreams into concrete strategies for program improvement.

Being a center director has never been easy, but it seems the increasing demands of the accountability movement—quality rating systems, accreditation, performance standards, credentialing—have created even greater pressure on program administrators. I believe the lopsided focus on school readiness and outcomes has had the unintended consequence of stifling directors' creativity and innovativeness, dulling their dreams and aspirations. Don't get me wrong, I'm all for standards and accountability. In fact my colleague Teri Talan and I wrote the Program Administration Scale (PAS) as a guide for measuring early childhood leadership and management practices. But even the PAS will fall short as a blueprint for improving program quality if directors can't elevate their leadership mandate beyond just complying with standards. More than ever before, the central message of *The Visionary Director* is needed to help directors avoid feeling overwhelmed by traditional bureaucratic approaches to quality improvement and the new tensions around standards and outcomes.

Visionary directors give voice and unleash the passions of their teachers. They understand that the heart of their enterprise is nurturing collaborative partnerships with families. And most of all, they recognize their enormous potential as advocates for social change. These are the qualities we need in every early childhood director. *The Visionary Director* is an inspiring resource to help directors embrace this higher calling.

Paula Jorde Bloom, PhD
Michael W. Louis Endowed Chair
McCormick Tribune Center for Early Childhood Leadership
National-Louis University

Foreword to the First Edition

Even after a short time in our field, it would be relatively easy for most people to list what's wrong with child care programs in the United States—poor salaries and benefits, too few materials, damaged equipment, unmanageable adult-child ratios, extraordinarily high staff turnover, a dwindling pool of reliable substitute teachers, gaps in language and culture between programs and the children and families they serve, and not enough training that meets our day-to-day and on-the-job needs. Every day, we witness the direct results of drastic neglect and underfunding of our child care system. We're pretty good at agreeing on the problems.

Over the last two years we have been working at the Center for the Child Care Workforce to conduct a series of trainings with center directors and teaching staff called "Taking on Turnover." Participants are quite forthcoming when we ask them to describe their problems at work. It's when they're asked to conjure up a vision of a good child care workplace—and to set priorities to bring the vision to life—that the trouble often begins. Perhaps tensions arise among directors, teachers, and aides about where the solutions lie or what should be addressed first. The process of creating change in any kind of organization can be painful and slow. But I suspect that most of all we have trouble because as a field we are so used to settling for what we can get, and "coping creatively" with too few resources, that we don't ask the fundamental questions about how child care ought to be. We don't raise enough challenges. We forget to dream.

Imagine the child care of our dreams, not just child care that's good enough. Imagine if people working with young children received adequate professional preparation, opportunities for ongoing professional growth, and earnings equal to their investment in their careers. Margie Carter and Deb Curtis invite us to imagine and dream, and they assist us in the process. They help us see how settling for the current situation dulls our enthusiasm and ultimately diminishes our efforts. Ultimately, they invite us to create an environment in our programs where the adults, not just the children, continue to learn, grow, and use their imaginations to guide their work, family, and community life. And they offer an array of strategies toward that end.

Why does using our imaginations matter so much? On the most basic level, this is a critical task. Our current work environments, more often than not, fail to attract and retain highly skilled teaching staff. The most recent follow-up to the National Child Care Staffing Study found that only one-third of the teaching staff in a sample of centers rated higher than average in quality had remained in their jobs for at least five years. Such high turnover signals inconsistent care for children and demoralization for staff and parents.

It is a steady combination of using our imaginations, enhancing our skills, and mobilizing our collective will and political clout that will move us beyond the basics to create child care programs that really nourish and strengthen children, families, and staff. If we are to address the real issues in our programs and the early childhood field and, as Deb and Margie suggest, have our work influence the larger social change required, it is essential for us to reach a common understanding of goals. Otherwise, we will pull ourselves in opposite directions, leaving no one with a sense of accomplishment or satisfaction. We can start on a practical level. For example, if we can agree on how much paid planning and preparation time the caregiving and teaching staff really need, we can take steps—even if they are small at first—toward implementing a policy that's closer to our goals. But first and foremost, we have to have a vision. Without one, it is mighty hard to reach a destination and easy to get where we never intended to go.

I came to child care in the early 1970s, a time when envisioning alternatives was the name of the game. For myself and many of my peers, child care held the promise of the future. As I phrased it then, child care was the key to women's liberation and the path to a more just world. A good child care system, we reasoned, would enable women to help support their families and feel secure in knowing their children were well nurtured. Children would be helped to reach their full potential. Our society would recognize child care and other forms of traditional "women's work" as highly skilled professions. It was probably a good thing that I didn't know how formidable the barriers would be to realizing this vision, or I might have never begun! Although I have been exceedingly frustrated over the years at the slowness of progress in improving our child care services and jobs, I still find nourishment and direction in that early vision of child care as a service that supports parents, nourishes children, and rewards practitioners for the complexity of their work. Indeed, it is this shared vision that has helped me and others get through the hard times, put disagreements in perspective, and, most important, keep reflecting on how best to do our work.

In the 1990s developing the Worthy Wage Campaign has served as another vision to guide our efforts to create quality, affordable programs for families and fair and decent employment for child care teachers and providers. The goals and growth of this campaign parallel the picture Margie and Deb paint on these pages—all that can happen when people germinate a vision together and roll up their sleeves to make it happen. The underlying idea of the Worthy Wage Campaign is to engage everyone involved or affected by child care in understanding that a skilled and stable workforce is the cornerstone of a good child care system. But stabilizing and adequately compensating the workforce only addresses the basics of what we really long for. Our dreams reach far beyond. The Worthy Wage Campaign aims to build a critical mass of people who begin to see issues about affordability and compensation in child care as political, not just personal issues. As people become engaged in seeking solutions, they will see the connections that ultimately suggest a vision and demand for larger social change. The vision of the Worthy Wage Campaign has not only sustained many of us "old-timers" but generated a new generation of advocates and activists willing to take on the challenge of improving child care jobs and services so that we can move a step closer to our dreams. For those of us working on child care issues over the last quarter century or more, the most heartening development is this group of new folks committed to refining and carrying forward the vision.

In this book, Margie Carter and Deb Curtis help take the "envisioning" process out of the realm of tasks that sound too overwhelming and impossible to begin, let alone complete, and in their inimitable way, they make it not only manageable but creative, inspiring, and playful. They are guided by a vision of child care that acknowledges the importance of both child and adult development, recognizing that adults, too, must be acknowledged as individuals, respected for their points of view, and challenged gently to see things in new ways. Their vision affirms the right and responsibility that we have as adults to make the world a better place, and they remind us that this vision underlies why many of us chose to work in child care in the first place. *The Visionary Director* offers us an essential tool for affirming and renewing our commitment to child care and to meeting the challenge of nurturing our society's future.

Marcy Whitebook
Codirector, Center for the Child Care Workforce
May 1998

Acknowledgments

To the directors, caregivers, and teachers who have lent their stories to this book we extend sincere appreciation. They represent programs large and small; diverse and homogeneous; serving middle-class, upper-class, and poor families; private, parent cooperative, or sponsored by Head Start, government, corporations, school districts, or colleges; and located across the United States and Canada and on U.S. military bases in Europe.

Special thanks to Laila Aaen, Amy Baker, Pauline Baker, Sabina Ball, Ruth Beagleholz, Diana Bender, Sarah Bishop, Julie Bisson, Ron Blatz, Cathy Burckett-St. Laurent, Caren Burgess, Wendy Cividanes, Marcela Clark, Jim Clay, Christie Colunga, Dana Connoly, Anne Marie Coughlin, Ellen Dietrick, Lisa Dittrich, Linda Duerr, Kathleen Gonzales, Leanne Grace, Mary Graham, Charlene Grainger, Bill Grant, Karen Haigh, Pamela Harris, Leslie Howle, Joy Humbarger, Susan Dumars Huvar, Kathryn Ingrum, Barb Janson, Jennifer Kagiwada, Linda Kern, Michael Koetje, Becky Krise, Carmen Masso, Laura McAlister, Meg McNulty, Paula McPheeters, Paul Moosman, Leslie Orlowski, Paige Parker, Ann Pelo, Jan Reed, Alice Rose, Caron Salazar, Teresa Senna, Margo Shayne, Linda Skibinski, Alicia Smith, Dorothy Stewart, Teri Talan, Alicia Tuesta, Mayela Visconti, Marlys Vollegraaf, Julie Weatherston, Wendy Whitesell, Carol Anne Wien, Ellen Wolpert, Angela Woodburn, Adina Young, and Billie Young. While many of us have removed ourselves from the day-to-day work of leading programs, these folks remain on the front lines pursuing their vision with great tenacity. We see them as inventors, craftspeople, cultural workers, and artists.

Thanks to Jeanne Hunt and Lonnie Bloom, who put up with us once again as we abandoned them for another big writing project, and to Beth Wallace, who served as a fine editor in our revisions work. For this second edition, we appreciated the behind-the-scenes work of the people of Redleaf Press, especially Carla Valadez, Laurie Herrmann,

Kyra Ostendorf, Andrea Hanson, and David Heath. We continue to extend gratitude to Bonnie and Roger Neugebauer of *Child Care Information Exchange* for publishing the articles that were later incorporated into this book. They have spent the last thirty-some years bringing ideas and directors' voices together and have expanded their efforts to create a global community of early childhood educators.

We want to again thank Marcy Whitebook and Rosmarie Vardell for their exceptional leadership and contributions to the Worthy Wage Movement and the first edition of this book. Though the Worthy Wage Movement has sadly faded away, the work to address equitable compensation remains an ongoing call to action, as does crossing racial and cultural barriers to support the expansion of the leadership and advocacy base for our profession. We extend our deep appreciation to those who take up this work in earnest, especially our new partners at Harvest Resources Associates, Wendy Cividanes and Debbie Lebo. Please stay in touch with us by visiting www.ecetrainers.com, where you will find ongoing discussions and examples of what we are up to.

Introduction

Most directors of early childhood programs find themselves working in a climate of ever-increasing regulations and standards, brought to life by mounds of required paperwork. Many come to their positions with little administrative experience to prepare them for the awesome task of trying to run a quality program with less than adequate resources. They may have a handful of promising seeds, but before long they are stretched too thin, frantically patching the holes that continue to appear in their watering can. We wrote a new edition of this book because we believe early childhood program directors more than ever need to systematically develop their leadership and organizational systems in relationship to a clear vision and set of values. Otherwise they will easily lose their moorings and their hearts for this challenging work. If directors are to be successful and satisfied with their work, they need not only skills and expertise but a way to get a handle on their jobs and a replenishing source of nourishment for themselves. Their professional development must not only include the skills of administration, business and finance, supervision, and human relations, but also the arts of dreaming, designing, organizing, and improvising.

Since the publication of the first edition of this book in 1998, the early childhood field has seen a number of exciting efforts aimed at enhancing the skills and leadership potential of program directors. We welcome these efforts and list but a few examples in the last chapter of this book. These examples address what we have intuitively understood and what research now confirms: the director's leadership is the primary nutrient for growing a quality program. We hope that this book will contribute to the ability of directors to summon the resources and skills to be visionary leaders for their programs—to "find the fire and pass it on."

How Can Directors Become Leaders?

It's easy for directors to feel helpless and victimized under conditions that include an ever-growing body of standards, required measurable outcomes, and a faltering economy. There are so many factors that seem out of control. While this feeling of helplessness is understandable, we also know that directors seldom claim the leadership potential their position offers them. Instead, they let the limitations and pressures of the current conditions constrict their imaginations and creativity. Under the "be realistic" or "meet the standards" banner, directors tend to stay focused on how things are, rather than on a vision of how things could be. They hope that somehow more checklists and accountability systems will "fix" the problems of trying to provide quality in a service that is underfunded, undervalued, and operating with an inadequate workforce. All too often, however, this added paperwork simply increases the barriers to quality instead of helping directors surmount them. It is unusual for early childhood program directors to imagine a different course or use their leadership to pursue a different vision. Our hope is that *The Visionary Director* will spur you into developing the leadership to pursue a new vision of early childhood.

Whatever the external factors, you have the power to shape the environment around you. If you do this thoughtfully in your role as a director, you'll find that your early childhood program can transform the sense of powerlessness and isolation that prevails in the lives of caregivers, teachers, children, and families. Your leadership toward that end has the further potential to influence larger social change, as Valora Washington quotes in one of her own articles:

> Transformation of the social order often begins with an act of imagination that elevates a startling dream of change above the intimidating presence of things as they are. Further, if such dreams are passionate and clear, and if they can call a great many people into their service, they may ultimately give shape to the future. (W.K. Kellogg Foundation 1996, 3)

This is the message you will find in the pages of *The Visionary Director*, along with numerous strategies to move your program in that direction. While we have been discouraged to hear many directors describe their vision for their programs in narrow terms, such as improving their playground or getting accredited, we have also been heartened to meet others who have bigger dreams for the role their programs can play in reshaping the communities where they reside. Some have made significant changes in transforming the organizational culture, physical environment, activities, and interactions that shape quality in an early childhood program. Others have taken steps toward creating a community of dreamers who are on the road to making changes.

Imagination and Activism Are Key

If you see yourself as the developer of an organizational culture, your leadership will extend beyond managing an early childhood program. As you create a culture of safety and respect, alive with a sense of possibilities, your program will attract staff and families longing to be involved in this kind of community. And if your policies and actions go beyond lip service to diversity, you create the potential for using that diversity to transform the fear, alienation, and despair that are so pervasive in our wider community.

Cultivating imagination is as critical to a director's success as acquiring skills. So much in our world conspires to take away our dreams. With all the tasks you as a director need to accomplish, it's easy to get consumed by the daily details, neglecting your heart and mind. New energy comes when you step outside your "to-do" lists, make time for activities that call forth your creativity, and do things that intellectually stimulate and nurture you. It's equally important to

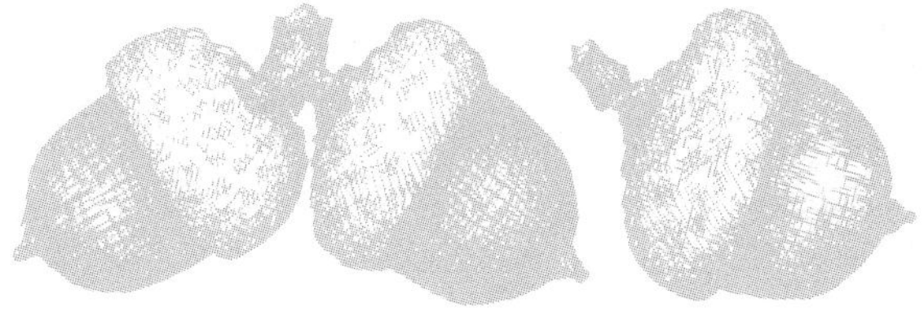

involve yourself with people and efforts working on behalf of social change, inside and outside the early childhood profession. Some of the most promising efforts in the profession have come when directors begin linking up with others for support and action.

The Director on Fire

It's not uncommon to hear the words *program director* and *burnout* in the same breath. Our goal in writing this book is to help you avoid burnout by setting your heart on fire. We've come with kindling that has proven reliable. You can fan the flames with the beating of your own heart. On these pages you will find the spark of a guiding vision for directors of early childhood programs. We have seen what a difference it makes when directors give attention to shaping an organizational culture of collaboration and excitement. Rather than just running a program, this kind of director is creating a learning community and spurring others into activism on behalf of social change in the world. You will hear the voices of directors like this throughout these pages.

Over the past ten years we have encountered an expanding number of directors who have worked with a fierce fire in their hearts and sparked big dreams among the teachers, children, and families with whom they work. Those who have created lasting results have started by forming a strong organizational system to underpin their dreams. We've seen those who haven't taken this step lose heart, lose their valued staff, and ultimately lose even their own health and well-being trying to single-handedly keep their program on course with their vision. With this as a backdrop, our revisions in this edition of *The Visionary Director* include a stronger emphasis on creating organizational structures and systems to support your vision.

The prevailing approach to quality enhancement suggests that requiring more standards, documentation, and training will improve outcomes for children. Apart from the salary issue, what about the foundational elements of a structure that provides more time and space for teachers to plan, organize, think, meet, and talk about the complex tasks of caring for and educating groups of young children? Our experience suggests that organizational budgets and infrastructures contain the elements that indicate program quality. In this edition we offer ideas for organizational structures to orient new teachers to the program philosophy, pedagogy, routines, and culture.

This can't be a one-shot run-through of regulations with the director, but a process over time with the director or a designated mentor helping new teachers fully integrate and learn how to think through the daily complexities of caring for and educating young children in group care. In today's climate, an organizational system must be in place to mentor teachers to see how standards and outcomes that reflect the director's vision of an expanded definition of quality can be met in the course of daily routines and planning. Directors must work with their budgets to create an organizational structure that provides teachers time to meet together in teams to discuss what is unfolding, build meaningful relationships with the children's families, and pursue professional development goals for themselves.

We once heard Carol Brunson Day speak of strengthening the power of children to develop through their culture. This not only influenced our thinking about the role of ethnic culture in shaping development, but also inspired us to imagine the kind of early childhood program culture that would support the power of the staff and families to develop. There are no quick fixes with this approach. It is steady, patient, improvisational work. You have to invent it as you go, shaping your program around the events and lives that come through your door each day. *The Visionary Director* offers a framework for thinking about and organizing your work. In these pages we suggest principles and strategies to cultivate the kind of thinking and activities that support a vision of early childhood programs as learning

communities. We believe the dreams and inventions you draw from these ideas will surpass any specific formulas or directions we could offer.

Using This Book

The chapters of this book focus on a conceptual framework and self-directed activities to help you develop your own understanding and possibilities for working with the framework. Chapter 1 offers our vision of early childhood programs as the new neighborhoods of the twenty-first century, poised to transform the cultural ills of our society with genuine, mutually respectful, empowering relationships. Included are lessons from African proverbs, organizational development theory, and our own childhood memories of life in a neighborhood or community. In chapter 2 we propose thinking of a director's work as a triangle, carefully balanced on all sides. Here you get a taste of "systems thinking" as it pertains to developing the culture of early childhood programs.

Chapters 3, 4, and 5 offer more details about working from each side of our triangle framework, with principles and strategies to consider. For this edition we have added a new chapter 6, with four composite stories of directors working to bring a particular vision to life in their programs. Here you will find detailed examples of how to translate your values into innovative practices for your center.

At the end of this book there is an afterword with snapshots of promising initiatives around the country, appendixes that offer sample forms for some of the strategies we describe, and lists of references and recommended resources.

What you will not find on these pages is help with budgeting, fund-raising, or financial management. We know there are other valuable resources to assist you in these areas, and we have included some of these in the Resources section.

The Visionary Director focuses on the strategies to light your fire and the vision to help you clear the smoke. For the ideas in this book to become part of your approach to directing, you will need practice making them yours. Each chapter of this book concludes with a practice activity for further reflection on the ideas just discussed. It might be tempting to skip over this section, but we advise you to reconsider. We encourage you to use this book for more than inspiration or reference. Make it a workbook that you return to on a regular basis. For over a decade, administrators have sent us stories of how studying this book as part of a directors' support group or class has helped them apply the principles and strategies to their work. You could be one of those people. May we all stay strong and live with joy, intention, and gratitude.

Chapter 1

Guiding Your Program with a Vision

Before you begin reading our ideas about being a program director or supervisor, take a minute to consider yours. Which of the answers below best match your thinking regarding the purpose of an early childhood program? Check the box that represents your highest priority.

- ☐ To provide a service for parents while they work
- ☐ To give kids a head start to be ready for school and academic success
- ☐ To enhance children's self-concept and social skills as they learn to get along in the world
- ☐ To ensure that children have a childhood full of play, adventure, and investigation
- ☐ To create a community where the adults and children experience a sense of connection and new possibilities for making the world a better place
- ☐ ____
  (add your own words here)
  ____

We start this book where we hope you will start—describing what you see as the primary purpose of your work. There is no right or wrong answer in the choices above. Your view of your work may encompass some version of each of these ideas. Most likely you go through your days with a general sense of purpose. We recommend taking the time to be specific about your purpose and vision because your image of an early childhood program shapes the way you guide your program, consciously or unconsciously. Your vision plays the same role in your program as your breath plays in your body—distributing the life force of oxygen throughout your system, exploring where things are tense and need some attention, and providing a rhythm for your muscles to do their collaborative work.

How often do you pay attention to your breath? Right now, for instance, have you noticed how you are breathing? As you read these words, does your breath feel rushed, tight, or even hard to detect? Are you aware of where your breath is in your body? Take a minute to check this out. Likewise, consider how frequently you do your job as a director with a vision flowing through your mind. Developing a regular awareness of your breath in your body cultivates mindfulness for all parts of your life. Similarly, when you move through your days with a vision of how things could be, you'll approach directing tasks and decisions in a thoughtful manner.

You may have come to this book searching for answers, for solutions to the stresses and strains of directing an early childhood program. We suggest you start your search by finding your breath, not only because this is literally a good thing to do, but also because this action symbolically represents the essence of what this book has to offer. With all the pressures surrounding a director's job, no doubt you barely have time to catch your breath, let alone read a book. This means you probably spend most of your time reacting to how things are, rather than developing new ways of being. Consider the smoker who relies on cough drops to soothe a scratchy throat and neglects to find support for changing habits and healthier living. This is akin to directors who rely on management tips to survive instead of taking stock, reorienting their approach, and claiming their power to create something different.

Searching Your Heart for What's Important

When it comes down to it, looking for quick answers and formulas to run a child care program is like turning to diet pills and beauty products to improve your health. It's just not that simple. To be sure, it's important to acquire skills and learn the how-tos of developing a well-functioning management system, and a growing number of resources can help you with this. *The Visionary Director* suggests something books on supervision rarely discuss:

- finding the heart of what brought you to the early childhood field
- remembering the vision you've had for how it could be
- drawing on this vision as you move through your days
- creating an organizational culture and systems to support your dreams

As you take time to find your breath, literally and metaphorically, you will begin to discover deeper longings that live in your body, such as

- a desire for meaningful work that makes a difference in the world
- time for joy and laughter
- a place where you have genuine connections with others
- a community where you feel safe, have history, and enjoy a sense of belonging

When you embrace rather than ignore this longing, it can shape a vision that guides your work as fundamentally as your breathing guides your body.

Around the country, directors are attending conferences, seminars, and classes in search of ways to improve their work. We've discovered that although at the surface this appears to be a search for some quick ideas, a much deeper need often brings them together. Directors long for a place to unload the heavy burden they carry. The reality of their work is often different from what they imagined it to be. People usually come to the work of directing early childhood programs eager to make a difference in the lives of children and families. Faced with the current conditions, many directors are aware of a lot of "if only" feelings lingering below each breath—if only we had more money to pay the teachers, if only we could improve the facility, if only there weren't so many regulations and so much paperwork, if only we could offer more scholarships, if only we could just get parents more involved, if only people understood the importance of this work.

Beyond the need for a steady paycheck, most of us seek jobs in early childhood care and education because it is work with real meaning and real people, and it offers the possibility of making a difference in the world. Yet all too quickly external pressures and the demands of this work make us lose sight of our original motivation. Budgets, regulations, reports, perturbed parents, and shrinking substitute lists soon overwhelm our hearts and minds. There is hardly time to get to the bathroom, let alone to that stack of reading to be done and papers to be filed. Before long, we find ourselves moving from crisis to crisis, too frazzled to remember all those time-management techniques and exhausted down to our bones. The original dreams we brought to our job can easily fade or seem totally out of reach.

This book is meant to rekindle a sense of new possibilities. Rather than help you get better at working with how things are, *The Visionary Director* offers you a framework and beginning strategies for transforming the limitations of your current mind-set and conditions. At the heart of this book is a vision of early childhood programs as active learning communities both for children and adults. It's easy to talk about your problems and the things that bother you in your work, but too often directors neglect to describe how they would like their work to be, the specific elements of their vision. It's a challenge to let your mind spin out new possibilities when you are so used to adapting and accommodating yourself to how things are. Breaking out of these confines can stir up old longings and remind you of how little you've settled for.

Imagining How It Could Be

The vision we have for early childhood programs replaces the institutional feel of items from an early childhood catalog and the lifeless description of standards with materials from the natural world that keep us in touch with the life cycle of living, growing, and dying and with the interdependence of living things. The walls are adorned not with commercially produced displays, but with images from the lives of the people who spend their days there together. There are a variety of interesting textures, colors, and things to discover and investigate. Inviting smells of food and flowers overtake the odors of stuffy rooms, urine, and disinfectants. Natural light and soft-light lamps create comfy places for people to enjoy each other's company. Staff members and children have a place for their things, their meetings, and the tools they need for their work and play, as well as a quiet place for when they need a break away from each other. People build genuine relationships across differences in age, economic class, gender, and culture. They actively listen to and learn from each other, show their passions, feel safe in expressing disagreements, and negotiate problems with remarkable creativity. Mutual admiration and appreciation flow between the staff, children, and families. No one shies away from hard work and challenges, as they have come to understand that these can deepen people's connections with and commitment to one another. Respect from others translates into respect for oneself and a desire to make a contribution in righting the wrongs of the world. The way people learn to listen, talk, play, think, negotiate, value, and care for themselves and each other in these early childhood programs spills out to other lives in the surrounding community. People have a taste of a different way of being and are no longer willing to settle for the inadequacies and injustices of how things are.

Our intention in writing *The Visionary Director* goes beyond trying to make your job easier, though we certainly hope it does that. We believe early childhood programs are in a pivotal position to foster relationships that can heal the rift all people feel between themselves and others and between themselves and the natural world. We can address issues of bias and inequality in our thinking, actions, and structural arrangements. Early childhood programs can give the children and adults involved an experience of empowerment, of democracy in action, so that they have the will and know-how to make this a priority in our country. On the whole, most early childhood programs haven't been developed with this vision. They've been focused on the more limited goals of keeping children out of harm's way or getting them ready for school. There is so much more we could be reaching for, seeing the connection between our work and larger social change. That vision could mobilize enormous energy and turn us into a force to be reckoned with.

> If I hadn't maintained my vision of how this place could evolve, I could not have stayed in this job as long as I have. It's your vision that gets you through the very rough times.
>
> **—Paul**

Fortifying Yourself with a Vision

In visiting directors around the country, we've found that those who actively work with a bold vision create programs that stand out from the grim statistics on mediocrity in child care. Think of your vision like the breath in your body. The more attention you give to it, the more it fortifies you. When programs are led by directors who breathe a larger vision into everyday tasks, people feel more alive in their bodies, and their spirits lift with a new sense of hope. This is one of the greatest antidotes to burnout.

Ante los horrores que veo que ocurren diariamente pido por un milagro. Un milagro para que nunca más se le dé una paliza a un niño, que nunca más los niños sean golpeados ni abusados. Vivimos en una época en la que la violencia es aceptada como algo normal. Debemos cuestionar las golpizas y humillaciones a los niños así como las expresiones violentas de rabia y frustración de la misma manera que cuestionamos el tratamiento sexista y abusivo a las mujeres.

Cuando tuve la oportunidad de abrir un programa de cuidado infantil para madres adolescentes, sabía que la realidad de esas injusticias no se podría evitar en nuestro programa. Sabía que me agotaría muy rápidamente si no tenía una visión clara. Quería crear un lugar donde la gente pudiera participar en la lucha por la no violencia y en terminar con esa conspiración silenciosa que acepta, por ejemplo, darle una golpiza a un niño porque no quiere ponerse los zapatos. La clave para comprometerse a practicar la no violencia se basa en comprender el desarrollo del niño y aprender a tener paciencia.

La visión que tengo cada día cuando vengo al trabajo es ofrecer a las madres un santuario de paz y de liberación del dolor de traen de afuera. Un santuario donde se acepten sin juicios las historias de cada una de las adolescentes. Un lugar de recuperación y cambio. Cuando las adolescentes vienen a nuestro programa, deben aprender que está mal ejercer la violencia hacia otra persona. Todas estas madres han vivido bajo la violencia la mayor parte de sus vidas. Ellas tienen que aprender a hacer las cosas de una manera diferente, aún cuando todavía no sean capaces de hacerlo. Nosotras les decimos, "No las vamos a juzgar y ustedes no van a mentir ni quedarse calladas acerca de lo que les sucede. Pueden enojarse o pueden odiar lo que les pasa, pero siempre sin violencia." Ese es nuestro lema.

Es tan difícil y tenemos tantos contratiempos. A veces me canso y me pregunto a mí misma, "*¿Cuántos años más de todo esto?*" Y, sin embargo, este es el trabajo que me hace sentir que puedo influenciar y ejercer un cambio. Y así lo hacemos. Cada año vemos como estas jóvenes madres se hacen más fuertes. Observamos como comienza a aparecer la esperanza seguida de la compasión. Aprenden a apoyarse las unas a las otras y nosotras vemos cómo cambian su manera de ser. Creo firmemente que luchan por ese cambio porque buscan tener esperanza para sus hijos.

—Ruth

With all the horrors one sees in our popular culture, I have a dream. If I could create one miracle before I die, it would be to stop children from being spanked, hit, or abused. We live in a culture where violence is normalized. We must question the cultural edicts that condone spanking and the humiliation of children, just as we must question the abusive and sexist treatment of women and the expression of frustration or anger in the form of violence.

So when I had the chance to open a child care program for teen mothers, I knew I couldn't divorce the politics of the wider injustices of the world from our program. Without a clear vision to focus on, I knew I would burn out very quickly. I wanted to create a place where people would take on this struggle for nonviolence and step out of this conspiracy of silence around such things as spanking toddlers for not wanting to put on their shoes. The key to making a commitment to nonviolence is through understanding child development and through learning patience.

The vision I form each day I come to work is to provide for teen mothers a sanctuary of peace and freedom from the pain of the streets. A sanctuary of acceptance without judgment, where each teen's story is her own. A place of healing and change. When teens enroll their children in our program, they have to buy into this notion that violence toward someone without power is wrong. All of these mothers have been living with violence most of their lives. They have to want to do it differently, even if they aren't able to yet. We say to them, "We will not judge you, and you will not lie or keep silent about what's going on. You can be mad, you can hate what is happening, but no violence." That's our mantra.

It's so hard, and we have so many setbacks. Sometimes I get so tired, and I ask myself, "How many more years can I do this?" Yet this work is what makes me feel like I can have some influence, create change. And we do. Every year we see these young mothers get stronger. Hope and compassion emerge. They support each other, and we watch them change the tide. I firmly believe that ultimately people will fight for change because they want hope for their children.

—Ruth

Over the years, we've asked directors to describe the vision that is guiding their work. To our surprise, many have a limited response. Some talk of a new playground, more scholarship dollars, or an active substitute teacher list. We see these responses as goals or items on a wish list, possibly indicators of a dream not yet fully articulated. A surprising number of directors point to NAEYC accreditation, Head Start Program Performance Standards, or scores on an Environmental Rating Scale (such as the ITERS, ECERS, or PAS) as their vision. To be sure, we have great respect for these guideposts and have used such things for many years in our own work. But as we begin to look around at the classrooms that only follow these standards, and when we assess the focus of the curriculum and interactions between the staff, children, and families, our hearts sink. Somehow the idea of a vision for a program has been reduced to a set of goals, standards, and regulations—lots of paperwork, checklists, and rating scores. Our concern about vision begs other questions. Where are the heart and vitality in these programs? What gives these programs life? Who spends their days here, and what are their hopes and dreams? How are they learning to be citizens in a democracy?

In the early years of developing programs for young children whose mothers worked all day, the vision was to create a home away from home. Teachers and directors took inspiration from the philosophies of early nursery school and kindergarten educators, as well as child psychologists—people such as Caroline Pratt, John Dewey, Maria Montessori, and Jean Piaget. The supervisor's focus was on providing meaningful play experiences for children, not managing complex programs with multiple demands. Time, history, and economic, political, and educational trends have brought us to a new place.

Over the past thirty years, the early childhood profession has come of age. Early childhood caregivers and teachers have now become a full-fledged workforce with standards, a code of ethics, a shared language, definitions of core competencies and best practices, and a huge selection of conferences and resources. An ever-expanding body of research-based knowledge includes professional development and accreditation systems. The federal No Child Left Behind Act (NCLB) of 2001, along with the emergence of state-funded prekindergarten programs and the 2007 reinvention of the NAEYC Early Childhood Program Standards and Accreditation Criteria, has brought the field to a crossroads. Indeed, Stacie Goffin and Valora Washington (2007) describe the first decade of the twenty-first century as a defining moment for the field's future with a tremendous amount at stake. These leaders have outlined adaptive leadership challenges for the early childhood field that resonate with our belief that the profession urgently needs a clear vision about its purpose, identity, and responsibility. Rather than leave this work to some outside experts, we believe program directors can take responsibility for growing a vision right where they are, joining with others in shaping the profession's future.

Can directors develop a vision that holds strong standards for their work without homogenizing their programs or standardizing childhood and curricula? Carol Anne Wien asks the question this way: "Are teachers able to find meaning in their work, to find relevance to children's lives and love of the world and its ecological diversity, beauty, pattern, and texture? How do teachers sustain themselves through mechanistic, competitive, production-driven processes?" (2004, xv). In early education policies in state governments across the United States and in the direction professional organizations in early care and education are moving, quality improvement seems tied to an ever-expanding set of requirements and expectations placed on teachers. Wien states her position clearly: "The use of prescriptive processes in education is misplaced because humans, who include intention, ethics, and creative joy in their ways of being, cannot be reduced to machines carrying out someone else's prescriptions for teaching" (152–53).

Visit a newly accredited early childhood program in any region of this country and you will likely find any number of thick binders documenting how they meet the criteria defining best practices. On the one hand, we feel proud to be part of a cadre of people determined to see that young children in group settings are educated and cared for with accountability to high standards. But for all their good intentions, we get the impression that most of the folks who are developing these new standards haven't recently been directing a program, let alone been responsible for a classroom of active young children. We want to ask some additional questions. Do directors experience current quality enhancement initiatives as worth the amount of time and focus they require? Are new standards improving working conditions and salaries and supporting responsive pedagogy to engage teachers, children, and families in learning together? Do new resources infringe on or enhance the vision teachers and directors are building?

We welcome the efforts of publishers and companies to provide early childhood educators with better equipment, multicultural materials, curriculum frameworks, and child guidance strategies. On the other hand, when we visit exhibit halls at conferences, we fear our profession has lost sight of the need for a vision to guide our work. Many early childhood educators seem to have fallen prey to strong commercial interests and misguided pressures to prepare kids for school at younger and younger ages. How has this happened, and what does it mean? Recognizing the importance of the early years has become a mandate for instruction in "readiness" activities, overtaking the view that children are born ready and eager to learn and their childhoods are to be respected. The prevailing outlook on children, families, and teachers is that they are deficient and need to be fixed with educational products so they can further serve the nation's larger economic agenda. Desired outcomes then focus on children and adults becoming consumers, not creators, of culture and knowledge.

So, for instance, in large and small programs, for-profit and not-for-profit, from Florida to Alaska, and on U.S. military bases around the world, accredited child care and Head Start programs are all starting to look the same. Most are furnished with items from the same early childhood vendor catalogs and have the same bulletin board displays and curriculum plans posted on the wall. Criteria and standards, originally developed as guidelines for quality-care hallmarks and educational benchmarks, have now become narrowly interpreted rules to enforce. Though they pay lip service to the concept, most programs are missing the heart of a caregiving partnership with families. We see teachers offering parents dutiful communications about whether their children ate, slept, or had a good day. Most of these daily report forms end up stuffed in the bottom of a bag or on the floor of the car because they convey little about what families really want to know about their children's time spent away from home.

Children spend more of their waking hours in these programs than with their families. What families really need are snapshots (descriptions and photographs) of how their children are developing and making friends, what they are doing and thinking, liking and avoiding. A daily form with perfunctory information doesn't make up for what families are missing. Because parents often lack the experience to find significance in their children's play, they add to the pressure teachers feel to provide them with traditional signs of their children's academic progress. They like to see art projects, worksheets, and checklists indicating what they think of as school readiness. Teachers striving to be developmentally appropriate get frustrated with these requests. Requirements for formal assessments of children's progress often feel disconnected from the daily life of the classroom and a distraction from being more engaged with the children. Caregivers and parents want assurances and appreciation from each other. Often both groups feel unsatisfied with what they get.

Meanwhile, from the children's perspective, life is getting more crowded, rushed, and regimented into scheduled, short blocks of time. Children spend too little time outdoors, in the world of real work, or with meaningful relationships and a sense of community. They rarely get to be alone, to play for as long as they like, or to be with children who are not their own age. Caregivers and teachers come and go, and no one takes a special interest in children for long or gives them a sense of history or belonging. Most of the adults in their lives seem obsessed with whether children know their colors and numbers. Talk of getting "big enough to go to school" sustains little hope for engaged interest or meaningful learning.

Early care and education programs are a daily fact of life for children and families in the United States. On the way to work each morning, most parents leave their children in the care of someone outside their families, usually in settings that look far more structured and institutional than where they spent their own childhoods. Some children are fortunate enough to be in quality family child care, but before long, the provider goes out of business or parents move their children into a preschool setting they believe will help the children be ready to succeed in school. Well-meaning parents focus on their young children's education in a narrow sense, not considering the larger picture of their childhoods and the real experiences needed for success in life.

Rethinking What We Need

It is estimated that young children today spend approximately twelve thousand hours in group care and institutional settings before they even get to school. This means that children are spending the bulk of their childhoods in our programs. Childhood in the last few decades looks different from what most people reading this book remember. Growing up in a neighborhood; roaming freely on the block; climbing trees; playing street games; making creations with logs, stones, or found junk; having regular family gatherings; playing with children of all ages as the neighbors watched out for everyone—these are things of the past. The experience of participating in the daily life and meaningful work of the community is less and less available to young children. Instead, most children today spend their days in programs with large groups of children the same age, isolated from their families and the real world, surrounded by institutional walls and chain-link fences, playing with single-purpose plastic toys, and spending time with underpaid, often unresponsive or disgruntled adults. As Jim Greenman (1992, 22) asks, "Is that what we want for the one childhood allocated to our children?"

I want every room in our program to be one I would love to put my own child in. Each new baby I enroll in our program I personally take into my arms and say, "I will do my best to see that every day you are loved by someone here. In every way possible, we will find ways to let you know how special and important you are to us."

—Laura

Early childhood programs are microcosms of the larger world. Often they are devoid of spirit and meaningful connections, plagued with crumbling infrastructures, and distressed with lives on the brink. Staff, children, and families are filled with stress and assaults to their physical and mental health. To cope, we become desensitized and think of this way of living as "normal." Living with an unacknowledged but nagging discrepancy between how things are and how they could be easily leads to cynicism or depression. We lower our expectations to avoid deep disappointment. Any vision we may have started with gets sacrificed in the name of saving our sanity.

Visit any early childhood center and you will find that everyone needs more support. Scratch the surface and you find a profound need for a place to be nurtured and appreciated. People desire more than reminders to have a good day. They yearn for fuller connections with others and more meaningful daily exchanges. Why don't needs assessments acknowledge this human longing for connection as people's most vital need? This acknowledgment would be a wake-up call that educators could respond to with commitment and know-how. The early childhood profession knows about nurturing human development. Within its control are buildings where people of different ages and, in many cases, different cultures come together each day with the potential of real interchanges of ideas, needs, skills, and resources. Everyone comes together with a clear focus on children. Everyone acknowledges that these children are the future. They represent people's hopes, promises, and deepest longings. Ask yourself this question: Am I using this daily opportunity to its fullest potential?

The often-quoted African proverb "It takes a village to raise a child" is an important reminder. But perhaps in this consumer-oriented, technologically advanced, fast-paced culture, it will take a child to raise a village. When people genuinely come together around their hopes and dreams for children, a sense of possibility can be rekindled. This goes far beyond providing a service or a school readiness program. Early childhood centers can play a central role in recreating the new village, the new experience of neighborhood for daily life. They can become places that respond to the longings for community, meaningful relationships, a sense of belonging, and an exuberant experience of learning about the world. This is a real vision you can have for your programs, not just words on paper. Your actions, your policies, and the pulse of your organizational culture can reflect and embody this dream.

Distinguishing a Mission from a Vision

The early childhood profession gives periodic lip service to the idea of having a vision, but it is uncommon to find much time or space devoted to this topic in literature or professional development offerings. More typical are discussions of appropriate practice, standards, regulations, and rating scales. Though these certainly may be part of one's vision, they are not usually discussed in this context. With all our profession's emphasis on the components of quality child care and best practices, specific mention of working within a larger vision is usually missing. Is this because we don't understand the concept or role of a vision in our work, or are there other explanations?

Many early childhood programs have something written on paper about their purpose. Often this is in the form of a mission statement outlining their intent to serve children in need of care, to treat them respectfully, and to meet their developmental needs. But directors hired into programs are seldom asked how they would like to see the organization's purpose brought to life. Mission and philosophy statements are occasionally posted in programs and are usually found in handbooks or the organization's literature. Rarely do these statements make their way into the hearts and minds of the staff or in any way become a guiding vision for program environments, policies and procedures, or daily decision making.

A mission statement is usually about purpose, but it is seldom about a dream. Typically, a mission statement tries to address a problem with a statement of services. A vision, on the other hand, goes beyond how things are to describe how we would like them to be. In the words of Susan Gross (1987, 25–26), a vision is "what the world or society or an environment or community would look like if that purpose were realized."

There are a number of reasons why the early childhood field has focused more on the delivery of services with educational outcomes and has neglected to project a larger vision. As the field has grown beyond the part-time nursery-school model of providing enrichment experiences for children and has battled the notion that full-time child care is just babysitting, the bulk of attention has been on learning how to use curriculum and assessment tools and developing an agreed-on body of professional knowledge and ethics. The primary focus has been on the child's learning experience, and secondarily on parent involvement. While a growing emphasis has been placed on staff qualifications and training, with more and more job requirements, little attention has been given to the working conditions and resources caregivers and teachers need to do their work well. If we projected a picture of the work environment and professional support that is really required, we'd have to admit how woefully inadequate our programs are.

The members of our profession are predominantly female, and in a world where resources are controlled by predominately male priorities, we struggle to be taken seriously. To get the recognition and support they need, women tend to do what is expected of them—color within the lines and play the game according to the rules. In early childhood care and education our message is often, "We are doing such a good job with children; please give us more recognition and resources." If we spoke the bigger truth and acknowledged that most of our programs are mediocre at best, we'd feel like failures. Politically, we'd be shooting ourselves in the foot. Most of us early childhood professionals prefer to confine our sights to what seems possible, rather than face the pain of what Langston Hughes called "a dream deferred." Thus we strain under multiple stresses and minimal resources, and our workforce continues to turn over at a disturbing rate.

As children and their families come to us increasingly needy, with their family life and communities under assault from commercial interests, media culture, violence, economic downturns, poverty, and racism, we frantically put our fingers in the leaky holes. We have failed to mobilize a vision that would hold back the floodwaters, let alone dismantle the dike and build a new structure that would universally meet the needs of children and families.

Peter Block reminds us in *The Empowered Manager* (1987, 107) that

> a vision exists within each of us, even if we have not made it explicit or put it into words. Our reluctance to articulate our vision is a measure of our despair and a reluctance to take responsibility for our own lives, our own unit, and our own organization. A vision statement is an expression of hope, and if we have no hope, it is hard to create a vision.

Are there places in our profession where a larger vision is central to the discourse and is actively generating hope? The early care and educational systems of the schools of Reggio Emilia, Italy, and of schools in Sweden and New Zealand show us a vision of how programs could be if we genuinely dedicated ourselves to the lives of children. These schools take the view that children are today's, not just tomorrow's, citizens and deserve our careful listening and attention for what they offer us in the here and now. In the United States, alongside the standardization movement, programs inspired by the Reggio approach have been diligently demonstrating a different vision of the teaching and learning process. When you visit a program that is deeply studying and translating Reggio ideas for their settings, you are immediately struck by the intentionality, intellectual vitality, and collaboration that is inherent in the Reggio approach. Directors guiding their programs through this exploration are less buffeted about by external requirements and standards because they are confident about the vision they stand for. Their hearts and minds are focused on a philosophy and pedagogy that promote critical thinking, and they continually examine the assumptions they work with.

The heart of the Reggio model includes not only an image of children who are creative and capable, but a culture that is family-centered and attentive to sensual pleasure, reflection, intense discussion, and collaboration. Schools following this model have grown from a vision of social justice in the politics of the Italian town for which they were named. The adults have created early childhood programs out of the real lives and values of children. If we are to draw inspiration from these Italian schools, we can't simply imitate their culture but need to find our own way. It helps to study how this approach has been interpreted in other countries, such as Sweden and New Zealand, and in states and provinces across Australia, Canada, and elsewhere. Researching these examples helps us understand values and principles and avoid a superficial adaptation. We learn to dive under the profit-driven popular culture of America and bring forth the values and practices we know nurture children and family life, such as having relationships with real people rather than television personalities, slowing down to notice and celebrate how the light changes with different seasons, and taking time to create lasting traditions and memories. The challenge is to create a program culture with systems and structures that supports these values and practices.

I work in an inner-city setting that is often stereotyped because it is riddled with all the problems of poverty. It's easy to have low expectations and become immobilized by the difficulties. But if you want to find them, there are still many possibilities for the people who live in these communities.

From the beginning of my directing work here I knew my challenge was to go beyond just meeting the standards, which is what most people reach for as a goal for an inner-city program. I had a driving belief that children, families, and staff members all have the potential to continually learn and grow. With this in mind, I began to think in terms of instilling a sense of hope as a primary goal. Most inner-city child care and Head Start programs don't get access to progressive, visionary ideas. The focus is usually just about needs, deficits, and survival. My search for a way to change this led me to the schools of Reggio Emilia in Italy.

At Reggio, I found an extraordinary set of infant, toddler, and preschool centers founded by a small group of determined people after their country had been ravaged by war. Over the years, they got their municipal government to fund these programs. At first I was hesitant to try to use Reggio as a model for our programs. Reggio Emilia and the inner city of Chicago are so completely different. I knew we would have to invent our own way, and I questioned whether we could.

I had to learn how to focus on opportunities and not obsess over the barriers and obstacles or allow ourselves to get stuck there. My dream is to create a different example of quality for others to see, especially in programs such as Head Start and subsidized child care. Rather than seeing our children as just needing more social services, we have begun to recognize that despite the hardships in their lives, these children come to us with ideas, interests, and curiosities that we need to help flourish. Reaching our vision is an ongoing process, and we are figuring it out as we go. I don't think it will ever end. There are peaks and valleys, but we are continuing to move forward.

—Karen

Cultivating a Vision

How much of your time as a director is spent nurturing hope and giving a sense of possibility to those in your program? Are there ways in which you are cultivating a vision as part of your regular conversations, parent orientations, and staff development efforts? *The Visionary Director* contains ideas on how to move in that direction. Throughout this book are snapshots of the many different ways directors are making this happen. As you hear their voices, let them strengthen your ability to guide your program with a vision and deepen your desire to be part of this spreading movement to turn early childhood programs into genuine caring and learning communities.

Go back to why you're doing what you're doing. I don't mean going back to the regulations. Don't be outer-defined. Do not allow the regs to define who you are. Do not allow any outside forces to define who you are. Allow for the possibility that the regs may actually catch up with your vision. There will be a flicker of fire that's very exciting.

—Dana

Going Beyond Managing to Leading

Guiding early childhood programs with a vision requires more than management skills. A manager is focused on the people, problems, and tasks at hand, using technical skills to address them. Beyond that, working with a vision requires developing oneself into a leader who inspires others to participate in and expand the vision. Of course, early childhood directors who are leaders attend to management concerns, but they also bring these concerns into a group focus through vision building, what Peter Block calls "convening, valuing relatedness, and presenting choices" (2008, 85). Leaders create management systems and structures to support a visionary organizational culture. Linda Espinosa, who embodies these dimensions of leadership, says, "Leaders are those who provoke or nudge or elevate others into thinking, feeling, or behaving in ways they would not otherwise have demonstrated" (1997, 97). Growing yourself as a leader goes hand in hand with growing a vision.

It's pretty easy to be a star if you are a hard-working director with aspirations. You can create some innovative things in a program and then move on to the next phase of your career. I strive to be a leader, not a star. A leader plans for what stays when they leave. The big difference between a leader and a star is in the size of a person's ego. I know that as I provide leadership, people won't always love me and be happy. But I'm trying to build an institutional structure that will outlast any focus on me.

—Laura

A vision can't be handed down like a mission statement or a memo. The ground has to be prepared, seeds have to be planted, and tender shoots have to be protected from destructive pests and early frosts. This requires what Sharon Kagan and Michelle Neuman call "conceptual leadership," which they say is "more about how we think together about the field's destiny and the role that early care and education must play in a democratic society" (1997, 59), a theme echoed by Stacie Goffin and Valora Washington (2007). As conceptual leaders we continually step back and look at the big picture. We need a working knowledge of systems thinking, human development, pedagogy, and group dynamics. Where can we find models to adapt for this kind of leadership in our field?

Looking for Models

Surprisingly, it is outside the field of early care and education where we find the most literature and training with an emphasis on leading organizations with a vision. For the past thirty years, the vision of workplaces as learning organizations has been advancing in the business sector, but it is only occasionally found in early childhood programs. Corporate consultants and CEOs have been influencing the direction of for-profit business using ideas that seem intrinsic to the early childhood field: ideas of human development and the processes of teaching, learning, and teamwork. Yet it is the business world that has taken off and prospered using these concepts. Since the 1990s, a proliferation of corporate business management books, trade journals, and now Web sites and blogs have been discussing ideas that should be the foundation of the work in the early childhood care and education field—build from people's strengths, acknowledge contributions, develop shared visions, do systems thinking, see empowerment as the key to success, provide for and reward collaborations, and celebrate often. Shouldn't these concepts be filling our literature, conferences, and professional development seminars? The corporate world has created a vision and mobilized a workforce around a strong sense of purpose, ultimately to enhance profit margins. What are equivalent actions we can use to become powerful in the world?

One voice in the field, *Child Care Information Exchange*, has consistently tried to bring the lessons of the business world to the field of early childhood care and education. As early as 1987 they featured an article by a business management consultant alerting us to the way organizations become powerful. Here's a taste of what Susan Gross has to say in her article "The Power of Purpose" (1987, 25–26):

> What we mean by purpose is the end or result at which an entire organization is aimed. Purpose is the organization's driving force and reason for being. It is always translatable into vision—that is, an image shared by the organization of what the world or society or an environment or community would look like if that purpose were realized.

For early childhood programs, Gross is describing something different from uniting a center around the self-study for NAEYC accreditation, as important and rewarding as that might be. She is suggesting using our imaginations, not our checklists, to define dreams that linger with us as we move through our days of stress, chores, meetings, and to-do lists. Her point has to do with how we cultivate our hearts, make connections with other people, and create a desire to reach for something better. Gross goes on (25):

> The most potent ingredient in organizational effectiveness is a clear sense of purpose shared by every member of the organization. Organizational problems, including nasty interpersonal conflicts and wrenching internal schisms, can literally begin to dissolve when people in an organization rediscover the depth of their common vision.

Susan Gross and other people in the business world are reminding us that vision is central to organizational effectiveness. Another business management consultant, Peter Senge, in his seminal book about systems thinking and learning organizations, *The Fifth*

Discipline (2006, 9), explains that the very definition of leadership in an organization is tied to working with a vision:

> If any one idea about leadership has inspired organizations for thousands of years, it's the capacity to hold a shared picture of the future we seek to create. . . . When there is a genuine vision (as opposed to the all-too-familiar "vision statement"), people excel and learn, not because they are told to, but because they want to. But many leaders have personal visions that never get translated into shared visions that galvanize an organization. . . . What has been lacking is a discipline for translating vision into shared vision—not a "cookbook" but a set of principles and guiding practices.

To develop yourself as a leader, you need to work with a clear set of principles. Each chapter of this book offers principles that are valuable for early childhood programs, and strategies to bring them alive. Below is the first principle—the foundation of your work to come.

Principle

Create a Process for Developing Your Vision

A vision for an organization can't be just one person's idea. As a director, you may have the initial inspiration for your program's purpose, but for these ideas to grow, you must steadily invite the interest and involvement of others.

Because many early childhood program directors are inexperienced in working with a vision, they may be uncertain how to talk about it and bring their vision into focus for others. We recommend developing a vision-building process that is regularly revisited and invites people to reflect, engage, and challenge each other to connect their values and beliefs to their daily lives.

Vision statements grow by involving people in activities that help them name what they find most meaningful and memorable from their own family lives, and together examining real-life examples using stories, poems, and other media. These two approaches can help determine the values and concepts that are important to people's lives and could become a part of your vision.

Collaboratively developing a vision takes time and involves many twists and turns. The following pages contain strategies that have proved useful as directors have developed their leadership skills in guiding the process.

Strategy Regularly share memories of favorite childhood experiences

Whether our childhoods were generally positive or negative, most of us have some favorite childhood experiences to share with others. When adults take on teaching jobs in early childhood programs, the primary memory bank we draw on is a school setting. But deep within us are other memories that fill us with warmth, giggles, and sensory details we love to talk about. These can become frequent discussion starters to generate ideas about the activities and relationships that are valuable for children.

In the initial process of working with a staff to build a common vision for the program, it's useful to devote a large block of time to some specific storytelling about childhood memories. This gets people in touch with a vital set of experiences that have lasting meaning for them. Devoting precious staff development time to this sharing communicates the priorities of the program and the value that is placed on people's own lives as a rich source of learning. It also sets the tone for creating a "storytelling culture" in the program.

The way you launch an activity of sharing childhood memories among your staff depends on your assessment of who they are. Getting to know your staff will help you determine how to set the stage and introduce the activity. If you have a large staff, you may need to allow more time or you may want people to share their stories in pairs or small groups. If people are hesitant to talk in a group, bringing in some objects and pictures can help spark people's memories. When people have good listening skills and feel at ease with talking in group settings, this activity usually runs smoothly. If one or two people tend to dominate the discussion, you will need to monitor the time and structure of the activity so everyone has a turn. If you have a group that seems hesitant to talk about themselves, you might do better to keep the talking in pairs or have them make some written lists.

This idea might be introduced during a meeting by asking the staff to separate into pairs and having each share a favorite memory from childhood. Acknowledge that some may have had difficult childhoods, but nearly everyone has something special they remember. Tell the group you will give each pair about ten minutes for sharing. After the first five minutes, alert them that it's time for the second person to share. When you reconvene the whole group, ask for reflections on what they heard. Rather than having them repeat stories, ask them to name the themes they heard. This process of analyzing and drawing out the meaning of the stories is where "ah ha's" happen. Many people have memories of endless hours playing outdoors without any adult supervision. Others remember playing with kids of all ages in the neighborhood, eating peanut butter sandwiches out on the steps, turning found objects into toys or inventions. As you list these kinds of themes—endless hours outdoors, no adults around, making mischief, make-believe—consider which are currently available to children in your program. Obviously you can't do some of these things, but can you find ways to create similar memories for children today?

Discussions like this are the tender shoots of a growing vision. As the months go on, you can further develop this aspect of your organizational culture by devoting ten to fifteen minutes of each staff meeting for continued storytelling. What you want to cultivate is a climate in which stories are everywhere in your program, reflecting a genuine enthusiasm and engagement with what is happening. This initial story-sharing practice will lay the groundwork for giving attention to the details of children's conversations and their play. It will further the respect and appreciation staff and families have for how stories offer a window into who they are and how they think.

Sometimes it helps to suggest a specific focus for a childhood memory, such as remembering a time when you took a risk. You can experiment with free-form sharing, letting anyone who is ready have a turn to speak, or you can just go around the room, giving everyone a turn. Use these questions with any childhood memory activity to generate the components of a child- and family-centered program:

- What were the themes in the stories you heard?
- If you were going to give this story a three- or four-word name, what would it be?
- Which of these themes would you like to be part of the children's and families' lives in our program?
- How can we simulate some of these experiences within the confines of our safety regulations?

One director we know wanted to build a playground that would provide children with opportunities for risk taking and adventure. She used childhood memory activities to raise funds and design a playground built for risk and adventure in her program. In meetings with her staff, child care licensers, local businesspeople, and parents, she asked them to recall their fondest memories of being outdoors. Their memories included lots of sensory elements, such as water, dirt, and even prickly bushes. With fondness, most of them recalled favorite hiding places, taking risks, and doing things their parents might not have allowed had they been around. After brainstorming lists like this, the director suggested they compare their experiences with the lives of children in full-time child care today. The contrast was striking enough that she was able to mobilize the support and resources to build a playground that simulates many elements of these childhood memories. It is designed around nature and adventure, with more money put into landscaping than plastic, immovable climbers. For a fuller account of this inspirational story, see our book *Reflecting Children's Lives: A Handbook for Planning Child-Centered Curriculum.*

Strategy *Represent childhood memories with found objects or art materials*

We've also found that caregivers and teachers respond well when asked to use open-ended materials such as toilet-paper rolls, wire, and blocks to represent their favorite memory or a favorite place they remember from their childhood. This often generates creative thinking and playful interactions, reminding people of the spirit of childhood.

Strategy *Use children's books to unearth childhood memories*

If you have a group that is slow to participate in sharing memories and stories, you might want to launch this activity by reading a children's book that captures some aspects of your vision. Some books that work well in launching childhood memory activities are listed in the strategy that follows.

Strategy *Use children's books regularly in staff meetings*

There are a number of reasons to read children's books in staff meetings and workshops. One, of course, is to help unearth childhood memories, as described previously. Overall, we need to improve the way we typically use picture books with children. Books are usually given to children as a holding pattern, a way to keep them occupied during transition times, with little support for any real interest in the books. Often a requirement is to put them away when the teacher is ready for the next activity. Story reading in many early childhood programs often happens in large groups at circle time, with repeated reminders to sit quietly and not interrupt. This habit is counter to much of what we know about helping children become lifelong readers and book lovers.

To explore a child's perspective on books, ask the staff to share their favorite childhood book memories. They most likely will share stories about curling up with a book and a flashlight under the sheets or in the closet, or sitting outside on the steps or under the trees. Or they may remember being snuggled in the lap of a family member, perhaps at bedtime, with few distractions and ample time to talk about the pictures and share wonder and related experiences. Sharing these memories and regularly using picture books in staff meetings can alert you to changes you might want to make in using them with children.

If you model book reading or invite teachers who are expressive to do this, reading books in staff meetings helps cultivate good story reading voices and listening habits. Books are also a terrific way to jar people's memories of what things are like from a child's perspective. Stories told from a child's eye not only are useful in consideration of issues like child guidance, but often provide an opportunity to dream a little and to remember the kind of environment and experiences that create close relationships, a strong sense of identity, and the wonder and magic of learning in the company of people who love you. Choosing picture books with childhood themes nudges you to explore their implications for your program. They are great vision-building tools.

A good story to start with is *On the Day I Was Born* by Debbi Chocolate (1995). The text of this book is simple but uses engaging language to accompany the rich texture of the illustrations. The child in this story talks about being wrapped in a soft cloth, being adored by his family members, and making his father stand tall and proud. Read the book with expression, as you would with children. You can read the book all the way through or stop after a few pages. Use the following questions for discussion of the themes in this beautiful book:

- How does our program reflect the feelings of the child in this book?
- What is our softness curriculum? Can you describe specific things we do that make children feel they are wrapped in a soft cloth?
- Do we convey to the children and their families that they make us feel proud? If so, how?

Another book that helps teachers explore the specific components of childhood that their programs should provide is *Roxaboxen*, a true story by Alice McLerran (1991). It is filled with images of children engaged in meaningful, self-directed play that involves all the goals you have for block and dress-up areas, for nature and science activities, and for physical, social, emotional, and moral development. Together as a group or in pairs, ask staff members to reflect on questions like:

- When the children in our program grow up and think back on their time with us, will it be with the same fondness and meaning that *Roxaboxen* offered? If not, how can we make it so?
- What are the elements of childhood portrayed in *Roxaboxen*, and how can we recreate or simulate them in our program?
- What are the jewels that children find in our program? Are there enough to go around?
- Where in our program do children experience the sensation of riding fast like the wind on a pretend horse?

Miss Tizzy by Libba Moore Gray (1993) offers another wonderful picture of how children and adults could spend time together. Many aspects of a vision for early childhood programs becoming genuine caring and learning communities are in this book. Miss Tizzy is part of a neighborhood and engages children in predictable routines and unexpected treats. She shares herself fully with the children and involves them in meaningful work and joyous play. In her care, the children learn to make a contribution to the neighborhood and ultimately to Miss Tizzy herself. To guide the discussion of this book, ask staff to reflect on the specific things Miss Tizzy does with the children that make her so wonderful. Consider questions such as:

- How do we connect children in our program with nature in the spirit of Miss Tizzy with her garden and cat and songs to the moon?
- What special things from home do we bring to work to share with the children?
- What risks do we take in sharing ourselves with children, like Miss Tizzy having a house and garden that looks different from everyone else's or being willing to sing even when she is slightly off-key?
- How do children in our program experience a similar sense of neighborhood when they are in our care?
- How do children in our program learn to make a contribution to those around them?

Sylvia Long (2000) has adapted the traditional "Hush Little Baby" lullaby into a delightful book that demonstrates how you can better align your values with traditions. She introduces the book with the story of how she grew up with this lullaby and wanted to pass it on to her children. But when she listened more carefully to the lyrics, she realized they didn't represent her values. Each verse of the original song suggested comforting a child with an offer to buy something. Long's new lyrics offer comfort to children by connecting them with the natural world and with music by showing the child a hummingbird or pointing out the evening sky. You can "sing" the book to the group and then ask them to write a verse or two of their own.

Each of these books generates wonderful discussions and provides twinkles and tears for your eyes. They help you remember how childhood can be and inspire everyone to move in that direction. If you spend much time in the children's section of a library or bookstore, you will likely find other books to use in your vision building. Consider children's books not only for meetings with staff, but also for gatherings with families, board meetings, or even hearings with licensers or legislators.

Having tried this strategy of reading children's books, many directors have shared exciting results. In one program, some of the staff were so inspired by *Roxaboxen* that they put all their plastic, commercial toys in storage and replaced them with open-ended materials from nature, such as driftwood, rocks, shells, and old wooden boxes and baskets. The quality of play among children that followed was unlike anything they had seen before. When shelving units and furniture needed replacing, they began shopping at garden stores and IKEA, instead of using the traditional early childhood educational supply catalogs. The atmosphere became more relaxed, and parents started lingering more at drop-off and pickup times. Soon they began to find parents snuggled with children on a wicker love seat looking over children's artwork or favorite books, while others helped add finishing touches to a fort made of bedsheets and driftwood pieces.

Since we read *Roxaboxen* to a group of licensers, several of them have remarked that they now regularly read children's books in their office meetings. A family provider called and told us her licenser had a sudden change of heart after rereading *Roxaboxen*. She decided the huge pile of dirt in the backyard didn't really constitute a health and safety hazard. In fact, she thought it might be an exciting playground if the children were given some natural props and simple tools like sifters, pails, shovels, and rakes.

Strategy *Get to know families' dreams*

Each family enrolling a child in an early childhood program has hopes and dreams for their child. This is easily overlooked as schedules and fees are negotiated. To coax these aspirations out of families, put something in your application form that asks about their hopes for their child as they form relationships with caregivers and teachers. During home visits, interviews, and orientation sessions, respectfully raise questions that get to the values and longings they have for their children.

Make families' values and dreams for their children visible to the staff and others in concrete ways, such as bulletin board displays that feature different families every month. Put interviews and photographs that tell a family's story in your newsletter or in a homemade book for others to read. To make this welcoming for everyone, be sensitive to issues that families may feel awkward disclosing, such as the configuration of their home life, economic circumstances, or health. These strategies and your sensitivity go a long way to create an inclusive environment that acknowledges that all families have strengths, just as all families struggle. The Tucson Children's Project (see Afterword) is an inspiring example of how a program used families' hopes and dreams to advocate for respect and support in the larger community.

Nuestra labor comenzó cuando descubrimos que había pocas opciones para las familias que necesitaban programas bilingües. Mi esposo y yo teníamos una visión. Habíamos decidido que el español sería el primer idioma de nuestros hijos. Queríamos un ambiente que valorara la cultura puertorriqueña. Otros padres de diferentes culturas o grupos étnicos también querían tener esas oportunidades para sus hijos; nuestra dedicación a estos valores nos llevó a un compromiso y un sentido de comunidad.

Descubrimos que nuestra visión no es estática y que ha sido moldeada, modificada y puesta a prueba por los niños, maestros y agencias reguladoras con los que nos relacionamos a través de los años. El interés mutuo de los participantes por el bienestar y la supervivencia del programa ha sido el impulso que nos ayudó a realizar lo que nos habíamos forjado. Hemos hecho grandes cambios en el ambiente físico, en nuestro currículum, en nuestras políticas, en superar los problemas económicos y todavía nos mantenemos como una agencia independiente y privada. Esto nunca hubiera sido posible sin el sentido de comunidad que hemos forjado en nuestro Centro.

—Carmen

Our journey began because there were very few options for families looking for bilingual programs. My husband and I had a vision. We were really determined to maintain Spanish as the primary language for our children. We also wanted our children to be in an environment that validated their Puerto Rican heritage. This vision was shared by many other parents across racial lines. They too wanted a program that would provide these opportunities for their children. Our commitment to these issues created a bond and sense of community.

We have discovered that visions are not static. Our vision has been molded and put to the test by the many children, parents, staff, and regulatory agencies that have been involved over the years. The vested interest of all the participants in the survival and well-being of the program has been a very powerful force in accomplishing what we have. We have made major changes in our physical environment, curriculum, and policies. We have overcome financial hardships and have managed to remain an independent and private agency. This never would have happened without the sense of community that has emerged at our center.

—Carmen

Strategy Reinvent the idea of quilting bees

Bring people together for meaningful tasks that aren't always about cleaning, painting, and repairing. Entice them with an enjoyable and useful activity, such as organizing their family memories into scrapbooks and photo albums. With busy lives, this is something most people don't make time for. They are usually grateful for the opportunity to rekindle memories at this type of bookmaking party.

Suggest that families and staff members bring photographs, special mementos, or just their memories to create visual stories about their lives. Offer a variety of colorful background papers, magazine pictures, stickers, and old greeting cards. Get a frame shop to donate a supply of recycled mat board or foam core. Provide glue, markers, scissors, and other tools for making bulletin boards or homemade books.

Offer initial ideas to get people started. They could create a book or display board around the topic of family history, favorite memories, holiday celebrations, or special accomplishments. Not only do you end up with visual stories of people in your program, but as they work on these projects together, staff and families learn about and from each other, thus building a caring community.

Strategy Seek the children's ideas

We so often do things on behalf of children while neglecting to get their direct input. Part of your vision-building process should include ways to solicit the perspectives of children on what they value most in their time with you. Try asking them to draw their favorite places or activities in the center. Play a variation of the "I spy" game, asking them to offer responses to statements such as:

- I spy something that makes me feel better when I'm sad.
- I spy a place to go when I want to feel powerful.
- I spy my favorite place.
- I spy something that reminds me of something we do in my family.
- I spy a tool I want to be able to use.

Strategy Put images and words together

We have offered you a vision of early childhood programs as learning communities that can serve as the cornerstone for larger social change. Take some time now to gather your own thoughts and reactions to this idea. If your program was to move closer to this vision, how might this look in your particular setting? Remember the words of Sylvia Ashton-Warner: "Dreams are a living picture in the mind generating energy" (1972, 87).

Try to imagine the feel, the look, the sound, and even the smell of such a place. What words would you use to describe this picture? Jot down some phrases that describe how the environment would influence the interactions and activities of children, staff, and families.

Now look over your list. Do any of your words match your image of a school? Are they similar to any elements in your current program? Go through the list again. Can you identify three things you could do, with negligible impact on your budget, that would reflect some of the elements you pictured? Perhaps your list would look something like this director's list:

- soft music and seating in our entryway—set up tape player and wicker love seat by sign-in table
- chocolate-chip cookies baking—have potpourri or scented candle for interim
- small groups of parents talking about weekend plans together
- monthly toy and clothing exchange for families
- community garden in a section of our play yard
- hosting ESL and citizenship classes for the community—call Refugee Alliance to discuss and offer space

Strategy Develop a vision statement together

After you have spent time with some of the previous strategies, you will be ready to create a public declaration of the vision you are trying to build. When the ground has been adequately tilled and fertilized with activities such as those previously discussed, invite people to collaborate on writing a vision statement. With help from the accumulation of notes from your childhood-memory sessions and input from staff, parents, and children about their values and what's important to them, invite people to collaborate on writing a vision statement. Here are some possible approaches to use.

Create a three-column chart like the one below.
Working in three different groups, one group for each column, have people begin to generate words and phrases for their column. Then bring everyone back together to compare what each group came up with, and begin to build sentences from these bones for your vision statement.

Children deserve	Families deserve	Staff deserve

Ask people to look over the other lists and visual representations created in earlier activities.
Begin to put these words into concept groupings, perhaps through word webbing; encourage people to brainstorm specific images to add more detail. During this process, suggest that they think of the special things they already experience in the program, and then add more ideas about what else they would like see.

Ask for volunteers to record what is being said.
Assemble all the selected words, phrases, and sentences, and choose some opening phrases to capture concepts to include in your vision statement.

Have small groups flesh out short paragraphs for each opening phrase.
It might take a couple of sessions to come up with a statement that sounds pleasing to everyone, but keep at it. The process itself continues to feed the vision.

Here's an example of a vision statement created by a program in Seattle:

Hilltop Children's Center

A Learning Community for Children and Adults

Where children are valued for their ability to do meaningful work, their wonder and curiosity, their perspectives, and ability to play—

Where families are valued for their bonds and traditions, their ability to play, their commitment to work, home, and community, and their dreams for their children—

Where staff are valued for their vision, their delight in children, their skill, heart, and knowledge, a commitment to families, and an ability to play—

We cherish what we learn from one another.

At today's teacher meeting a teacher led us in singing the John Lennon song "Imagine." After singing, we took some time to reflect on the program of our dreams. What would it feel like for teachers? Children? Parents? Inspired by Margie and Deb's books, I asked the teachers to use as many sensory and emotion words they could think of to describe their dreams. Then I handed out strips of paper and asked them to fill in the blanks:

> Imagine a school where teachers . . .
> Imagine a school where children . . .
> Imagine a school where families . . .

We then gathered into small groups to organize the small strips onto large sheets of paper to create poems. One teacher volunteered to take all three poems and synthesize them into one poem. I was so thrilled with the results. The poems were amazing! I've tried visioning exercises before, but it was always difficult to get people to see beyond the details to the big ideas. The "Imagine" framework allowed them to think in a different way.

—Ellen

Strategy Represent pieces of your vision with blocks

People need to see examples of what your vision looks like on a daily basis. After some initial time spent identifying and working toward a vision, get your staff focused on how they see this shared vision in action. Bring a pile of blocks and sticky notes to a staff meeting. Ask people to look over the components of the vision again, and then think of an example they've seen lately. Have them write a story (a brief description) on a sticky note, put it on a block, and then place the block so as to begin to build a foundation that represents the vision. As the foundation gets built, have each story read aloud so that the examples are visible to everyone. You might even find a way to display this block foundation on a table with a sign for parents and staff members to continue to add more story blocks as they see the vision coming alive.

Practice Assessing Yourself as a Visionary Leader

Management consultant Carl Sussman once suggested that the typical early childhood environment does not cultivate the kind of risk-taking behavior that is needed to conceive and carry out an expansive vision (1998). Inherently, the work of taking care of children involves patience, consistency of routines, the utmost vigilance over safety and health, and gentle, accepting, nurturing behavior. Perhaps because of this, many of us in the early childhood profession have a temperament less inclined toward risk. In fact, most directors associate the idea of risk with liability and strive to keep everything safe, literally and figuratively. But if you are to be a leader and move your program toward a larger vision, you will need to cultivate yourself as a risk taker.

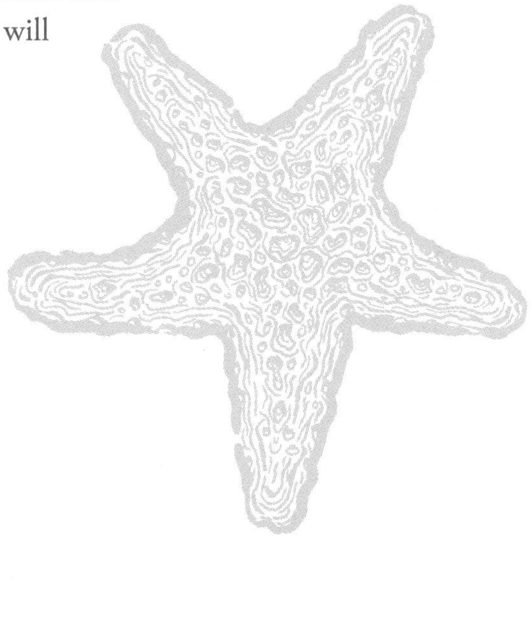

I didn't always know this. The learning took years. But once I learned how to make army regulations work for us rather than letting them work against, I felt powerful and helped the people who worked with me feel empowered.

Yes, we do have to be 100 percent in compliance with army regulation 608-10 in order to maintain our Department of Defense certification (the army equivalent to state licensing). But what I've discovered is that somehow rules get "made up" that are not and never were in the regulation. Why this phenomenon of making-up rules occurs in early childhood programs might make another whole story. Maybe we make them up because we're inventing our profession as we go. Maybe we do it because we're scared of inspections. Maybe it's because we have such different levels of understanding about best practices for early childhood programs. It could be a combination of all of these.

For example, when I was a preschool teacher there was a "rule" among the child development centers and family child care homes in our community that said the children must wear their shoes at all times, even during naptime, because there might be a fire drill. Does that make sense to you? Did you ever try to sleep comfortably wearing your shoes? Did you grow up never being allowed to go barefoot? It made no sense to me, but we did as we were told by our directors and kept the children in shoes.

So how did we work through this in my program? We began to question the rules—the ones that didn't make sense to us. We began to expect inspectors to "show us where it says that in the regulation." We learned that the army regulation actually stated the intent for each rule. When we found that out, we began to work with rule makers to develop plans and solve problems. Our goal was to meet the intent of the regulation rather than continue to comply with arbitrary rules. We began to feel that we were in control of the rules, not that the rules were in control of us. We began to feel powerful. We began to think for ourselves. We became thinking people caring for our nation's children. We began to be creators rather than followers of regulations that didn't make sense.

—Kathleen

Take a minute to assess yourself. Do you see yourself as a risk taker? A visionary? Are you satisfied with how things are in your program, in your profession, and in society at large? How close to your dream are you? Which one of the following statements feels most like you?

- ☐ I avoid taking risks and tend to put my head in the sand when it comes to big changes that are required.
- ☐ When I feel something really needs changing, I'm willing to stick my neck out.
- ☐ I'm always ready to challenge the status quo, to speak up or advocate for something that obviously needs changing.
- ☐ My program is pretty close to how I want it to be.
- ☐ I have a list of changes that need to be made if our program is going to meet our profession's definitions of quality.
- ☐ My vision for our program goes far beyond what is typically discussed in our professional literature. I have big dreams and am willing to work to achieve them.

Getting the most out of this book will require you to take some risks. Lay aside any skepticism or list of "yes, buts." Approach the coming chapters as a dreamer, making notes about what appeals to you, what you'd like to try. Let your mind stretch to spin out possibilities, your spirit fill with courage and determination, and your heart draw strength from your breathing. It's possible to change how things are when you remember and recommit yourself to how they could be.

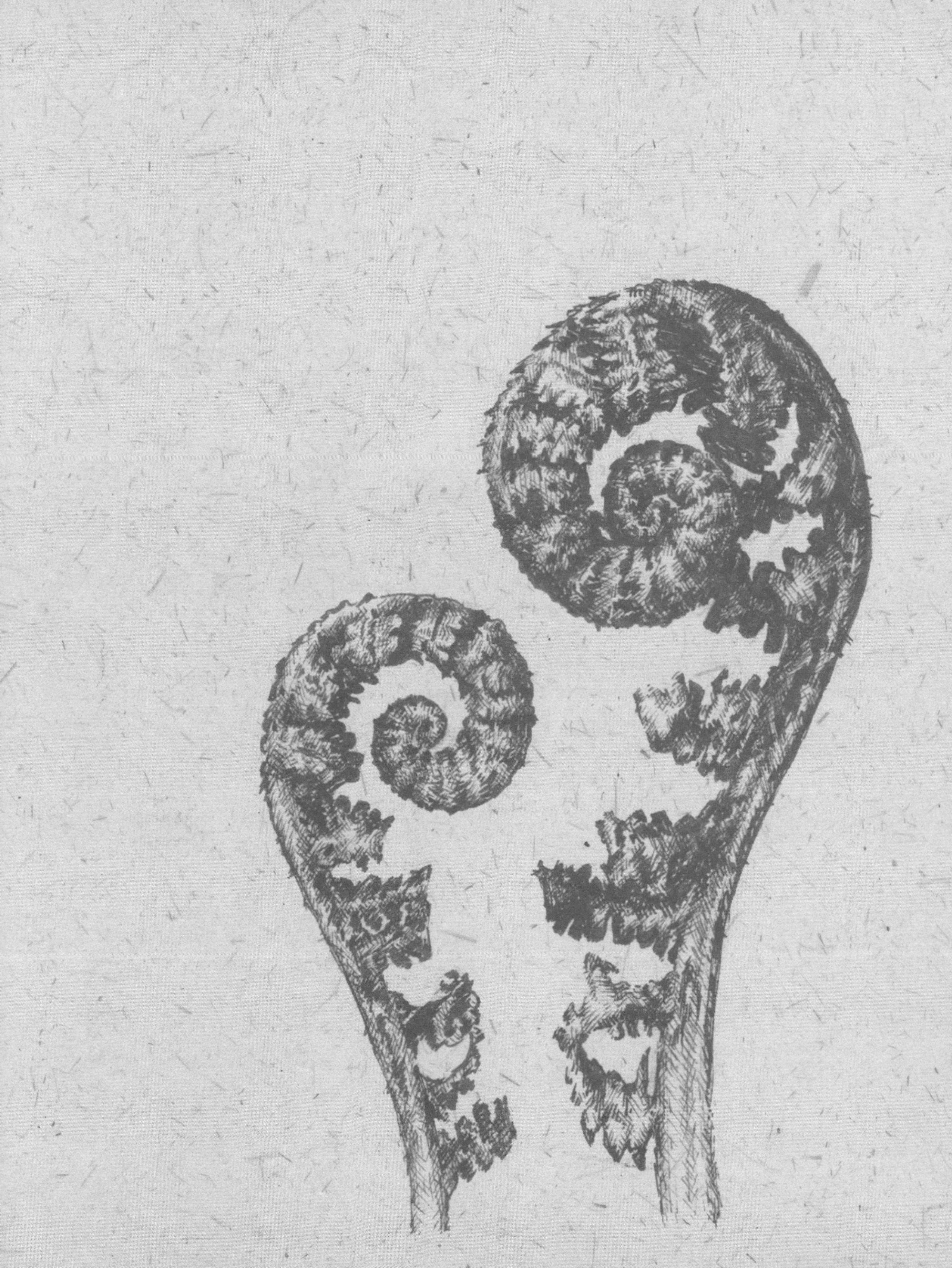

Chapter 2

A Framework for Your Work

The job of directing an early childhood program has many faces. Whatever your intentions on any given day, the ebb and flow of events at your program places consistent demands on your time. Consider how your time has been spent over the last few weeks, and place a check in the box below that most closely represents how you have felt.

Currently, most of my time at work is spent as:

- ☐ an air traffic controller
- ☐ a welcome-wagon hostess with the mostest
- ☐ a midwife
- ☐ a police chief
- ☐ ______________________________

(add your own images here)

____

When you begin the work of directing an early childhood program, you may have a strong sense of purpose and be clear about your vision. Perhaps the first chapter of this book has sparked some new awareness for you, and your mind is full of ideas. But consider this scene, which is no doubt a familiar one for you:

On the way to work this morning you've been thinking about the growing vision you have of your program becoming a caring and learning community for all involved. There are signs that many of your teachers are understanding the significance of their work in the larger context of changing the culture of consumerism and violence that surrounds us. Parents, too, are beginning to recognize the contrast between how vibrant it feels at your center and the environments where they live and work. They see how much people at the center seem to enjoy each other's company and help each other out. You feel inspired and resolve to work on behalf of this vision, knowing that it will make a difference in the lives of the children and adults.

Walking in the door, you learn that one of your teachers has called in sick and no substitute has been found. A parent approaches, impatient to speak with you before she heads off to work. In the back of your mind you notice the payroll accounting begging for attention so checks can be cut by the end of the day. On your desk you find a long to-do list that must be accomplished before your board meeting this evening. The glow of your morning thoughts fades as you face the pressing issues of the day.

In scenes like this, how do you keep hold of your dreams as you move through your day? Do you have strategies that keep your head above water, your mind focused, your sight clear? Your work life as a director is so encompassing, so filled with squeaky wheels and daily crises, that it's easy to lose sight of where you want to be going. Building and sustaining your vision takes more than your imagination or a head full of dreams. You need a structure and systems to help you organize the tasks that lead to your vision, one that keeps you acting intentionally in your planning and responses. Directing with a vision requires a conceptual framework and a practical grasp of effective tools to meet the multiple demands of this complex work.

Looking for Tips and Techniques

When you seek out resources to help you in your work, what is usually on your mind? Are you looking to acquire particular skills such as budget development, time management, or delegation of tasks? This know-how is obviously important for program managers, and you need a number of other competencies to be an effective supervisor. For example:

- recruiting, orienting, supervising, and evaluating staff;
- marketing and advocating for your program with parents, potential funders, and policymakers;

- writing handbooks, correspondence, and newsletters;
- meeting standards and maintaining contracts, policies, and documentation;
- solving problems, managing conflict, and accessing resources.

The good news is that there are management books, assessment tools, and resources designed to assist you with the day-to-day activities of your job. You can find these within and outside of the early childhood field, and we have listed related ones at the end of this book (see Resources).

Along with management tips, most directors are seeking ideas to cultivate their leadership skills. As we discussed in the first chapter, learning to lead as well as manage is what makes it possible to bring a vision to life. If you are a leader, you work with a larger framework for thinking and responding. At any given time you intentionally choose which of your management roles is most likely to bring you closer to your vision. You need an approach, a presence of mind, that keeps your attention on the process of nourishing the vision you're after. This obviously involves more than checklists, good software, and management techniques. While you work to uphold standards, you translate them into meaningful concepts to guide the everyday activities in your program. Human development and making connections are as central to your thinking about quality as those rating scales and component checklists. With each situation you encounter, you find a way to frame your thoughts, tasks, and decision-making process in the service of your vision. When you organize your work with attention to a vision, you find yourself moving forward, not spinning your wheels. Your spirit is awakened rather than drained.

What framework makes sense to guide your work as an early childhood program director as you seek to lead with a vision? Without funds for an ever-expanding administrative staff, how can you fulfill your multifaceted responsibilities? The ideas and inspiration you need are often found outside the typical early childhood publishing house: you might try visiting a magic shop, becoming an understudy to the sorcerer's apprentice, or perhaps contacting a laboratory specializing in clones. Keeping a sense of humor is essential to maintaining your sanity. Equally important is finding a way to think about the many aspects of your job. You need a framework that gives you a picture of your leadership tasks, one that keeps your work in a balanced perspective as you take on the discrepancies between how things are and how you envision they could be.

In recent years, our Head Start has grown exponentially. Like every other Head Start program, we had a hierarchical structure. This worked fine when the problems were simpler and only required limited intervention, like speech services. What started to change were the growing needs of children and families. The numbers of families needing intervention grew, and their problems became more involved and complex. I remember very clearly a defining moment during a staffing, where we assigned eight to ten program people to intervene and address the problems in one family's life. I remember thinking, "This is stupid. This is the most fractured family, and this approach will disrupt their lives enormously." As a director, you have to stop blaming and listening to excuses and start assessing what change is needed. You must learn to discern the difference between idiosyncratic blips and problematic structural patterns.

At that point we had to redefine how we wanted to deliver services. The performance standards were segmented into many components, and we had to find a more holistic way. We had to back out of the existing model and reorganize ourselves from the family's problem, rather than from the institution's structure. This change process included the entire staff. We were committed to this vision, and we had to create an organizational structure to support it.

The beginning of the process was very hard. There was old baggage among staff members, and they were unable to let go of past injustices. But we stayed with it, and the outcome has been very positive. People were able to create a new structure that has worked very well for us. They believed in it; they owned it; they developed better working relationships. They had experienced a crisis, worked through it, and saw they could come through with good results.

As a result of this experience, I tried to build into our system more opportunities for collaborative planning, reflection, and problem solving. This involved restructuring our staff scheduling to create more paid time away from children. We ran up against a number of barriers, and we are still working to bring them down. There are no easy solutions to limited funds, time, and know-how, but we are determined to create a way out of no way.

—Dana

One of the definitions *Merriam-Webster's Collegiate Dictionary* offers for the word *framework* is "the larger branches of a tree that determine its shape." Many management frameworks are designed to help you make the current shape of your organization work better. What we are suggesting is that you consider a new shape for your early childhood program, one that nurtures the growth of individuals and their community in a way that transforms business as usual in the wider world. A framework such as this infuses everyday tasks with opportunities for collaboration, reflection, and the discovery of other perspectives on children and families. Developing this kind of framework will most likely require you to shift some old habits and ways of thinking. To get off the typical treadmill of directing from crisis to crisis, it is helpful to step outside the early childhood field for some fresh ideas. We recommend turning to sources that may not have occurred to you, ones that offer you a new way to conceive of what you need to do. For instance, consider the concept of balance, which is so critical to your thinking and functioning.

Learning about Balance

Learning to effectively juggle all the aspects of your work requires some understanding about the notion of balance. What will keep things from spinning out of control or, conversely, prevent your spirit or your program from shriveling up and dying from inertia? How do you balance sanity in your life with expediting quality in your program?

Balance is more than an abstract idea of how to lead one's life. *Balance* can be defined as the equality of totals in the debit and credit sides of an account, and you know this refers to both money *and* energy. The *American Heritage College Dictionary* includes definitions of balance such as "a stable mental or psychological state; a harmonious arrangement of parts or elements, as in a design; the difference in magnitude between opposing forces or influences"—a daily way of life for early childhood program directors. The demands and details are so plentiful that you find it hard not to be in a continual reactive state. Taking time to compare and prioritize may seem like a luxury, given all those fires to be put out. On the other hand, balance is certainly a key factor in staying healthy and effective as a director. You need models who have mastered the practice of balance, who have strategies you can adapt for your work. Where can you find those with examples you can use? Take heart! There are people whose lives depend on a precise understanding of balance, and they have lessons to share.

Expand your mind's eye and consider the work of jugglers, figure skaters, whirling dervishes, and gymnasts. Perhaps this suggestion makes you chuckle, but here's what jugglers tell us about their art. The trick to keeping all those balls in the air is to find one spot to focus on as all the balls are tossed in a path. If your eyes shift as they try to follow the individual balls, all that dispersing movement will cause you to lose concentration. You'll drop the ball. (Ever had this experience during your days of directing?) Figure skaters offer us a similar message. They say they are able to keep their balance while doing those amazing twirls and spins by focusing on one spot. They train their eyes to immediately find this spot as they make each whirl and turn.

Are you familiar with the mystical branch of Islam called Sufism, whose members are called whirling dervishes? As they dance into a trancelike state, they too follow this approach. When you watch dervishes dancing, you see them simultaneously whirling in individual circles while moving as a group around a big circle. They do this for up to an hour without ever losing their balance. Dervishes explain this practice as one of complete abandonment to their spiritual focus.

During one of the Olympic games, a gold-medal gymnast described her success as more than a matter of skills and techniques. She said the most important thing is to get an image in her mind of what she wants to achieve. She asks herself, "What does it look and feel like, going up in the air, over the bar, and landing on my feet?" Similarly, you can create specific images in your mind of what your center might look, feel, smell, and sound like when your vision is accomplished. The images will guide you as you master the techniques to get there.

Try asking yogi masters how they manage to keep a sense of balance while stretching their bodies into seemingly unimaginable positions. Their response will start to sound familiar. Yogis say one strategy for maintaining balance is to find a spot on the ground to focus on as you begin to position your body. They stress that this approach to physical balance helps to empty your mind of clutter so that you can find an internal place of balance. As you store a physical sense of balance in your brain's memory, it helps nourish this balance in your mental, emotional, and spiritual lives.

The lessons from all these folks have a common thread. There is a relationship between their ability to use their imagination, find a focus, and keep themselves in balance. More than maintaining a yoga stance or doing triple toe loops, they develop an internal sense of strength and an ability to stay focused and clear about where they want to be. Furthermore, their bodies teach their minds about balance. Translating these lessons to your work as an early childhood program director suggests two things: it is essential to find a focus and return to it again and again, and you need to give attention to your body as well as your mind. A program director using these notions of balance is attentive to what nourishes people, not just whether they are meeting the requirements.

Mary Catherine Bateson, author of *Composing a Life* (1989), suggests that you should explore the concept of balance by looking at a tightrope walker. Many people use the term "walking a thin line" to refer to some aspect of their work, but have you ever watched closely to study how those on a high wire do this? The tightrope walker usually carries a thin rod and continually moves this rod while walking along the high wire, changing the angle to maintain balance. This rod is equivalent to the framework you use to keep yourself balanced in your work. A conceptual framework is something you can continually hold onto as you move through your daily tasks. It helps you know what shifts and adjustments you need to make to stay on track.

Bateson also suggests you consider music composition and visual arts for insights into composing a life of balance. Musicians and artists are skilled at finding a way to fit things together—different movements, forms, and colors—into a composition that is balanced, pleasing, and nourishing to the listener or viewer. Learning how they think and approach their compositions could be useful for you as you face parallel challenges of combining disparate elements into an engaging work of art. Directing really is a creative process, a pulling together of different elements to create a tapestry. You can approach your work not as a dot-to-dot worksheet of meeting requirements, but rather as an ever-changing, ever-growing canvas on which you make bold strokes all the while paying attention to details and the creative process.

We recommend that you continue to explore insights in the worlds of the physical, spiritual, and visual arts. You are likely to always find metaphorical, if not practical, ideas that will help you shape an approach to your work. Metaphors can help you learn to shift your thinking and discover new insights. They help you access a different part of your brain. With metaphors you can find personal meaning and connections with something outside your normal frame of reference. For instance, if you begin to think of your work as a director as similar to that of a gymnast, inventor, or landscape architect, your mind begins to reorganize understandings and possibilities. Metaphors are useful in creating new emotional as well as cognitive associations. They help you redefine the familiar and make sense out of the unfamiliar. You can find new ideas for your work by exploring new words to describe what you do.

Searching for ideas in unusual places isn't just a wild idea from Deb and Margie. You find recommendations like this in established icons like *Fortune* magazine. For instance, in an interview, business consultant guru Tom Peters said, "The point is that in any business it's a matter of breaking completely out of familiar ways of thinking, of not limiting yourself to what is comfortable or comprehensible to you" (Fisher 1997). He goes on to suggest that it's critical to find places where you experience a different kind of learning, such as going dog sledding at the North Pole, rather than attending a management seminar. For early childhood educators, this suggestion might actually sound more appealing than exploring the business strategies of transnational corporations. People like to play, express their creativity, and take new field trips!

Taking Bright Ideas from the Business World

Because their world is so different from ours, perhaps it hasn't occurred to you to seek out ideas from the corporate sector of society. Certainly they have resources far beyond those of early childhood educators, and goals that are often antithetical to your values and priorities. How surprising, then, to discover the familiar concepts and language of human development in corporate literature and seminars.

As the early childhood profession has grown and changed over the past thirty years, so has the approach to corporate business management. So-called innovators in the business world continually speak of whole systems thinking, and what was once called the personnel department is now referred to as human resources. The literature for corporate managers is filled with charts illustrating various conceptual frameworks for roles, functions, human dimensions, and processes that must be considered while effectively leading an organization. Managers are encouraged to focus on systems thinking, team building, and diversity training, to be risk takers and visionaries, to think outside the box and consider the unthinkable. We were surprised to find corporate consultants who emphasize eliminating hierarchies and bureaucracy, strengthening the imaginations and autonomy of employees, and creating permanent flexibility. Much of their talk is what you would expect to find in early childhood management literature because these are the values that seem inherent in your work with children. Though the early childhood professional literature now includes a range of resources for administrators and teacher educators, few of them call for the kind of innovation you can read about in the business world.

If you browse the business management shelves of your local library or bookstore, you are likely to find books by Peter Block, Stephen R. Covey, Tom Peters, Peter Senge, and Margaret Wheatley, all highly regarded business management consultants. Consider what they have to offer us. For instance, in his book *The Empowered Manager* (1987), Peter Block stresses that all management structures and systems reflect a framework for the distribution of power. This is the foundation for an organization's culture. Block describes how managers can use their power to advance an organization to be a place where employees are pleased to be spending the best days of their lives. He presents the fundamental choices managers must make as those between maintenance and greatness, caution and courage, dependency and autonomy. Block's discussion of the kinds of mentalities that hold managers back from greatness, that have leaders slip into bureaucratic and narrow thinking systems, matches much of what we have seen in large early childhood programs. We've seen directors more focused on maintenance than greatness, cautious about stepping out and trying to reach for something currently beyond their reach, and often waiting for someone else to address the larger economic and political constraints that surround them. With the overwhelming forces marshaled to distract and drain them, early childhood directors would do well to heed Block's reminder that creating a vision of greatness is the first step toward empowerment. He hits the nail on the head when he says, "The struggle to create a vision is the struggle with hope" (1987, 124).

Expectations for early childhood programs, accompanied by required documentation, have grown faster than most directors' visions or their capacity to design systems that respond to the real lives of children, families, and employees. Taking some cues from innovators in the world of business, as well as the valuable standards in the early childhood profession's Program Administration Scale (PAS) (Talan and Bloom 2004), directors need a conceptual framework for organizing their thoughts, roles, and tasks so they can steadily build and sustain a vision for their programs. Keeping in mind the ideas about balance discussed earlier, we can conceptualize the work of early childhood directors in terms of a triangle.

The programs I see that are in trouble are ones where directors are not willing to be unpopular and make hard choices. Someone has to make hard choices. It's not fair to leave that to be resolved by the group. When you are a leader, you have to learn to live with discomfort. It's easy to lead when things are going well. What's not so easy is to make hard decisions to push forward change.

Change involves a dynamic process that people have to go through. Unless things become uncomfortable, nothing changes. If directors insulate themselves, they can become too complacent. When you are complacent, you aren't moved to see any discomfort there might be in your program, let alone get beyond it. Discomfort is fertile ground for change. Allowing yourself to be uncomfortable is where vision comes from.

—Dana

Considering a Triangle Framework

A number of years ago, while consulting with a Migrant Head Start program, we worked with our colleague Gloria Trinidad to draw on the image of a triangle as a simple framework for conceptualizing the work of program supervisors and directors. Our experiences as a child care director, bookkeeper, and Head Start education coordinator, along with our understanding about cultural diversity, group dynamics, and pedagogy for adults, led us to the idea of an equilateral triangle, with three sides equally balanced and focused on our vision of early childhood programs as learning communities for children, families, and staff. Each side of the triangle (managing and overseeing, coaching and mentoring, and building and supporting community) is integral to the whole and incorporates our values of progressive education and antibias practices, as well as the pedagogical principles of social constructivism, inquiry, and critical thinking.

The image of a triangle to represent this framework works well because we believe that each side of your management work is of equal importance. Keep in mind the notion of balance. If attention isn't given equally to all the sides of the triangle, it becomes lopsided. At that point, both director and program are in danger of collapsing. What follows is an overview of this triangle framework as it pertains to your human resources work. We conclude this chapter with an opportunity to practice applying this framework to your current work as a director. The next three chapters will explore each side of the triangle in depth, offering strategies to build and sustain the vision of early childhood programs as caring, learning communities.

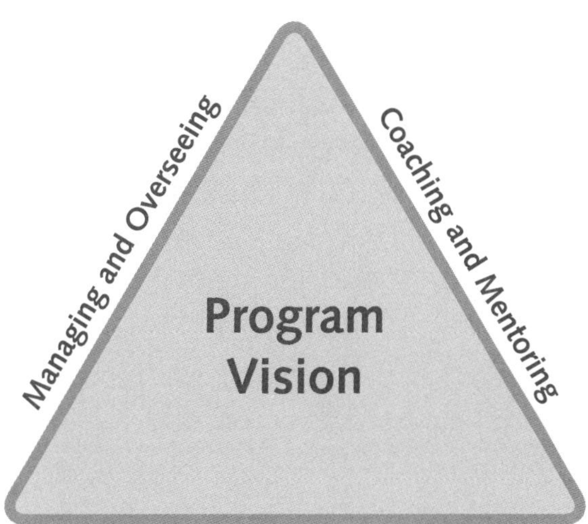

The Roles of Managing and Overseeing

All you have to do is look around your office for concrete representations of this side of the triangle. Perhaps you'll find the alphabet soup of rating scales such as PRISM, ITERS, ECERS, PAS, or QRIS, accreditation criteria and guidelines for Developmentally Appropriate Practice (DAP) from the National Association for the Education of Young Children (NAEYC), or your state's early learning standards for desired outcomes. Your particular program probably has a handbook of policies and procedures, and no doubt there are personnel files in your cabinets and on your computer. Maybe you've been working on your current staffing patterns, drafting a caregiver's performance evaluation, or processing a teacher's request for supplies from an early childhood supply catalog. The managing and overseeing side of the triangle involves many of these kinds of tasks. For staff supervision it includes things like:

- maintaining contracts and accountability systems
- clarifying professional standards and expectations
- developing a salary scale

- arranging staffing patterns and schedules
- establishing effective communication systems
- organizing training options and meetings
- conducting performance reviews and evaluations

The numerous activities related to managing and overseeing are critical to the functioning and well-being of your organization. If you do not have clear accountability standards and effective systems to guide your program, it is on very shaky ground. Any dreams you have of creating a learning community will be undermined if you aren't well organized and guiding your program with a strategic planning system and policies that reflect this vision.

As a director or supervisor, you are probably most familiar with the work on this side of the triangle. Most administrators approach their jobs through these tasks, because they are so demanding and lend themselves to a checklist. If you are mainly operating from this side of the triangle, you find yourself constantly dealing with paperwork as well as assessing, reminding, evaluating, and reporting. These are important management tasks, but in and of themselves they don't lead to a program in which the children and staff are learning and thriving. Your managing and overseeing role has limitations when it comes to applying what is known about adult learning theory and effective staff development work. Just because they've read your manual or attended some early childhood classes, caregivers and teachers don't necessarily understand how to genuinely meet children's needs. Effective staff development requires a different mind-set and a different set of behaviors than managing and doing performance reviews. The tasks of mentoring teachers to learn and grow belong on another side of the triangle. But your managing and overseeing role is about creating structures and systems to support your mentoring and professional development efforts for your staff.

The Roles of Coaching and Mentoring

Directors and supervisors often bring us complaints like these: "I've developed a really good staff handbook, and I regularly send out memos and have conversations with my staff. Still, no matter how many times I tell them, they just don't seem to get it." Or "I've spent a lot of money on a curriculum with clearly spelled-out guidelines, but I'm not seeing the promised outcomes." Comments like these come from the mistaken notion that if supervisors can just get their staff to remember all the regulations and guidelines, or if they purchase a research-based curriculum, they will have a quality program. This reflects a managing approach to teachers' learning. Not only is this approach ineffective for staff development, it reinforces ideas about teaching and learning that you would never want teachers to use with children. Most directors would be aghast to hear this sentence coming from a teacher: "If I can just get the children to recite their ABCs at circle time, then they'll learn how to read."

Here's the fundamental difference between your managing and overseeing role and your coaching and mentoring role. As a manager, your starting place is your standards and policies. As a coach, you start with the learning style of each staff member. Adult learning theory suggests that as a director you must be mindful of the family and cultural backgrounds and the life experiences that the staff bring to your program. These are as influential in their learning process as any guidebook we might offer. Adults also learn more enthusiastically and effectively if they are taught in a way that is meaningful to their needs and interests. When you work from the coaching and mentoring side of the triangle, these ideas about pedagogy, family, and culture-of-origin systems are central. You use multifaceted strategies to meet the needs of your program's staff, including:

- creating coaching methods for diverse learning styles
- offering opportunities for self-assessment and goal setting
- allowing time to practice new skills and apply new understandings
- nurturing dispositions favorable to effective teaching
- provoking new insights with questions
- inviting staff to do research
- providing a protocol or Thinking Lens (see p. 157) for reflection
- giving feedback and support for growth and change
- fostering mentoring relationships

When you cultivate your ability to work from the coaching and mentoring side of the triangle, you have more success with staff development. The roles you play here strengthen people's own power to develop, a central theme in strong and caring learning communities. You help them learn a way of thinking about the teaching and learning process.

The Roles of Building and Supporting Community

Because building and supporting community are at the core of our vision and our beliefs about what is important in early childhood programs, we put these roles at the base of our triangle framework. When staff and families identify themselves as a strong community working together on behalf of children, the program has a solid foundation. This side of the triangle is critical for all your human resources, bringing connections and liveliness with meaningful activities and interactions to everyone's time together.

Most early childhood directors operate from this side of the triangle in an intuitive way. Do you see your work of building relationships and offering support and recognition to the children, families, and staff of your program as part of your "real" work of managing human resources? You probably do nice things like periodically putting treats in the staff room, organizing secret pals for staff birthdays, and hosting occasional potlucks or special events for the families or staff. These should not be seen as extra tasks outside your regular role as a program director. Rather, we encourage you to see your community-building work as central to your role. You should regularly devote time to be intentional about the efforts needed in this area.

The building-and-supporting-community side of the triangle includes activities such as:

- designing an environment that promotes a sense of belonging
- developing a shared vision with empowering roles for staff and families
- acknowledging and respecting each individual and the contributions each brings to the group
- learning the family contexts and cultural frameworks that shape the individual lives in your program
- helping people make connections and establish bonds with one another
- creating opportunities for shared experiences that establish traditions and a sense of collective history
- linking the people in your program to the wider community around them

Building and supporting community requires more than good intentions or an annual celebration. It's important to develop processes for bringing people together and to harness your negotiation skills for the times when increased investment and collaboration inevitably lead to disagreements. This side of the triangle requires a commitment to collaboration and a persistence in working with conflict and across different cultural perspectives. Sometimes the work is difficult and goes slowly, but the fruits of your labor will sustain you through other difficult times.

Consider How Different Directors Respond

Early childhood professionals are such seasoned problem solvers that they have a tendency to want to jump in and "fix" things immediately. A quick fix may offer a temporary solution to a problem, but it usually doesn't build the deeper foundation necessary for a caring, learning community. If you don't have a framework for moving toward your vision, you probably often use knee-jerk responses to situations. This results in a hit-or-miss approach and doesn't create a sustaining organizational culture.

To explore how this might look in action, consider the different approaches to a common early childhood scenario described below. Which director's approach is similar to your instinctive response?

The Scenario

Teresa is a hard-working assistant teacher. She's a cooperative team player on the center's staff and is extremely gentle and nurturing with the children. Teresa is private about her family life, but the director knows that Teresa's husband works the graveyard shift and that she has three kids to get off to school each morning. She is often late to work, showing up anytime from ten to thirty minutes late. Teresa's tardiness is a problem for the other teachers and for the director in maintaining appropriate adult-child ratios. The director has spoken with her about this situation on several occasions, and she always promises she won't be late again.

Rhonda's Approach

Director Rhonda has just about had it with Teresa. When Teresa again arrives late to work, Rhonda stops her in the hall and tells her, "You've been hired for the morning shift. It is your responsibility to be on time! I could understand if this happened only once, but it's a regular habit with you. I know you have a lot to do at home in the morning, but you have assured me you can be here on time. Our policies are very clear about this. Your lateness jeopardizes the safety of the children and puts other staff members in a very difficult position. I'm putting you on probation. If you are late one more time, you'll be fired."

Teresa meekly continues down the hall to her room. Overhearing this confrontation, two of her coworkers comfort her: "We don't want her to fire you! You're a member of our team, and the children would be so sad. We have to get Rhonda to back off. Let's talk during naptime and figure this out."

Donovan's Approach

When director Donovan approaches Teresa about being late again, he asks, "Teresa, how can I help you overcome this habit of being late? You're a valuable member of our staff, and I don't want to lose you."

Teresa, who doesn't usually share much about her personal life, bursts out, "I just wish I had more time in the morning with my children. We always have to rush, and I get so stressed out. Today we ended up yelling at each other, which woke up my husband, and then I had to calm him down. We just never have an easy morning, and it makes me cranky and late. I just don't know what to do."

Donovan's face shows he has empathy for Teresa. "I really want to help. There are some good articles on time management and balancing work and family life in my office. I'm sure you'll find some good tips in them." Later that day he brings the articles to Teresa's room. Teresa smiles politely and accepts the articles, but thinks to herself, "I don't know how reading is going to help me find more time."

Maria's Approach

Director Maria loves Teresa. She values her ways with children and sees the quiet, calm strength Teresa brings to the dynamics of the staff. But Teresa's tardiness has been contributing to large group sizes and unacceptable adult-to-child ratios in the mornings. To address the problem, Maria has been arriving early so she can cover for Teresa if she's late. This makes Maria's day really long, but she knows Teresa has her hands full in the morning and doesn't want to put more pressure on her. She wishes Teresa would figure something out soon because the staff is starting to grumble about it and Maria's getting a bit resentful herself.

Analyzing the Three Approaches

Rhonda's response to this situation shows her emphasis on the managing-and-overseeing side of the triangle. She sees her job as creating systems to make sure the standards and regulations are followed, without regard to the impact this approach has on the climate in her workplace. Rhonda certainly has legitimate concerns about Teresa's tardiness. Required adult-to-child ratios have been developed to keep children safe and to enhance opportunities for individual attention.

Donovan, on the other hand, started on the right track by indicating to Teresa that he would like to help. He is working from the coaching-and-mentoring side of the triangle. But in the end, he didn't prove to be an effective listener. From Teresa's perspective, the issue is not about time management but about the stress in her family life and having someone to talk to who really understands. Donovan thinks he can fix Teresa's problem by giving her something to read.

Finally, Maria's efforts to fix this problem rely on her own good will and a "finger in the dike" model. She is primarily working from the building-and-supporting-community side of the triangle. She has genuine empathy for the stress in Teresa's family life, but her neglect of the other two sides of the triangle keep her from finding a balance that works for her whole program. Ultimately, Maria's approach backfires, creating a disgruntled climate among the staff and the conditions for her own burnout. Rather than supporting Teresa to take action on behalf of her needs, Maria is trying to mop up behind her.

Each of these approaches to solving the problem of Teresa's tardiness is constrained by the limits of the director's vision. These examples demonstrate that no single side of the triangle is adequate to handle the complexities of the human challenges that face directors. Only by thinking through the problem from all three perspectives can a workable solution be reached that furthers the vision of the program as a caring, learning community for all the children and adults involved. Each director has a piece of the puzzle but is missing the overall framework.

For example, Rhonda has a good handle on management and is clear about the limits to acceptable behavior in her program. She knows what the standards are and is not afraid to name them. Nevertheless, because Rhonda limits her focus to Teresa's behavior as an employee, she misses an opportunity to enhance her program. Rhonda might find it useful to think about the problem from the other sides of the triangle. If she were actively growing a vision of a caring, learning community, she could work from the building-and-supporting-community side of the triangle to try to discover a way to support a change in Teresa's behavior. Keeping the coaching-and-mentoring side in mind, she might find a way to work with Teresa that is less stressful and isolating for both of them. This in turn might lead her back to her managing and overseeing roles with the goal of designing more flexible systems for the real lives of her staff members. With such a vision, Rhonda would be modeling respect and active listening. If she turned to the staff for their ideas, she would also be creating a climate for collaboration and problem solving.

Donovan's response reveals some understanding of the coaching-and-mentoring side of the triangle. He knows Teresa needs some help and is trying to think in terms of resources. He would be more effective if he worked with Teresa to identify what kind of help would be meaningful. Together they might consider strategies to meet Teresa's family needs and enable her to be responsible on the job. An effective coach knows that people learn best when they build from their strengths. If Donovan acknowledges the importance of Teresa's family life and explores ways to reduce her stress there, he will be a more useful mentor. A vision of workplaces as caring, learning communities must recognize the needs of whole persons, even as employees are coached to let go of behaviors that undermine their work. Donovan could also work from the building-community side of the triangle to involve other staff members and perhaps parents in finding a solution to heavy enrollment at the beginning of the day. Like Rhonda, he might also find himself moving to the managing-and-overseeing side of the triangle to rethink staffing and enrollment systems.

Maria is right in valuing Teresa's contribution to her team. But she takes an intuitive approach to the building-and-supporting-community side of the triangle and seeks to avoid conflict by taking the sole responsibility to mediate the consequences of Teresa's tardiness. If Maria were approaching this side of the triangle thoughtfully instead of instinctively, she would use this as an opportunity to work with the staff to support Teresa through this stressful situation. Maria's approach, too, would be strengthened by attention to the two other sides of the triangle. Working from the managing-and-overseeing side would help her set clear limits for staff members, including Teresa and herself. Taking up the slack for Teresa without a plan to improve the situation is not a sound management technique, because of the stress it places on Maria and the other staff members. Her coaching and mentoring skills could also help her work with Teresa to build from the strengths Maria sees so clearly to address the stress in her family life.

Using the Triangle Framework

With the myriad tasks and decisions you face each day as an early childhood director, it is useful to have a framework for choosing your responses and the role to play in each situation. The triangle framework offers a balanced approach to analyze and respond to the daily demands of your work. The intent of this framework is not to lead you to the "right way" or to a "right answer." Rarely are the choices simple or clear-cut. Any number of responses may help fix a problem, but using the triangle as a framework can help you clarify your priorities and spot how a response might either undermine or grow your vision.

In formulating an approach to something like Teresa's tardiness, it is helpful to analyze the issues from all three sides of the triangle. Some questions and considerations follow that you might pose for yourself, using the particulars of your program and the staff and families involved as the context for your thinking. Once you've clarified the issues as they relate to each set of roles you have, you can determine the responses that will best serve your vision.

Building and Supporting Community

- What impact does Teresa's tardiness have on the staff, children, and families and all the working relationships?
- Are there contributions that Teresa brings to the community that offset the problem with her tardiness?

If Teresa's tardiness creates problems with ratios and tasks to be accomplished, her coworkers are likely to become disgruntled and children will show signs of stress. The issue then goes beyond an employee's tardiness and job performance. Are there any signs that families are beginning to question Teresa's reliability and viability as a caregiver? If not, working on this issue in the context of staff problem solving seems a more suitable approach.

If Teresa is a valued and well-liked caregiver, the parents and her coworkers would be upset if she were dismissed rather than given some alternative options. Because Teresa is an employee who brings many positive, tangible qualities to her work, her director might prefer to work with her rather than find a punctual employee who offers less to the children and her program. These issues must be weighed against a hard-and-fast rule about dismissing anyone who is tardy to work.

Coaching and Mentoring

- What are Teresa's views and values about balancing work and family time?
- Does she understand the impact her tardiness has on the program?
- Have we helped her understand this issue as it relates to her own needs, values, and learning style?
- What skills, knowledge, and resources might be helpful to Teresa in balancing her work and family life?

Many times, early childhood program regulations are unconsciously designed around one cultural framework. If Teresa's lifestyle, values, and cultural framework are different from those of the overall program culture, it is important to examine cultural assumptions and consider other possibilities for regulations that allow for real differences and more inclusiveness.

Asking Teresa to share her perspectives, what she values and thinks is important, is a good starting point for solving this problem. Exploring the goals she has for herself and how she goes about learning new things will help her identify what needs to be addressed, what can be compromised, and what can't. This approach focuses on Teresa's learning rather than immediate compliance. On some occasions a director can make this choice.

Managing and Overseeing

- Do the regulations and standards for quality on this issue support our program's vision?
- Does Teresa's tardiness negatively affect the quality and safety of the program for children?
- Are the expectations, policies, and job descriptions related to tardiness clearly formulated for the program as a whole and for Teresa in particular?
- Is there any flexibility built into our system of staff scheduling to respond to people's real lives?
- What resources are available to help address this problem?

If a vision of a learning community guides your thinking, your management systems and responses from this side of the triangle will keep the whole picture, not just a particular rule, in mind. If you choose to take disciplinary action toward Teresa or move quickly to fire her, the impact both on Teresa and the overall program climate could be quite negative.

Some personnel issues require immediate corrective action in order to keep children safe and parents confident in your program. This should be a thoughtful and timely decision as opposed to a knee-jerk reaction. In Teresa's case, you can examine the ratios, staff scheduling, overall morale, and communications to determine your priorities for action. Reexamine your orientation procedures for new staff members, as well as your written and oral communication systems, to make sure expectations have been clear, rather than left to general assumptions.

If you consider Teresa's contributions, her stage of development as a teacher, and her cultural framework, you may conclude she is a bigger asset than liability to your program. There may be possibilities for reassigning your human resources, schedules, or training dollars. All of these are considerations of the managing-and-overseeing side of the triangle.

Looking at issues from each side of the triangle may initially seem daunting for day-to-day situations. You will find that as you practice using the triangle framework, analyzing the issues from all three sides becomes second nature to your decision making. This kind of intentionality will strengthen your competency as a director and make it easier to grow your vision.

Practice Using the Triangle Framework

Before going on to a more in-depth consideration of each side of the triangle, practice analyzing the issues in each of the following scenarios, using the chart provided. Try formulating and answering questions related to each side as demonstrated in the previous examples. This will help you overcome the urge to respond with a quick fix for the situation. Once you've identified the possible issues related to each side of the triangle, consider responses and strategies. Pay attention to how each of your strategies may undermine or enhance the vision of a caring, learning community.

Scenario 1: New Director Dilemma

Mary Beth and Katrina have worked together in the two-year-olds' room for the past eight years, and they run a tight ship. Everything looks neat and tidy in the room, and the children are always kept busy with activities. Still, you can see some need for improvement. Charts, pictures, and toys in the room look like they have been there forever. The curriculum is organized around art projects and seasonal themes, and though the children will do these activities, they seem meaningless and not very engaging.

Recently hired as the new director, you have gotten a cool reception from Mary Beth and Katrina. They tend to ignore you and go about their business when you enter the room. You have tried making a few friendly suggestions but can't tell how they are being received. Another teacher, Doreen, has let you know that Mary Beth and Katrina have been complaining about you and are trying to get other teachers to do as they are doing and not respond much to your suggestions. Doreen herself has only worked in the program for three months. She is enthusiastic when you are in her room, and she seems eager for your suggestions on how she can improve.

Use the chart on page 67 to answer these questions:

1. *What issues are raised from each side of the triangle by this situation?*
2. *What strategies from each side might you use to address the issues?*

	Managing and Overseeing	Coaching and Mentoring	Building and Supporting Community
Issues			
Strategies			

Scenario 2: Messing with Michael

Michael works as the lead teacher in the four- and five-year-olds' classroom. He has a strong philosophy guiding his teaching style and approaches. One of the beliefs he often mentions is the importance of giving children meaningful responsibilities and decision-making opportunities in their day-to-day lives. Each of the children has his or her own large cubby located in the school entryway. This is the main walkway used by parents dropping off and picking up their children. Michael leaves the care and ownership of these cubbies and what is put in them entirely up to the children.

You often notice that the cubbies are in a complete shambles, with papers, toys, clothes, and various other items overflowing into the hallway. Michael's classroom is often in disarray as well. You've discussed this issue with Michael once before, suggesting that he spend more energy keeping these areas clean. You dropped the subject when he strongly objected and stated this was an important learning experience for the children. Michael has resisted other suggestions from you, citing his teaching philosophy as the reason. Today the cubby area is a real mess. You notice the smell of rotten food and have to step over items as you go through the walkway.

Use the chart below to answer these questions:

1. *What issues are raised from each side of the triangle by this situation?*
2. *What strategies from each side might you use to address the issues?*

	Managing and Overseeing	Coaching and Mentoring	Building and Supporting Community
Issues			
Strategies			

Practice Assessing Yourself

Reflect on the analysis you did of the two situations on pages 66–68. What side of the triangle felt more familiar to you or was easier to generate responses for? Which side seems more difficult for you to work with? After this exercise, consider any goals you want to set for yourself to cultivate a more balanced approach to directing from each side of the triangle. The following chapters are designed to help you explore how to better use each of the three components of our triangle framework. The ideas and strategies offered may help you move closer to your goals.

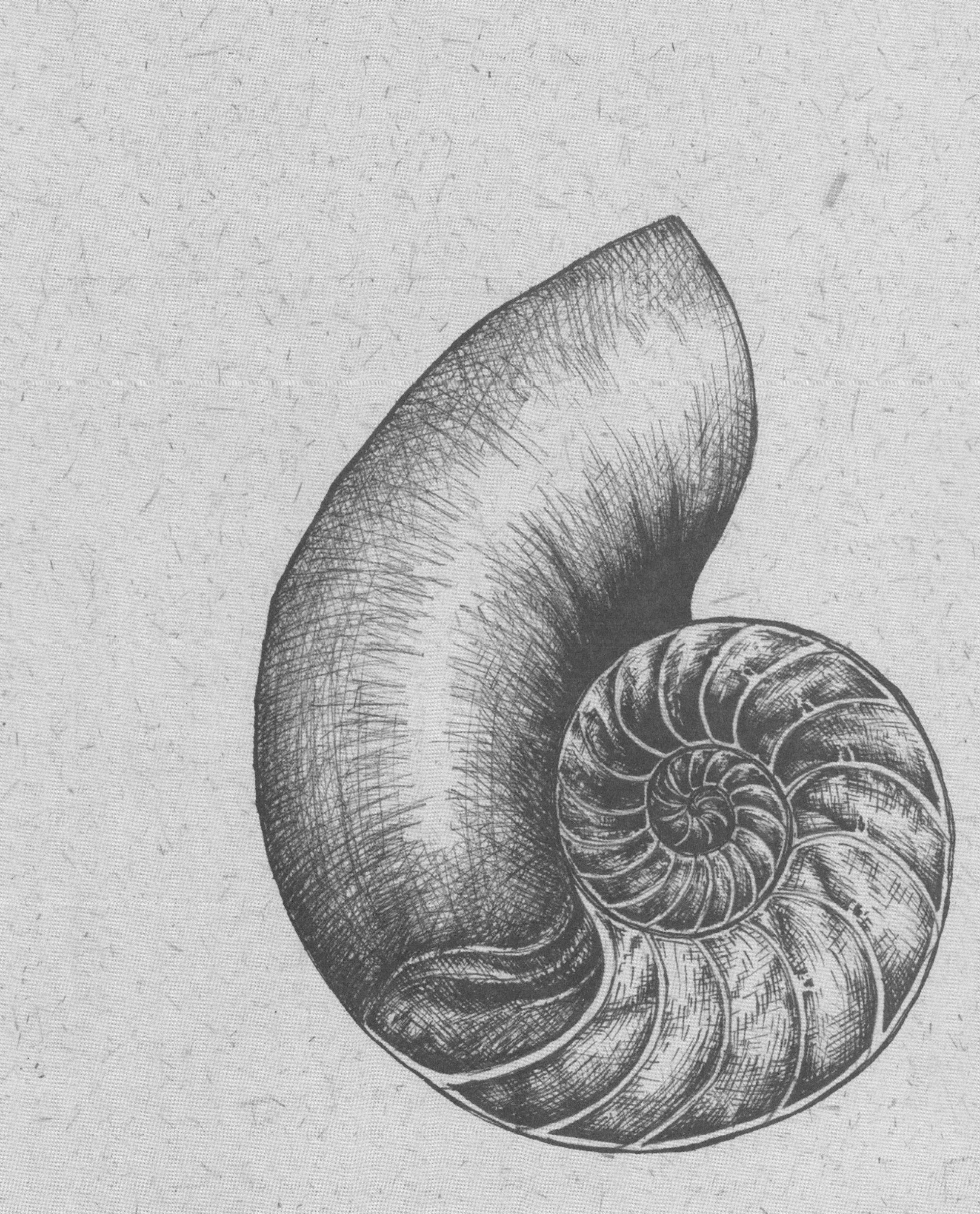

Chapter 3

Your Role in Building and Supporting Community

Kianna and her dad, Jackson, have planned to arrive early at the center today so they can have breakfast together. As they walk in the front door, an inviting smell of apple muffins greets them. "Ummm," Jackson hums softly to Kianna as he carries her to the booster seat at the table, where a few other families and staff have already gathered. "It sure smells like we're having something good for breakfast today."

It's midafternoon and director Sandria has some errands to run for the center. On her way to the bank and post office, she stops by to pick up the two preschool children whose turn it is to ride with her in the school van today. Abby and Rochelle are eagerly waiting at the door. On the way to the van, they chatter excitedly. "Do we get to help put stamps on the letters? Can we put them in the mailbox?"

After a tense day at work, Maia is delighted to find that the children and staff have lemonade and snacks waiting for families at pickup time. As she enters the gate, Maia's school-age daughter, Audrie, proudly greets her. "Hi, Mom. Come on and sit under the umbrella, and I'll bring you some snacks we made." Maia sits on the lawn chair right next to where her baby, Ronnie, is sleeping in a baby seat. Maia relaxes and smiles as she joins the other parents enjoying this special treatment.

On a sunny Saturday morning, Alexis, a staff member, and Darcy, a center parent, are weeding together in the child care center's pea-patch garden. As they work, they can easily watch their children playing nearby. Developed by staff and families who didn't have their own space or who wanted to work with others, this is an impressive garden of vegetables and flowers. A small section is designated as the children's garden, while the rest is tended by center staff and families.

As you read over these scenes, what was your first response? Are there elements described that sound similar to your program? Did you think to yourself, "That sounds so wonderful, I want to try that!" Perhaps you found yourself immediately reviewing all the reasons why this couldn't be done in your program.

It's true, few early childhood programs have typical scenes like these. Most attempts to define professional standards and risk-management practices have all but eliminated the home or neighborhood feel to child care. Instead, the atmosphere in early childhood programs feels more institutionalized, either cluttered and dreary or brightly colored rooms where play is orderly and controlled and lessons are taught. Your reaction to the scenes described above probably reveals the vision or mind-set you bring to your work. When you think of a desirable early childhood program, is it an institutional model like school, or does it include elements of childhood, family gatherings, and life in a neighborhood?

The scenarios above are glimpses of real programs whose directors and supervisors are breaking away from the institutional model that has become the norm in the early childhood profession. These snapshots reflect programs that not only are designed for children, but also are places for families and provide an experience of community. The emphasis in these programs is on strengthening the bonds between children and their families and creating positive connections with other children and adults. The directors at the helm realize that when adults and children are removed from each other's daily life and work, neither develop or live as fully as they could. The approach these directors take reflects their understanding that children today are spending the majority of their childhoods away from their homes and neighborhoods. They are trying to respond to the lack of support families with young children receive in the larger popular culture of this country. These directors have a vision that goes beyond how things are. They want children in their programs to experience growing up in families with an extended kinship network and a revived sense of neighborhood and community.

Bringing a vision like this to life requires a shift in how you think about your program, the role you play as a director, and the way you spend the bulk of your time. This vision suggests that you consider all who cross paths in your program as a part of your community. When you are planning and carrying out various aspects of your job, all these players are included in your thinking. You are consciously helping each individual feel included and recognized. Your program culture intentionally shapes shared experiences that cultivate a sense of belonging and evolving history together.

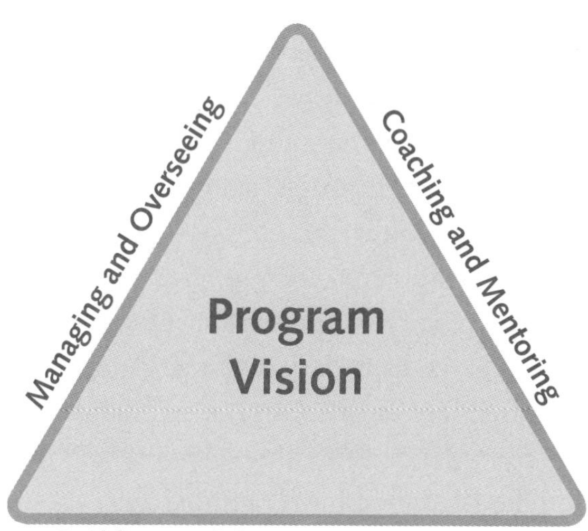

If you use our triangle framework for thinking about your directing job, the tasks of building and supporting community form the base of your work. This requires more than an incidental or "get to it when I can" approach. You need strategies specifically designed to nurture the experience of community in your program. And you need methods to cultivate the skills required for collaborating, working with conflict, and handling differences such as culture, family structure, and communication styles.

You can think about doing this community-building work in ways that parallel how you think about planning for children. You give attention to organizing and maintaining the physical space (indoor and outdoor learning environment), you plan for engaging activities and skill development (curriculum), and you continually foster connections and the building of relationships (social, emotional, and identity development). What follows is a discussion of each of these areas with examples of strategies to help you carry out your role of building and supporting community.

CREATING AN ENVIRONMENT THAT NURTURES COMMUNITY

Americans live in a highly mobile culture; most people live far from their place of birth and extended family. They conduct their daily lives in cars, on the Internet, at jobs, or in schools away from home or a neighborhood. The environments in schools and workplaces often contribute to a sense of isolation, if not alienation. These places seldom offer any meaningful context for people to be fully human, to learn from or contribute to each other's lives. People usually feel more stressed than nurtured when they leave.

Early childhood programs can either contribute to or counter the effects of living in a culture that gives only lip service to family life and community. As you walk in the door, the organization and aesthetics of the environment communicate a program's culture. Is this a place where there are rules posted on the walls, along with commercial alphabet charts, calendars, and curriculum materials? Or are there things children have created on the walls and around the room, along with other materials inviting curiosity and investigation? Are there bulletin boards and cubbies crammed with papers you want to avoid, or do you see pictures and words that pique your interest? Do you find yourself ignored and uncomfortable or welcomed with a comfy place to sit and people eager to greet you? If you spent your childhood or adult days in this place, would it leave you cranky or satisfied, dreading or eager to come back?

The typical early childhood program is situated in a less than ideal space with more limitations than most directors know what to do with. In an inspiring article titled "Out of the Basement: Discovering the Value of Child Care Facilities," Carl Sussman describes the situation this way: "Years of budget balancing and the widespread acceptance of inadequate facilities [have] desensitized providers to their environment and created chronically low expectations" (1998, 15). This problem has been compounded as states create standards for school readiness, requiring more accountability from programs and often without the necessary resources to support the expectations. The standards movement has resulted in the growth of commercial products and furnishings that focus more on safety and school readiness, with little attention to aesthetics or imagination. Usually there are child-sized tables and chairs, primary colors, an abundance of plastic materials, commercial toys, and bulletin board displays. You have to search to find soft or natural elements, places where adults as well as children can feel cozy, alone or with a friend. The smell of disinfectant often floats in the air. Have people forgotten how a cluttered or tattered environment quickly seeps into their psyches? Do they know how a sterile and antiseptic climate shapes their souls? Most early childhood programs look alike, although there are growing exceptions in programs that have been inspired by the beautiful environments of the schools of Reggio Emilia.

Caregivers, teachers, and children are spending the bulk of their waking hours—living their lives together—in your program. The way you organize the space, create traffic and communication patterns, furnish, and decorate affect the experience people have in your building. To guide your thinking about a physical environment that connects and nurtures people, consider the elements of a comfortable home and a vibrant neighborhood.

Principle

Make the Center Feel Like a Home

In the early years of professionalizing child care services, a homelike atmosphere was often the emphasis. As early childhood education has grown to incorporate concepts of giving children a head start on school readiness, even family child care homes have been encouraged to look more like preschools. It is our belief that reversing this trend will provide a stronger foundation for children. Getting children ready for school is best done in the context of their full lives and developmental needs. The elements of a good home and community environment create the best conditions for their learning and thriving.

Strategy *Incorporate elements from home-design magazines*

You can create an inviting atmosphere in your program by thinking about what you are most drawn to in magazines that feature pictures of home designs. You could adapt ideas like these:

- Make spaces for children and adults that include more soothing and interesting hues than just the standard primary colors.
- Add a variety of textures and natural elements throughout the environment—plants, rocks, shells, baskets, fabric, sculptures, and other art objects to look at and touch.
- Create cozy lighting by using dimmer switches, floor and table lamps, mirrors, and other materials that catch, reflect, and disperse light and create interesting shadows to explore.
- Frame and display children's art attractively on walls, along with work from well-known artists.
- Find inviting ways to include photographs of families, children, and staff on tables, shelves, and walls. Change these in a timely manner.
- Engage everyone's senses with inviting aromas at the beginning and end of the day—dough baking, cinnamon- and clove-spiced cider simmering, peppermint leaves in the sensory table, extracts in the playdough.

Strategy *Explore professional architecture and design resources*

The professional resources you can turn to have been growing over the last thirty years. Adding to the earlier European influence of Maria Montessori and Rudolf Steiner, in the 1970s Elizabeth Jones and Elizabeth Prescott began writing for early childhood educators in the United States about "environments as regulators of our experience." By the 1980s and 1990s, Jim Greenman (1992), Gary Moore (1997), Anita Rui Olds (1999), and the educators of Reggio Emilia were adding to this body of literature, bringing us further insights from artists, poets, architects, researchers, and landscapers. In 2003 we wrote the book *Designs for Living and Learning* along with companion CDs offering study guides to early childhood environments, and in 2008, Rusty Keeler inspired attention to nourishing environments outdoors in his book *Natural Playscapes*. If you're not familiar with these works, full citations can be found at the end of this book (see References). It is resources such as these, rather than commercial catalogs, that should be shaping your thinking about the design of physical space and the materials you purchase. They remind you of the elements that support human interactions, invite curiosity, and sustain attention for problem solving and learning.

How does your program environment affect the people who spend their time there? Keeping this question as a focus, take a minute now to review your environment—in your mind or on your feet—with pen and paper in hand. Ask yourself questions such as:

- Is there adult-sized, comfortable furniture tucked in spaces here and there, where a staff or family member can spend a cozy moment with a child, or a child can curl up alone and be reminded of those cozy moments with an adult?
- Are there floor seats with back support so that adults can spend extended time at the children's eye level?
- Do you have a room away from the children with a couch and adult-sized tables and chairs where staff can relax, work, eat, and meet?
- Are families and staff members encouraged to add artifacts, photos, and things they treasure to the classroom, the staff lounge, and other gathering spaces so that the children, parents, and coworkers see each other as people with real lives, skills, and interests to share?
- Does your outdoor environment include gathering areas for children and adults?

Principle

Give the Program the Feel of a Real Neighborhood

Too many early childhood programs in the United States are organized like schools for older children—isolated classrooms where the same group of children, usually of the same age, spends the entire day playing, eating, and sleeping together. The doors stay closed to keep children in and others out. Often there are no windows to look out of, and time outdoors is limited by a schedule. Most other spaces in the center, such as the kitchen or office, are off-limits to children. Children rarely spend time with others of different ages, including their siblings, older or younger children, and adults in the program. Parents usually leave children at the classroom door, and there is limited time or encouragement to stay awhile to play with children or talk with other adults.

Is this your view of a real neighborhood? If you have managed to free your program from some of these dehumanizing constraints, take heart. You are already on the road to change. You have recognized that the isolation and disconnection that have come with urbanization, fast food, commuting, and technology shouldn't be replicated in your program. Instead you should be organizing time and space to build and enhance people's connections with each other. We have included some models to consider. Perhaps there are elements you can adapt further, even if your space is limited.

Strategy Use homebase rooms and make time for children to roam

Jim Greenman, Anne Stonehouse, and Gigi Schweikert (2008) promote the idea of homebases rather than classrooms for child care programs. Children have a homebase and primary caregiver or teacher, but doors are often open and hallways are designed like blocks in a neighborhood to be roamed and explored from time to time. Some of the centers Greenman has been involved in designing have the equivalent of indoor parks with play equipment, benches, large potted trees, and space for children and adults from around the center to come together to talk and play. Children often visit the kitchen, which is designed to accommodate their observations and conversations with the cook.

Strategy Set up larger programs as villages

Architect Gary Moore has written in *Child Care Information Exchange* about designing early childhood programs with a neighborhood concept (1997). He proposes interconnected houses or dwelling areas designed for smaller groups of children, all surrounding a common core of shared facilities. This design offers opportunities for interactions throughout the day with other people and spaces in the building. Moore reports that large child care programs built as villages or campuses offset the difficulties of maintaining a homelike sense of scale. When a center is conceived as a series of interconnected homes, staff are able to individualize their systems and schedules in smaller groups rather than following one large institutional model.

Strategy Design space to resemble a neighborhood

With the initial leadership of Karen Haigh, the Chicago Commons child development program worked to remodel one of their old school buildings by adding corridors that look like play streets, with classroom doors and windows opening out onto them. The corridor begins at the entrance to the building, where they have designed an indoor parklike play area with beautiful wooden climbing equipment and benches for adults to sit and watch the children play. The staff are thrilled that their goal of inviting families to come together and stay awhile is happening in this new approach to a neighborhood.

Strategy Use natural shapes and soft lighting

Anita Rui Olds, a developmental and environmental psychologist, pioneered the innovative design of environmental facilities for children. In her workshops and consulting with both architectural and child care businesses, Olds stresses the importance of creating spaces where people can heal, work, play, and grow. Her innovations include softening rooms by creating more organic shapes and lighting to be responsive to human's sensory needs, and moving human bodies to fulfill our need to gather, be comforted, rest, and explore. Olds reminds readers that innovations do not have to be expensive or splashy. By using elements of the natural world and adding things such as mirrors, ramps, and lofts to create different levels and perspectives on space, a building can be transformed both in its ambiance and its function.

Strategy Use the beginning and end of the day

The self-initiated efforts of smaller programs with fewer resources can inspire us as well. The opening scenes described in this chapter highlight a few. Remember Kianna and her dad eating breakfast together in the story at the beginning of the chapter? Her center has created a family-style kitchen and dining area with a designated morning time for families and staff to eat together. They also offer parents the opportunity to come for lunch or have a snack with their children. Wonderful aromas are an added benefit to this idea. Those who come to eat pay an extra fee to cover costs, but for busy working parents it's worth it. This is an opportunity to slow down and spend some quality time with their children and center "neighbors." When you revisit the opening stories, you'll find that Audrie's school-age program created a similar feeling with their end-of-the-day lemonade picnic.

The seeds for a sense of community are often found in the early and latter part of a day, when children are combined into one group as numbers dwindle. We know of a program that shifted this idea to include "open door time" for the first and last two hours the center is open. During these hours the reduced staffing pattern is spread between several classrooms and the hallway so that children can move throughout the small building. This "roam the neighborhood" model allows children, families, and staff to interact across age groups and become more familiar with what is happening in other rooms.

Principle

Involve Parents and Staff in Considering the Space

As you consider the physical space available in your program, try thinking in terms of creating community, not just maintaining ratios. Perhaps you don't have the luxury of removing all the barriers to creating your ideal building, but you can knock down walls in your mind and begin to think differently about how time and space are used in your program. Here are some strategies to try in staff or parent meetings.

Strategy *Assess how a space makes you feel*

To broaden your ideas about early childhood environments and begin thinking about a model other than school, gather a group of magazine or calendar pictures that include a range of environments, such as bank lobbies, high-tech office buildings, seascapes, forests, mountain ranges, health spas, cozy fireplace gatherings, temples, churches, sacred rock structures, Disneyland sites, toy stores, early childhood classrooms, playgrounds, and school catalog scenes. As these pictures get passed around, pose the following questions for discussion in small groups:

- How do each of these environments make you feel?
- What elements in this environment influence your feelings?
- How might you behave in this place?
- If you spent lots of time in this environment, how might it affect you?

Come together after this initial discussion and make a list of the elements that were identified. Place them in two columns, one labeled with a plus for positive elements, the other with a minus for negative elements. Most groups who do this end up with a list of positive elements that bear little resemblance to a school. Here are some examples of positive elements other groups have identified using this process:

- organization—a sense of order that makes it easy to get work done
- aesthetics—beauty, an invitation for curiosity and discovery
- softness—cozy places for the eyes and body to rest
- lighting and color—natural light and soft lamps in a range of shades, tones, and intriguing shadows
- things from the natural world—different textures, water, sand, rocks, plants
- flexibility—allowing for intimacy or expansiveness
- belonging—reflecting the lives of people there

Whatever elements you list, the next step is to use them as an assessment tool. Invite the participants to move around your building with these elements in mind. When you regroup, consider the following questions:

- What examples of these elements did you find?
- Did you come across anything from our negative list?
- What changes should we think about making?

This strategy provides a concrete way for staff and parents to see ways you can begin to transform your program. As you begin to create an environment that is less school-like and more cozy and beautiful, children, staff, and families feel immediate benefits. They want to linger, investigate, and enjoy each other's company and the work at hand.

Most programs wait until they have money before they work on clarifying their vision. I've learned how important it is to write down our vision and continually refine our goals and action plans. I don't want to settle for small results. We are going for more than what seems possible at any given moment. For instance, we have developed extensive environmental plans for each site. We have done this partly by having biweekly planning meetings with our site directors, coordinators, and an architect. When our state announced that it was accepting proposals for quality enhancement dollars, we didn't have to scramble to write a proposal that probably wouldn't reflect our real needs. We already had a thoughtful, well-researched plan to submit.

—Karen

Strategy *Explore the environment as a child might*

During a staff, parent, or board meeting, use this activity to explore your environment with a focus on childhood, neighborhood, and community. It will alert you to what your environment now offers as well as provide a way for the adults who participate to play together as a community.

Have people work in pairs or small groups. Give them the assignment to go on a scavenger hunt and bring back an example, representation, or story of each item on the lists below.

Find contrasting elements:

- something heavy/light
- something smooth/rough
- something dark/bright
- something natural/manufactured
- something huge/tiny
- something scary/comforting

Find four kinds of:

- holes
- sounds
- things that move

- smells
- places that challenge your body
- symbols or writing
- dangers

Find places for pretending:

- you are powerful
- you are small as an insect
- you are at home
- you are on TV
- you are a detective
- you are an artist
- you are a scientist

Find in the natural world:

- a new texture to explore
- an intriguing shadow
- something the wind does
- animal tracks
- something alive
- something dead

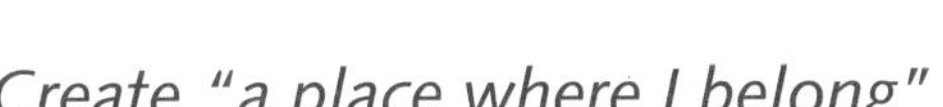 *Create "a place where I belong"*

You can also do a scavenger hunt to consider how your environment currently fosters or defeats a sense of belonging. Send small groups around the building to find something that represents each of the following:

- something that reflects what you like or are interested in
- something that tells who spends time in this place and what they do here
- something that sparks a favorite childhood memory
- something you don't understand

- something that makes you feel respected
- something that insults your intelligence
- something you would take to a desert island
- something that has at least three uses other than the obvious

The ideas, representations, and objects that get brought to the group discussion from both of these scavenger hunts will help you get to know each other better and provide a new look at your work and learning environments. End each activity by brainstorming a list of changes you'd like to bring about in your environments.

At one point we were starting to see a discrepancy in the quality of the environments in our classrooms. Rather than just pass this off to differences, we developed Saturday work parties where each room took turns getting ideas and help from the rest of the staff. The teachers in a room would explain what was working well and where they needed help. Other staff members would then choose different tasks to pitch in and help. Some cleaned, painted, sewed, or built things, while others shopped for needed items or brought lunch for everyone. This plan not only improved the look of our rooms but also our morale and sense of teamwork.

—Wendy

Strategy *Create the skeleton of a grant proposal or the inspiration for a work party*

Use a brainstorming process to ignite dreams that you can use as the basis for creating change in your environment through a work party or a grant proposal. Have handy some catalogs from garden and plant nurseries, architecture and home-design firms, and art and display suppliers to serve as resources in envisioning equipment that might be used in a home or neighborhood. Building on the elements described in the previous strategies or other discussions, ask key questions like the following to get creative juices flowing:

- If we were to knock out two walls, which should they be?
- If someone were to donate six large plants and three love seats or park benches, where would we put them?
- Where could we add some special lighting effects, with dimmer switches, lamps, ceiling spots, or wall sconces, in order to create some new atmosphere in our building?
- What are five things from the natural world that would enhance our program?
- Where would you put three new windows and four new mirrors?
- If we were to build a loft, a cave, and a corner café, where would we put them?
- What's something from your home or community you'd like to see included in our program?

If people are stuck in "yes, but" thinking, you may need to coax them along in generating a wish list. These questions are intended to help people think the unthinkable, to break out of the confines of the way they think about what's possible. It's important that all ideas in an initial brainstorm be considered of value so that the people involved don't censor their ideas before even raising them. You can create this feeling by including each one on your list. Then, as a group, conclude by doing some prioritizing and sequencing of the ideas on the list. Finally, take this list, get some cost estimates, and develop a grant proposal or plan for a work party to begin making some of these dreams come true.

People easily let their thinking get confined by the limitations of the space they are in. With each of the programs I have directed, I started by reconfiguring the physical space to create a sense of possibility that we could be something different. It's a way of raising the issue of working with a vision. I look for how to create a more open feeling, how to create special feelings with lighting and interesting visual elements. There are all these walls around how people think in this work. My motto is, "If it's not load bearing, tear it down." When the physical walls come down, it opens up the imagination, as well as communications.

—Jan

PLANNING YOUR COMMUNITY-BUILDING CURRICULUM

As an administrator, take a minute to consider the various activities you plan and oversee in your program. You'll probably list things such as staff meetings, where you review schedules and discuss policies, curriculum, and current problems. No doubt you plan parent meetings that you coax families to attend. If you lead a nonprofit program, there are board-meeting agendas to prepare and probably fund-raising events. With the exception of the latter, directors typically plan activities that reinforce a traditional school model, focusing on the tasks to be accomplished rather than the relationships to be built. Occasional events are for socializing, but these are usually seen as something outside the "real" work of managing a program.

Principle

Use Time Together to Strengthen Relationships

When you view your program as merely caring for children while their parents work, social events are seen as extracurricular activities. But if a primary emphasis of your work is building community, your focus will be on strengthening the relationships among staff members and between children, their families, and the staff. Consider the policies you develop and activities you plan as a form of curriculum that strengthens the social-emotional development of the adults as well as the children. Sometimes this requires special events, but mostly it's a matter of rethinking the ordinary events of the day. Here are some examples to adapt as strategies for your own program.

We are fortunate to have staff meetings every week in our program, short as they are. For a while we didn't realize how our time in these meetings could be better used for staff and community development. After we surveyed the teachers, we came up with a much more meaningful use of our time. Now only the first week of the month is devoted to center business. The second and third meetings are staff choices, where people do a variety of things, from requesting workshops to working on improving some aspect of our mission within their team. The last week of the month our staff comes together to work on creating documentation displays. We help each other with the writing and visual layout and simultaneously feel more connected to what's happening in our different rooms.

—Wendy

Strategy View staff meetings as circle time

Typical staff meetings in early childhood programs involve the director coming with a list of tasks, policies, and important dates to remember that she or he goes over with the staff. Rather than using the precious time you carve out for meetings on managing and overseeing tasks that can be handled in a memo, you can use this time for the important work of building community.

It may help if you think about your staff meetings the way a good teacher thinks about circle time with children. You know that good circle time with children builds a sense of belonging and a shared early childhood culture. Why not see your staff meetings as having the same goal? Good teachers also plan activities throughout the day that create a sense of respect and community. They invite individual children to talk about themselves and make choices, and they encourage groups of children to share their ideas and work together on projects. Rather than filling staff meeting time with announcements, scheduling details, and the authoritative voice of the director, can't directors use this time for genuine sharing, reflection, and collaboration? This might involve changing the idea of who's in charge, finding other means to take care of business, or creating an atmosphere that is physically comfortable, emotionally safe, and full of active listening.

Circle time is most effective when there is a welcoming leader, some thoughtful planning, and an opportunity for everyone to be acknowledged. Music and playful moments counterbalance serious stories. If your staff meetings have a different cultural feel, it will translate into a parallel experience for the children and their families.

My white-guy vision for an organizational culture that honors all people was deeply provoked when, in the early months of my work with Tribal Head Start, I was asked to attend a staffing, a pre-IEP meeting, for a young four-year-old Native boy. We were invited to stand while a drummer/spiritual leader opened with a blessing. "I want to thank you all for coming here today to this tribal center in support of one of our children. As you talk today, remember that this is a very important and special child to have brought all these important people from their jobs to gather in this place to talk to his family about him. He is honored that you have come together for him. I know that you will respect his culture, his family, and his person." He began a drumming chant, explaining that he was asking the spirits to bless our deliberations. We were then offered a feast, and the family—the grandfather, grandmother, aunt, father, and mother—were asked to serve themselves first, because we were there to help meet their needs. Then the professionals could serve themselves. We talked over lunch and developed a plan that all five family members and the agency people signed off on. There was a respectful and exceptionally considerate tone to all the conversation. Then we were invited to share our best stories about this child. The meeting ended with the grandfather thanking everyone for their support and an appreciation for the stories.

Imagine if every meeting that was set up by "professionals" to make plans for a child started with a reminder that this child is honored. We come together for his or her sake, and this child must be very important to have brought all of us together.

—Michael

Strategy *Learn about listening*

To build a community and work with the differences that exist in any group, you need to develop good listening habits. Introduce the following framework and activities to promote listening between staff, parents, and children. Begin by introducing the concept of three different kinds of listening:

1. Autobiographical Listening—You only hear things that relate to your own experience or perspective.
2. Merry-Go-Round Listening—You are waiting or biding your time until it's your turn to speak.
3. Deep Listening—You are genuinely trying to understand and learn something new.

Whether in a one-to-one exchange or during staff meetings, the practice of deep listening goes a long way toward enhancing the self-esteem both of the speaker and the listener. Develop this skill by devoting a few minutes of each meeting time to any of the following:

- Role-play the different kinds of listening, and discuss how each feels.

- Share a story in pairs, and examine the kinds of listening that occur.
- Point out the kinds of listening at work during a group discussion.

Strategy *Set ground rules, share feelings, and develop facilitation skills*

As a group, develop ground rules for behavior, communication, and decision making. Take time to draw in all the ideas and voices about this. Post these agreements, and review them regularly in the early months of this effort.

Devote some training to group facilitation skills so that responsibility for staff meetings can be rotated, allowing for individual style differences in facilitation. Post future meeting agendas with space to add ideas for discussions and who will plan them. Include some specific activities for getting to know each other and for building a group culture at every meeting.

> In our team meetings I have three goals for staff development. I want to create a climate where people become confident and excited about learning. I want to help them become more reflective in their work, to set goals and be able to explain why. Finally, I want them to share their thinking and hear other perspectives. In addition to our own viewpoints, we have begun to make sure we think in terms of three perspectives at each of our meetings: the child's, the teacher's, and the parent's. Sometimes the administrative perspective is needed as well.
>
> **—Karen**

Strategy *Use a fuss box*

It's also important to take time to acknowledge disappointments—things that are upsetting or make people sad. Periodically try using what Jean Illsley Clarke and Connie Dawson (1998) call a "fuss box."

Put a cardboard box, large enough for an adult to step into, in front of the group. Establish a few ground rules, and then invite anyone to step into the box for a bit of fussing. Ground rules should include a willingness to physically dramatize one's feelings as "fussing," an agreement to use "I" messages rather than blaming language, and a commitment to confidentiality and creative problem solving once the fussing is over.

Strategy Make tear-water tea

Owl at Home, a children's book by Arnold Lobel (1975), includes a short story titled "Tear-Water Tea" that provides another strategy for dealing with disappointments. Owl periodically takes a kettle out of the cupboard and sits with it, thinking of things that make him sad. As he calls them out, for instance, "Books that cannot be read because some of the pages have been torn out" and "Spoons that have fallen behind the stove and are never seen again," large tears begin dropping into the tea kettle until it is full. He boils it for tea and happily begins drinking, saying, "It tastes a little bit salty, but tear-water tea is always very good." You can read or tell the story, then pass around a tea kettle, asking people to acknowledge with an equally dramatic flare things that are upsetting them. Use the ritual of symbolically boiling people's disappointments to turn them into something good.

Strategy Become storytellers

To build a group culture and sense of community, the group needs to know who they are and why they are here and to begin to discover who they can be together. Devoting at least fifteen minutes of every staff meeting to self-discovery lays the foundation for this building process. Share childhood memories on various topics. Ask staff members to "tell a funny story about your family," "tell the story of how you got your name," or "talk about a time you were naughty." You also might use questions such as: Did you have a favorite toy, book, or song? How did your family treat a common cold? What celebrations were important to you?

A great resource for specific strategies on drawing out people's stories and using them for community building is *Telling Your Own Stories* by Donald Davis (1993). Personal stories help people get a fuller picture of each other. Bringing in actual photos or objects from childhood makes it all the more vivid. As people hear more about each other's lives, they discover how they are alike and different, weaving threads that tie them together in collective memories.

These stories may not always be pleasant, and that should be acknowledged as well. Suggest to staff that they choose a memory that will enhance their learning and not stir up emotional blocks. Remind them to keep their ears and hearts open to their colleagues, while being sensitive to confidentiality when it is needed. Shared stories and pictures are a vital part of any culture or community.

Strategy *Create visual stories of your life together*

In our book *Spreading the News: Sharing the Stories of Early Childhood Education* (Carter and Curtis 1996), we offer detailed instructions with examples of how to observe children and create a visual story display that reveals your understanding. This process is also a powerful tool for staff development as well as for learning to communicate effectively with parents.

You can put these stories into book form. Photographs of curriculum projects along with annotated descriptions from teachers can become handmade books that, when added to the reading corner, provide hours of continued revisiting and storytelling. Likewise, you can capture stories of the evolving development and thinking of individual children with handmade picture storybooks, and provide families with the impetus to create these at home for a wonderful back-and-forth storytelling exchange.

Amidst intense feelings about how we were going to handle holidays in our program, I introduced an idea I came across at a NAEYC antibias session. Each family and staff member at the center was given a piece of mat board to create a small display about how they celebrated the winter holidays. As we began to hang these in our vestibule, this became a new gathering place where parents lingered and learned more about each other and our staff. It was definitely a community-building experience that became an annual practice.

—Julie

Strategy Refocus parent newsletters

Many programs produce printed or electronic newsletters, blogs, or Web postings for staff communication with families. Typically these require teachers to write news about their curriculum and classroom events. For a teacher, this can be about as meaningful as preprinted worksheets, and parents respond with about as much enthusiasm as to a coloring-book page. Everyone is inundated with far too much to read. Unless it's real and meaningful to their lives, why go through the motions? Let's not waste this opportunity to have the teachers put forward their identities—who they really are and what matters to them.

Try having the staff write about things like:

- a favorite childhood memory that relates to their current work with children
- a person they look to for inspiration or leadership
- a book or author who has influenced how they see and work with children
- something metaphoric like a fable, poem, or song to describe how they experience their time with the children or respond to a particular event

Principle

Grow Community-Building Curriculum from the Lives Around You

If you work with a vision of creating a caring, learning community for your program, you see your role as director in some different ways. Just as the staff plans curriculum for the children, a good part of your work is planning "a curriculum"—systems, interactions, and activities that build relationships among all involved in your center. This takes time and specific strategies to ensure it occurs. You can draw upon the principles of good curriculum for kids:

- View curriculum as everything that happens.
- Arrange the environment and systems to bring people together around shared interests, curiosities, and reflections.

- Plan activities and responses from observing and listening.
- Facilitate interactions, mediate conflicts, and scaffold learning.

Here are some strategies, including examples of directors using these ideas to build community in their programs.

Strategy Rethink daily routines

Mull over a scene like this, and imagine it happening in your program.

Kali got to bed late last night, and her dad, Doug, wants her to sleep in as late as possible this morning. He packs her clothes for the day, and right before it's time to leave home, he gently wakes Kali, wraps her in a blanket, and puts her in her car seat. On the way to the center, he sings softly to her in the car. When they arrive, Kali's dad walks with her as she toddles through the hallway still in her PJs. He smiles at Kali's caregivers, grateful that later, during the dressing time, they will help her and the other children who arrived in PJs get dressed for the day.

The transitions and routines of your daily life with children are often the most stressful times for many people. Helping children separate and reconnect with their families is a critical aspect of your work. Too often programs view separation anxiety as a problem that children and parents must resolve on their own. Instead of viewing these times as something to endure, why not thoughtfully plan for them? Rituals and activities around pickup and drop-off times should be part of curriculum planning. Trying some of the following activities might encourage everyone at the center to slow down and use transition times as opportunities for connections and community.

- Include families in shared snacks or meals.
- Create consistent rituals for the beginning and ending of the day that families can participate in, such as singing, dancing, or playing music to signal these times.
- Design a cozy corner for families to read or cuddle together to ease the transition.
- Provide a dressing area for parents to help children who come early to change out of their pajamas and get clothes on or hair brushed.

This approach implies that the adults see themselves as partners in caring and educating children. It supports parents in talking with staff about their children, and encourages staff to be respectful of family values and routines. As these relationships grow, it will be easier both for family members and for staff to discuss any issues of concern with each other. From this kind of weekly communication a more meaningful curriculum can be developed for the children as well.

Strategy Grow curriculum from family life

Could you imagine this scene happening in your program?

Emily's mom is pregnant with a new brother or sister. It's a big event for Emily and her family. The children and staff are interested, too, as every day Emily talks about how big her mom's belly is growing. At circle time she reports on changes happening at her house to get ready for the new baby. Peter, the director of Emily's child care program, asks her mom to help create a display with photos of pregnant mothers, including one of her carrying Emily. The display soon grows with other center moms adding their pregnancy pictures. Emily's mom agrees to let the children trace an outline of her body on a large piece of paper. Each month they use string to measure around her belly to see how much it is growing. They label and hang the string next to the silhouette of Emily's mom. Soon families are found around the displays at the end of the day, sharing stories about births and how they handled the arrival of a new sibling. Excitement continues to grow as does this real-life curriculum.

As a program director, consider it part of your job to help teachers plan curriculum out of the children's family life. When real events and experiences in the lives of your families are the source of your activities, you never run out of curriculum ideas. Not only do you build meaningful curriculum, but a sense of community grows in the process.

Families, of course, do not always have happy events in their lives. It is just as important to acknowledge difficult ones. Sharing hard experiences is often not easy, but it can be the source of deeper connections and more meaningful relationships.

I really discovered how our center has become a community through a tragic event. A father at the center died suddenly, and what happened next still affects me. The morning we received the information, I was in the car and got the call on my cell phone. One of the staff asked another to call me because she was afraid she would be unable to tell me he had died. The first words out of my mouth when I heard were "Tell me you're lying!" She said, "No, I'm not. We just got the call, and we're concerned about how to give the information to the teachers and to others."

When I hung up the phone, I knew I had to deal with my own emotions quickly so I could be strong for the others. An hour after I arrived at the center, the mother called and said the two children had asked to come to school and what should she do. I assured her the teachers had the information and wanted to support the children. They would certainly welcome them that day. I also told her to let me know if there was anything she needed. After she dropped the children off, the mother came and told me the entire story. Through hugs and tears I comforted her as best I could. To take care of myself throughout the day I would close the doors of my office and allow myself to cry.

That weekend I went to the funeral home with some of the staff. Much to our surprise, there were many families from our center, both alumni and current children, parents, and staff. One parent came up to me and said, "I didn't realize until today that we really are one big family at the center." She then told me that her son said that the children who lost their father didn't have to worry because everybody at day care would take care of them. A food tree was set up for three months for the family, and the oldest son's class cooked dinner once a week. Other parents offered to take the children home with them so their mother could have time for herself. This support still continues for this family, even though it's been a year.

—Wendy

Strategy Grow curriculum from teacher passions

Teacher Gail is an avid recycler. She proudly boasts to everyone that she has recycling down to such an art that she only puts out half a can of garbage every week on her curb. Director Pam encourages Gail to bring her passion and knowledge about recycling to the child care program. Gail immediately begins planning a number of projects she can do with the children. First on her list is building a worm bin so the children can see composting in action. She tells Pam her big dream is to set up a recycling center for families in the program.

Jamilla is a talented craftsperson and artist. Recently she has been designing whimsical felt hats and selling them at street fairs. Director Rhonda encourages Jamilla to show the children how she makes hats. Jamilla brings in supplies for her own work and scraps and pieces for the children to try their hand at hat making too. Within a few weeks, the children are planning a hat sale as a fund-raiser for the new climber they want on the playground.

When you think about favorite adults from your own childhood, they are often people who shared a passion or skill with you. Children thrive when they are with adults who respect them enough to share things that are important in their lives. Apprenticing themselves to a mentor is a great way for children to acquire skills and a love of learning. As a director, are you interested in the skills and interests your teachers have outside of their work with you? Do you encourage them to find appropriate ways to share these with the children and their families?

Strategy Find curriculum in your wider community

Each year during the town Tulip Festival, many of the families and staff feel they don't have much time to get involved in the events. The director, Colleen, helps arrange for the children and staff to participate in the parade that goes down Main Street and to ride through the fields in Farmer Bob's hay wagon. She writes a newsletter sharing stories of the activities at the center, and invites the parents to share the newsletter at their workplace. This enables many of them to get time off to participate in the festival with their children and center staff.

A new hospital is being built down the street from the center. Most of the children and families pass this construction site on their way to the center and talk about it with great interest. Leon, the center director, contacts the construction company, requesting to have the children visit the site. He also invites a representative from the company to visit the center with some of their tools to talk with the children. In the meantime, Leon helps the teachers gather construction materials for their classrooms and designates an area on the outdoor playground for building.

As a director who seeks to build community and cultivate a program for childhood, your surrounding community is a possible source of rich experiences for curriculum. Your program and the larger community mutually benefit when children are visibly involved with their curiosity and contributions.

Strategy Connect people to one another

A strong feeling of community comes from the meaningful connections people have to each other. These don't just happen automatically, especially with the fast-paced lives people lead in today's world. Consider all the ways you as a director can help people in your program get more connected to each other.

Connect children to one another:

- Create opportunities for children to be in mixed-age groupings and to see each other throughout the day.
- Schedule regular opportunities for older children to help younger children—zipping, tying shoes, washing hands, serving food, rubbing backs, reading books, writing letters, making gifts.
- Develop a program phone book, listing children's and families' phone numbers and addresses so that they can visit with each other away from the center.
- Display photos of children and their families on walls around the center and in homemade books or photo albums.
- Share verbal and visual stories of the children's friendships and activities with each other.
- Design enrollment systems with continuity of care (looping) to keep children, families, and caregivers together over time.

I really wanted to do something different in our program, to create the feel of a family. To me this meant a wider age range in our rooms. There was resistance at first on the part of the staff and the parents. I had to hold fast to my vision and steadily grow the idea.

People were afraid that the toddlers and preschoolers might hurt the babies. Parents were worried that their older children might not learn as much if they were with babies. We had many staff discussions about the potential problems and benefits, and finally they agreed to try it. It wasn't long before we found that even young toddlers wanted to adopt the babies as special friends, someone they needed to watch out for. They would regularly put their arms around them and kiss them. I think it was my patience that ultimately paid off. A friend kept reminding me, "When you feed someone an elephant, give him one piece at a time."

—Leslie

Connect families with one another:

- Develop a skill and resource exchange bank, in which staff and families can trade skills, tools, babysitting, and other helpful resources.
- Organize family gatherings unrelated to the operation of the program, such as dances, book fairs, barbecues, and family field trips to museums, zoos, and places to swim.
- Arrange your insurance and janitorial services so that you can make the center available to families for other activities, such as gardening, aerobics classes, and birthday parties.

One of the children in our program lived with her grandmother. Her method of discipline was to swat the child, which we witnessed a number of times when they were at the center together. We wanted her to know that this was something we didn't want her to do while she was in our program and to suggest other options for discipline. We met with her and let her know that, of course, she could follow her own methods of discipline at home, but in our program swatting isn't appropriate. We shared other options for guiding children and the reasons we do things this way. This meeting was very difficult for us to think about and plan for. We wanted to be respectful, but also firm in our philosophy. Our concern and commitment must have come through because the meeting turned out really well for all of us. The grandmother shared her frustration and difficulty in controlling her anger with her granddaughter and asked for our help. She asked us to watch and help her recognize what was happening with her granddaughter and to tell her what else she could do. We also helped her contact and get involved in a program for grandparents raising their grandchildren.

—Paul

Connect staff with one another:

- Organize periodic outings and gatherings for staff and their families.
- Create visual displays around your building reflecting the lives and interests of staff members.
- Use part of each staff meeting for activities to learn about each other—life experiences, values, skills, and passions.
- Provide comfortable space and time for staff to have breaks and snacks, or perhaps exercise together.
- Give staff the equivalent of cubby space for personal belongings, treasures, photos, and books.
- Plan celebrations to mark special events and shared history.

Sin embargo, lo que más necesitamos es hablar y escuchar nuestras propias historias, y sentir el apoyo y amor entre nosotras. Al final del día de entrenamiento del personal, después de los talleres sobre diversos temas, terminamos con una ceremonia para sanar a quienes sanan, en la que encendimos una vela y nos lavamos mutuamente los pies. Hicimos esto por todos los pasos que nos esperan, por todo lo que debemos enfrentar para cumplir con nuestra filosofía. Eso tuvo un fuerte impacto en nosotras y nos llevó desde sentirnos cansadas y desalentadas a sentir que éramos siete mujeres con la fuerza necesaria para llevar adelante el cambio.

—Caron

Mostly what we need is to tell and hear our own stories and feel our love and support for each other. During our staff training day, after we had workshops on topics, we ended with a healing-the-healer ceremony where we lit a candle and washed each other's feet. We did this because of all the steps we have to take and how much standing up we have to do for our philosophy. It made a big impact, and we went from feeling tired and discouraged to feeling that we are seven women strong and able to change how things are.

—Caron

Connect with the larger community:

- Schedule regular opportunities for children to take the bus or walk to places in your community with you or other staff members—for instance, to the bank, post office, library, or grocery store.
- Invite members of the community to make regular visits or attend events the center offers.
- Arrange a monthly exchange with another early childhood program, a retirement home, or a youth center.
- Expand staff development opportunities to include attending a concert, museum, or local art exhibit.
- Arrange your insurance and janitorial services so that you can offer use of the center for community events such as classes or meetings.
- Offer your center's building for community events such as yard sales and book and art fairs.

Tratamos de crear un sentido de comunidad tanto dentro de nuestro programa como entre nuestro programa y la comunidad en general. Nuestra meta es ofrecerle a cada madre adolescente un tutor académico de una organización de mujeres de la comunidad y una mentora de la comunidad. Durante el "Día de llevar a nuestras hijas al trabajo", las mujeres de la comunidad llevan a una mamá adolescente al trabajo. Ponemos énfasis especialmente en los trabajos no tradicionales y en aquellos trabajos a los cuales no estarían expuestas de otra manera. A menudo las mujeres pueden ganar más dinero en oficios como plomería, electricidad o conducción de autobuses, que en los trabajos femeninos más tradicionales en oficinas o en el sector de servicios.

—Caron

We try to build community both within our program and between our program and the wider community. Our goal is to provide each teen parent with an academic tutor from a community women's organization and a woman in the community as a mentor. On "Take Our Daughters to Work Day," women in the community take a teen mom to work. We put a particular emphasis on nontraditional jobs or ones they might not otherwise be exposed to. Often women can make more money in trades like plumbing and electrical work, or careers like bus driving, than they can in more traditional women's jobs like office or service industry work.

—Caron

WORKING WITH DIFFERENCES AND CONFLICT

As you read the strategies above, you no doubt found yourself with some "yes, buts." Perhaps you wanted to say, "What about staff, parents, or children who are difficult to be with?" "What can I do when my staff members don't get along?" "How can I do this with a parent who does nothing but complain?" These are concerns common to most early childhood centers. They will periodically appear whatever your vision or the effectiveness of your community-building efforts. When you focus on the real lives and issues of the people in your program, there will almost certainly be conflict and difficulties. Group dynamics are seldom easy, even among people who genuinely like each other and share the same vision.

A community cannot be built overnight and certainly won't be built by directors who spend all their time managing and overseeing, to the neglect of mentoring, coaching, and building community. The tasks on this side of the triangle are probably not in your formal job description. They take time, intention, and hard work. You need to cultivate shared leadership and involve others in developing procedures, processes, and decision-making guidelines. From the beginning, set the stage with some specific strategies, anticipate where coaching and facilitation will be needed, and give attention to improving communication channels. When you take this approach and develop the skills for this kind of leadership, the payoff is enormous. You can feel it in the air, sense it in your heart, and see it in the living, breathing relationships among those in your program.

Our program is richly diverse with a large percentage of families having English as their second language. We have many Asian languages spoken and some Spanish, as well as English. At parent orientations and subsequent meetings I demonstrate our commitment to inclusion by offering simultaneous translation services. Initially the English-speaking parents were uncomfortable. They complained that the meetings take twice as long this way and suggested we have separate meetings. I helped them see the value and richness of the diversity in our program by sharing what is happening with the children. The children are very able to work through language differences, and in fact they are delighted in the many ways they can be with each other while learning new words to say. The adults have slowly come around to see that if the children can figure this out, so can they. We are committed to never separating our meetings.

—Mary

Principle

Acknowledge and Respect Differences

Whenever a group of people comes together, especially with the conscious intent of influencing the next generation, the personal and professional growth available to them is enormous. This is a disposition to continually cultivate, especially as you enter the troubled waters that are sure to come. Having some initial practice in consciously naming and working with different viewpoints establishes a foundation before the going gets rough. Over the years, we've seen successful strategies that create a climate in which people develop skills to work through the inevitable conflicts that are part of building genuine relationships.

Cuando se trata de seleccionar el personal de nuestro programa hago la selección basándome en la intuición del corazón más que en la educación. Me es más fácil entrenar profesoras que desentrenarlas. No encuentro a las profesoras a través de anuncios, sino pasando la voz. Cada profesora trae sus propios talentos y eso es lo que más nos interesa. Cuando alguien se va, no siempre encontramos una persona con las mismas características, sino a menudo, a alguien con talentos diferentes. Los éxitos que hemos logrado en nuestro programa provienen tanto de aquellos que han participado antes en el programa como de los que están trabajando actualmente con nosotras.

—Ruth

When it comes to staffing our program, I ultimately recruit staff based on heart, not education. I have found it easier to train teachers than to untrain them. I find teachers not by advertising, but by word of mouth. Every teacher brings their strength, and that's what we focus on. When people leave, we don't always get a new person with the same strength, but often someone with a different one. The tapestry of success that we have created in this program comes from those who have come and gone as well as those who are currently here.

—Ruth

Strategy Create a representation of a community

Sometimes the best way to learn about difference among us is to work as a group to create something. An hour to an hour and a half spent in the following activity and debriefing can illustrate the dynamics that are often present in working cross-culturally or with those who have different life experiences and values from our own.

Give the group an ample supply of scrounge materials (paper towel rolls, small boxes from food packaging, bottle caps, straws, newspaper, masking tape, wire, yarn), and tell them they have thirty to forty minutes to work together to create a representation of a community they all want to live or work in. When they are nearly finished, add the following tasks to their group work:

- Elect a mayor.
- Create laws and a story about the history of the community.
- Name the community.
- Decide how to present it to others.

At the end of the hour, have a debriefing that includes not only the presentations of the community but a discussion about how the group worked together. Focus the discussion around questions such as:

- Were they actively involved with each other or engaged in parallel play?
- Did they build a common vision together?
- Was anyone left out, marginalized, or made invisible?
- How were differences accommodated?
- What did the person do to get elected mayor?
- What does this tell us about leadership among the staff?

With an immediate experience to reflect on, new insights often emerge that are more difficult to get from abstract discussions. Helping teachers identify their own points of view and see why others might differ can lay the basis for respectful teamwork and conflict management. This activity also creates a sense of excitement and possibility for the vision of our programs as a community.

Strategy *Explore different values*

In many early childhood programs, some policies and practices are taken for granted with little discussion or questioning. Someone in the past may have set these up according to a personal preference, or the policies may have been adopted from professional definitions of best practices. In any case, it is useful to periodically explore the assumptions underlying certain practices so that everyone is clear about why the program has certain policies. A chance to discuss these issues also provides an opportunity to identify and manage any conflict of values among staff, and possibly between a teacher and a parent.

Teachers and caregivers benefit from the opportunity to examine and name the influences on their own values and preferred practices. A simple way to do this in a staff meeting is to write possible opposing viewpoints on policies on separate pieces of paper and then post them around the room. Ask everyone to find one viewpoint they wish to discuss, go to that paper, and talk with others there. They don't have to agree with the viewpoint, but they should at least have strong sentiments that they would like to discuss. Statements we typically write on these papers include:

- Children should be seen and not heard.
- Children should primarily be allowed to make choices and negotiate with adults.
- Children should primarily be offered limited choices and non-negotiable guidelines from adults.
- Children should call adults by their first names.
- Children should address adults by Mr. or Ms. or Teacher with her or his name.
- Children should usually be separated from the group or put in time-out when they don't follow the rules.
- Children should usually be redirected and involved in other activities when they don't follow the rules.

In the debriefing discussion following this activity, ask whether people found similarities or differences with others in their group. Did they choose their statement because they agreed or disagreed with the viewpoint? When teachers are asked to carry out practices different from their own belief systems, or when a family's practice differs from that of the early childhood program (for instance, in allowing a child to negotiate with an adult), this typically undermines the teacher's effectiveness with the child. In some cases, it may serve to discredit the parent's or family's values. Neither of these options is desired. Exploring the values and belief systems underlying practices with children can result in a willingness to accommodate a different viewpoint in order to create a better fit for a child, a family, and the program.

We started discussing our antibias work as part of our accreditation self-study. At one point I said, "We are going to have to deal with the gay issue if we are going to be truly antibiased." Several staff members were objecting to our need to take up this topic because we didn't currently have any children with gay or lesbian parents in our center. This could have gotten me off the hook, but I pressed forward and asked them how they knew that. I asked, "Do we feel confident that our center is a welcoming and safe place for a parent to tell us she is a lesbian or he is gay?" We took a walk through our center looking at the images and written materials around. We looked at our enrollment forms, handbooks, and newsletters to see if they gave any messages of inclusion or exclusion of families with gay or lesbian parents. It was a real eye-opener.

Several committees were formed to address our findings. Over the course of a year we struggled to develop several written statements. The first was our "we believe" statement, which was followed by a piece for our parent handbook that said our commitment to embracing diversity welcomed all kinds of staff and families to our program and would expose children to all kinds of families in our discussions and materials.

In developing the "we believe" statement we started with the idea that our program should be a safe haven for every child and family. As we got to the gay issue, I had to repeatedly clarify that we are not talking about sex education here, but rather an appreciation of diversity in the world. I had to help several teachers who had vocal religious objections to homosexuality see that they already knew how to keep their personal religious beliefs out of the program without compromising themselves. I told them I knew they had strong ideas about God, the Holy Trinity, being "saved," Bible reading, and prayer, but that they didn't impose this on the children, their families, or coworkers. I said, "You know how to keep these things separate, maintain your self-respect, and still respect those with different beliefs. You can do that on this issue too." It took some work, but we learned how to bring the concept of "agree to disagree" to life with what felt like genuine respect.

—Alicia

Strategy *Name your assumptions*

Even programs that pride themselves on having a great team spirit have periodic tensions. This may be a result of relationship patterns that stem from dysfunctional family dynamics imprinted on individuals at an early age. At other times, tensions represent the dynamics of power and privilege in the wider society. It is especially useful to identify your assumptions about working with diversity so that you have a frame of reference when conflict arises. Here is one way to frame your assumptions about working with diversity:

- Adults come to child care programs with a complex web of influences from backgrounds that must be untangled as they learn and unlearn across diversity.
- As adults come to deeper understandings about themselves and working with diversity, these understandings influence their work with children, helping them go beyond tokenism to counter biases and be culturally sensitive.
- Everybody has a culture; culture is learned and includes, but goes beyond, ethnicity.
- Bias comes in many forms; invisibility and lack of cultural relevancy are as detrimental as stereotyping.
- Antibias practices require that we recognize European American cultural dominance and learn how its assumptions become a bias when applied universally. We must learn new attitudes, information, and behaviors as we unlearn acquired biases.

- To be inclusive and genuinely multicultural requires that we make a place for those historically left out, misrepresented, or disenfranchised. Given the stakes, this will likely stir up emotions and conflict that we must learn to work with.

When I interviewed for the director position at our center, I was clear about my commitment to antibias practices and that I would want to immediately begin bringing more diversity to this white, middle-class program. At the same time, I had to be open if the staff had a different vision. To begin, I talked about how much my own life had been enriched when I diversified my circle of friends to include more people of color.

We began to discuss what would need to happen if our center were to become a place where families of color would feel comfortable. As we explored more what appeared to be the small diversity among us as a staff, some personal stories began to deepen understandings. We had great conversations about grandmothers, meaningful traditions, and religious issues. A Jewish teacher shared what it was like to be on the outside of the mainstream culture, as did one of our few teachers of color. Over time these stories chipped away at the mountainous task of rearranging understandings and attitudes.

It's a tricky thing to get a mostly white and privileged program to struggle around these issues. It takes way longer than you want. I had to keep tailoring my vision to a realistic time frame without ever giving up or diluting my vision. The success of small steps rewarded me and encouraged me to stay longer than I might have otherwise.

—Julie

Principle

Explore and Mediate Conflicts

Contrary to most people's instinctive feelings, conflict is not all bad. It has the potential to balance your relationships and expand your resources. When you stay on the surface and avoid or smooth over areas of disagreement, you rarely get to the depth of what you truly care about. Programs become richer when you can work through sources of friction caused by different perspectives, skills, and interests. Moving through bumpy times together forms deeper connections and more authentic relationships. The investment you make in really learning to work with other perspectives has a significant payoff. Here are some strategies to strengthen your ability to do this.

Strategy *Explore different communication styles*

Sometimes people make judgments about each other based on differences in communication styles. This could be a personal or a cultural issue, but whichever, it's useful to understand what's happening. Here's a playful way to explore how individuals send and receive information and feelings.

Ask your staff to consider possible labels for acceptable communication styles, and then choose four or five to work with. The term *acceptable* is a subjective one. Our intent here is to avoid negative labels such as caustic, attacking, manipulative, or defensive, and identify a variety of other styles that have a useful place in communicating. For instance, friendly, humorous, creative, decisive, analytical, direct, or indirect could be selected as styles for exploration. Spend a minute defining what is meant by each of these styles. Then divide the large group into as many small groups as there are styles, and assign one style to each group. Ask each group to generate a list of common phrases you might hear from someone who uses that style. For instance, the lists might look something like this:

Friendly style

- You have great ideas.
- I like what you said.
- They might not like that.

Creative style

- Anything is possible.
- Let's keep brainstorming.
- What if we flipped that around?

Decisive style

- Let's not waste time.
- We have to decide one way or another.
- I want to know what we're going to do.

Analytical style

- I think we should do a survey.
- The facts speak for themselves.
- We need more evidence.

Once you've given each group the time to come up with a list of three or four phrases, ask for a volunteer from each group and conduct a communications role play. Choose a topic that isn't emotionally loaded for the volunteers to discuss. Examples include what color the center should paint its walls, what kind of plants to get for the lounge, or what software should be purchased for your

computers. As you facilitate the brief discussion, ask each volunteer to try to use as many of the phrases on their list as possible in the discussion.

Along with being able to laugh and get a new perspective on how style might look in a group setting, you can debrief this activity to explore the strengths and weaknesses of each style and the barriers that can occur when you judge a person's contribution by their communication style. Staff members might enjoy identifying their own style and exploring how it can potentially conflict with another.

Building a community takes time. For me it took about eighteen months for the staff to know that when I say something, I mean it, and when I make a mistake, I'll admit it. I had to build trust before they would join me to form a community with a shared vision and purpose.

A lot of the staff had been there a number of years when I first arrived, and they had accumulated a lot of baggage. I wanted to start out with my vision of open and assertive communication to overcome the negative history. When I observed difficult interactions between staff members, I wouldn't walk away pretending I didn't see it. I would walk up and describe what I saw without judgment. I'd offer support and model conflict resolution. It took lots of work, and with each bumpy spot we had to come to new understandings and forge new agreements.

The staff came to understand that this was important to me. They slowly stopped complaining that their issues wouldn't get addressed. The whining mentality dwindled as everyone realized that they could articulate concerns and they would be heard and responded to in a safe and productive manner.

It's been a long haul, but we're ready now to do amazing things together. We're a team with a safe, supportive system in place. There's no limit to what we can do, because we won't be stopping ourselves anymore.

—Alicia

Strategy Design a conflict resolution process

With the demands and stresses of child care work, sometimes staff tensions can mount to an intense level before you know what happened. This is especially true when staff is paid from different funding streams with different qualifications, salaries, and benefits. As part of the list of working agreements you develop, it's important to include a process for how conflicts will be handled. Ideally, the expectations and approaches to conflict resolution you develop should parallel what you set out for the children in your program. For instance, you might have a general statement that would read:

> At our center we all share in caring for each other and for the environment. When someone forgets or breaks this agreement, we remind them of how it hurts the group, explore why this happened, and work together to help the person get back on track. We work out disagreements by taking turns listening carefully to each other, explaining what we understand, and exploring what changes are possible and acceptable to those involved.

You then need a clear process for how this takes place, and staff meeting time to practice on some minor issues. On the following page is an example of an agreement and process developed in a program Margie directed.

Any conflict resolution process should have at least the following elements:

- using active or deep listening, with the use of paraphrasing to check understandings;
- providing opportunities for each person to state needs and wants in the situation;
- generating an active, creative brainstorm of possible solutions while reserving judgment;
- evaluating possible solutions and choosing what to try;
- developing an action plan with specific details;
- evaluating the plan at designated intervals.

Examples of documents several programs have developed for their conflict resolution process may be found in appendix 12.

Agreement

When necessary, we will use a criticism/self-criticism discussion process to identify attitudes and behaviors that are negatively affecting our agreements.

Questions to ask oneself before giving a criticism:

- Is my criticism based on investigation or on assumption?
- What is the most important element in the criticism?
- What is secondary?
- What is my side of the problem, my responsibility, or my contribution to it?
- Are there any things I hide to avoid being criticized?
- Is my criticism intended to hurt, attack, or improve understanding and communication?
- How are our staff agreements hurt or helped by my criticism?
- How can I play a concrete, positive role in helping the other person change?
- What changes do I need to make in myself?

Stating a criticism:

- When you do ____________________, I feel ____________________.
- It hurts our agreements because ____________________.
- Therefore, I want you to ____________________.
- In the future I will behave differently by ____________________.

Discussions to investigate the criticism:

- Why do you feel that way? What happened?
- What other things were going on? (Include events taking place around you at the same time, as well as feelings and impressions happening within you.)
- What is the main thing that needs to happen here?

One of our infant caregivers had a style with the babies that many of our staff found offensive. She used inappropriate language, sometimes swearing in front of the children. Her sense of humor was often annoying rather than funny to most of the staff. We met as a team to discuss the concerns. This was a difficult discussion, as many of the staff wanted her to change immediately. Her response was "This is me; I can't change who I am." I tried to guide the discussion toward the tangibles of words to not use with babies. I reinforced that we didn't want to change who she was, but her language was inappropriate in this setting. This proved helpful, as she felt less personally attacked and more able to hear the specific criticism. The rest of the staff was also able to let go of the emotions around these issues and see her as a person beyond her language. She's made changes in her language with the babies, and staff relationships have improved tremendously. I believe this is the result of working through a conflict in a direct yet inclusive manner.

—Paul

Cultivating New Roles, Dispositions, and Skills

Your daily actions to build and support community in your program are some of the most powerful aspects of your job. It is easy to get overwhelmed and feel victimized in your work—and in the culture as a whole. When you create an experience of connection between people, you are creating a set of possibilities. When you view tension as a sign that people really care about what's happening, you can move past discomfort and fear to a place of discovery and integrity. If you dare to take up a vision and not settle for the status quo, you are on the road to nurturing it into reality. In the words of Peter Block, "the challenge is to pursue our vision with as much courage and intensity as we can generate" (1987). This is the heart of claiming your power and acting on it.

Think of yourself, not with the limited mind-set of a manager, but with the eyes and ears of a storyteller. Linda Espinosa reminds us that "storytelling is a means of communicating the substance of who we are and what we stand for. The vision we hold for children, for early childhood programs, and for families can be vividly captured in the stories we choose to remember and repeat" (1997, 100). Howard

Gardner specifically relates storytelling to the role of a director: "A leader is someone who has a compelling story to tell; he is able to forge a group identity and sense of community through his effective storytelling" (1995). When you see yourself as a storyteller, your tales will spread the news of what's happening in your program and shape its growing culture.

Practice Assessing Yourself

Spend some time considering other metaphors that help you assess how you are doing in your community-building roles. If you thought of yourself as an architect, what skills would you need to design plans for improving the physical and emotional space of your program? If you were a weaver, how could you cultivate your eyes and hands so that each day you could pull together threads for this tapestry you are weaving?

If you thought of yourself as a sculptor, a mediator, or a horticulturist, what skills would you need to learn? Use each of these professions as a heading, and make a list of skills and qualities that each might require or nurture in you. How do those skills apply to your work as a director? Consider what you already know about this work and what's not yet clear to you.

Set some goals for yourself, and step outside the early childhood field for some of the resources you might need. The act of moving across professional boundaries can be a community-building process in and of itself, making the world of early childhood care and education visible to others and bringing their knowledge and resources within your reach.

Chapter 4

Your Role of Mentoring and Coaching

Director LeAnn has a staff-training plan this year that includes the required health and safety review and how to identify child abuse and neglect. Because she has a number of new teachers, she has also planned an in-service on curriculum planning and assessing and individualizing for children. Even though they've covered this before, she thinks her long-term staff will still benefit from this training. Today, as she goes through her list of announcements at the staff meeting, LeAnn is discouraged, as several teachers mumble when they hear the training plans. She thinks to herself, "They don't know how lucky they are that we have money for staff training. I wish I could find some more enthusiastic teachers. They hardly pay attention at staff meetings, and no matter how much training I offer, teachers rarely change their behaviors."

Director Ramona is reviewing the required curriculum plans that her staff has turned in. Most of her staff complete these forms as directed, except for Lucy, a teacher in the preschool room. Her curriculum plans are always sketchy, and Ramona notices when she visits the room that Lucy never follows what she's written down. Lucy's children are always deeply engaged and happy, and Lucy eagerly shares detailed stories of what is happening with the children. The families love Lucy and the stories she greets them with at the end of the day. Ramona doesn't know what to do. She's talked with Lucy several times about her plans, showing her the plans that Brandi in the next room writes and follows so well. The truth is, Brandi's room—like most of the rooms in the program—doesn't have much depth, creativity, or child-initiated activity. Apart from issues of required paperwork, Ramona secretly wishes that Brandi and the other teachers were more like Lucy in their work with the children.

A director's approach to staff supervision and development has a significant impact on the culture of an organization and the quality of a program. We highlight this point not only because we know that everyone does their best work when they feel supported and respected by their peers and supervisors, but also because of what we know about how adults grow and learn. When your meetings and staff training are centered around checklists, rules, and regulations, you are operating from the managing-and-overseeing side of the triangle. Furthermore, by example you are demonstrating a way of teaching that you would most likely be critical of in teachers' work with children—teaching by lecturing, pointing out the rules, and requiring quiet, passive learners.

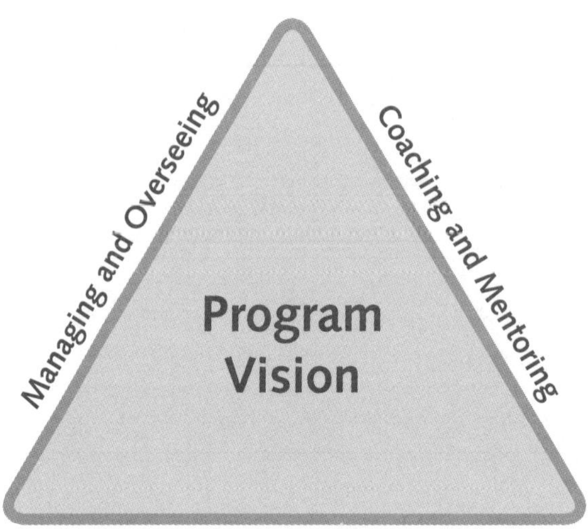

The models you see in directors LeAnn and Ramona will likely translate into a program culture where people are focused on schedules, curriculum plans to keep the kids busy, behavior management techniques, and compliance issues, because these are the things the director is focused on. If time spent together isn't viewed as precious and if conditions aren't conducive to self-reflection, collaboration, and excitement about children, staff tend to view training opportunities as requirements rather than opportunities. Like the director who is modeling this behavior for them, the teachers focus on the tasks and paperwork to be done. Rather than enthusiasm for new discoveries, tackling the deeper complexity of work with children, or the warmth of genuine community, the program culture is one of boredom, detachment, and going through the motions. Almost any director can create a program that technically meets the standards for quality, but where are the heart and spirit? How is the quality of life for the people in the program? Is there a sense of community with caring and intellectual vitality for all its members?

Yes, it's important for staff to follow policies and procedures and participate in ongoing professional development opportunities. But unless caregivers and teachers are exceptionally self-motivated and see themselves as lifelong learners, an approach like LeAnn's will be less than effective. As Ramona puts an emphasis on paperwork requirements, she fails to support what she sees as Lucy's strength. Ramona's actions will unconsciously uphold the lack of creativity that concerns her in the other teachers. Both directors may get staff to comply with regulations and standards, but this won't necessarily translate into high-quality work. Social constructivist and adult learning theories suggest that the learning that translates into improved job performance doesn't come from being told what to do. Rather, staff need coaching and mentoring for reflective practices; this implies a different approach to professional development.

People in early childhood education work in a profession with little public esteem, low wages, and inadequate working conditions. To make matters worse, there is an ever-growing set of expectations and requirements attached to the job. As a result, it is difficult for many early childhood programs to attract or retain people eager to learn and develop themselves, let alone think of themselves as qualified professionals. There are certainly a handful of wonderful exceptions, but many people do not enter this workforce as their preferred choice. They may come with no sense of personal agency, low self-esteem, and a long history of financial and personal struggle. When these folks work alongside more dedicated and professionally oriented staff, the climate is frequently tense. The group dynamics can exude a mixture of enthusiasm, victim thinking, blame, and defensiveness.

In hopes of better teacher performance and child outcomes, federally funded Head Start programs have been adding more regulations and education requirements for teachers. State-funded pre-K programs are also requiring degreed teachers and offering pay equity with their K–12 counterparts. But are these developments actually raising the quality of early childhood programs? Certainly pay equity is good news for those particular teachers, but it is leaving community-based child care programs with the less-qualified, non-career-oriented people, an experience Roger Neugebauer (2007, 4) terms "friendly fire." Degreed teachers who move into Head Start or school district pre-K programs discover they have inadequate preparation for the expectations that come with the early learning standards, and limited extra time or support to do the additional work. They often become discouraged, if not cynical. Rather than addressing the inadequate salaries, working conditions, and opportunities for meaningful professional development, school districts are compounding the problems with "teacher-proof" prescriptive curricula, imposing a barrage of commercially developed curriculum, assessment, and professional development packages, all purported to be research-based. Unfortunately, these same developments are making their way into community-based early childhood programs as well.

Along with continuing to address the external social, economic, and political agendas that shape early childhood education, the task of a director is to create a program climate that will nurture and stimulate the most skilled and dedicated staff and mentor and coach those not yet performing as reliably. Directors have to build self-awareness and reflection, confidence, and effective communication skills alongside a working knowledge of child development and learning domains. The goal should be to develop a workforce of reflective practitioners, not technicians. The tasks are pedagogical, not just managerial.

Coaching versus Managing Staff

We developed the triangle framework to help early childhood program directors understand the difference between their responsibilities as a manager and overseer and the skills of a coach and mentor. Keeping a clear distinction between these roles requires a commitment to integrity and staff empowerment. To be sure, there are contradictions inherent in having the role of manager and coach in one administrative position. The trust, open communication, and mutual respect required for healthy mentoring relationships are difficult to maintain when one party has the power to hire and fire. Nevertheless, given the financial resources and organizational limitations of most early childhood programs, these roles are usually combined in one person's job. Directors must and can learn to identify which role they want to work from on which occasion. In some instances you will feel that your priority is to immediately step in and exercise your power on behalf of a child or family, overriding a slower learning process for a staff member. In most cases, however, the investment you make on behalf of a teacher's learning process will lead to more meaningful understanding and reflective practices. When you coach staff members to become thinkers rather than rule followers, you are enhancing their power to respond on behalf of children and their families. This kind of teacher mentoring requires time and a trusting relationship, more than telling and reminding. It keeps you growing as a director, as you seek to understand your staff as adult learners and invent strategies to help them gain more knowledge and think for themselves.

When we think of a coach, we don't have in mind the person screaming on the field or in the locker room, but the one who takes the team through an analysis of the last game, spotting where the holes were, where things went wrong, and what strengths to build on. We picture the birthing coach who supports a mother through the labor and delivery process—watching; listening; sharing observations, skills, and resources; and providing guidance during the difficult time of giving birth. In many ways this is the director's coaching role—not punishing or admonishing, but focusing on the adult learner and his or her own power in the learning process while birthing new knowledge and skills. As a coach or mentor, your job is to develop strategies that will empower staff members to be autonomous and thoughtful in their work. This may involve addressing their lack of faith in themselves.

This field has its share of people who see themselves as victims and powerless over their lives. This may translate into passive and/or aggressive behavior and an abundance of "I can't" and "yes, but" thoughts. Being a coach may require you to renew your attitudes and approaches with a given teacher. For instance, instead of responding with irritation, you can be a patient listener, restating what you understand the person feels and then asking for a story about a time she or he learned how to do something difficult. Point out that even if it is hard to remember, this person has the strength and ability to learn and act on new knowledge. Consistently give the message that you have faith in your staff members and that you are looking forward to hearing their ideas, even if they are different from yours. Whenever you have the opportunity, point out examples of positive growth and change you see. This helps replace self-doubt with "can do" thoughts.

I hired Neil as an assistant teacher in my program because in our interview he said he really wanted to work with young children, and he would especially enjoy doing art projects with them. As I observed him with the children, I could see his skills were really lacking, and he seemed unfocused. He particularly had trouble guiding children's behavior and taking the initiative in managing a group.

After a number of failed attempts to help Neil improve, I felt I needed to talk with him about finding other work more suited to him. His lack of focus and difficulty in changing suggested to me that he wasn't really that interested in working with children. During our conversation he strongly insisted that he really did want to do this work and just needed more time. I agreed to keep working with him to see if he could realize the potential he saw for himself. I reassigned him to another classroom with a lead teacher who offered him the firm support and encouragement he needed.

It's taken quite a while, but he has now blossomed as a teacher. His skills have grown tremendously in many areas, and he continues to seek more training to continue his growth. He initiates and tackles complicated projects with children that are so rich and meaningful for our entire program. I am so glad I listened to him and gave him the time and support he needed to reach the potential he saw in himself.

—Jim

There are times you will need to respond to a staff member from the managing side of the triangle framework, and we offer suggestions for that role in chapter 5 of this book. As a coach, however, your job is to encourage and provide opportunities for defining and solving problems and for self-reflection and collaboration. It is important that you model the kind of behavior you want staff to use with children—providing for self-initiated learning, risk taking, and exploration. When staff members are involved in setting goals for themselves and in creating strategies for their professional development, they bring more energy to their work and contribute to the growth of your organization as a learning community.

What Do Adult Learners Deserve?

Many directors come to their jobs having been classroom teachers first. As a director, you have expertise when it comes to providing good learning experiences for children, and this is usually the focus when you seek to improve teachers' behaviors. It is less common for directors to have experience or consolidated thinking about providing good learning experiences for adults. You instinctively think of your job as making sure things go well for the children, and you may miss the implications this has for tending to the climate the adults experience and organizing activities for them.

The truth is that the better the environment is for the adults involved in the program, the better the care the children receive. The link between the quality of experience for the staff and the quality of care for the children has been made clear in a number of research studies in early childhood education. Several of these studies focus on issues of organizational culture and support for the staff, while the studies of Carol Anne Wien and the High/Scope Educational Research Foundation analyze components of pedagogy and effective in-service training. The findings of these studies forecast the benefits of coaching and mentoring programs that are now receiving more attention across our profession.

For a number of years, Paula Jorde Bloom has studied the dimensions of an organizational climate that lead to quality programming for children. Her book *A Great Place to Work: Improving Conditions for Staff in Young Children's Programs* (1997) translates these findings into a guidebook for directors. Bloom's studies make it clear that if working conditions aren't suitable for the adults, it is hard for children to thrive.

This understanding led the Center for the Child Care Workforce to conduct an informal survey and a set of focus groups asking child care providers and teachers to describe what they consider to be model work standards (1999). We discuss these standards more fully in the coming chapters, but it's worth noting here that teachers feel their ability to perform well and continue in their professional development is dependent on their working conditions and the support and mentoring they receive on the job.

In *Developmentally Appropriate Practice in "Real Life": Stories of Teacher Practical Knowledge*, Carol Anne Wien (1995) describes her research, which also involved extensive interviews with teachers. Wien's study was designed to learn why teachers educated in developmentally appropriate practice often fail to teach in this way when working in early childhood programs. She suggests that the organizational climate of a teacher's workplace is a significant factor in her or his ability to follow developmentally appropriate guidelines. Teachers working in programs that use a school-like framework, that emphasize time schedules and top-down administrative practices, tend to adopt these same behaviors with children. Wien concludes that when programs promote and provide for observation, reflection, and collaboration, teachers are supported in developmentally appropriate practices and are more likely to carry them out.

An earlier research project conducted by the High/Scope Educational Research Foundation predicted Wien's findings. To evaluate their extensive teacher training program, High/Scope studied the components of in-service training that resulted in teachers appropriately implementing the High/Scope curriculum. Their findings, published in *Training for Quality* (Epstein 1993), are summarized below. Their research demonstrated that effective training

- provided a focus over time, where knowledge was cumulative and followed a consistent theoretical framework;
- actively involved participants through interaction with the trainers and each other;
- allowed time for reflection;
- provided hands-on practice to try out new ideas and strategies;
- followed up with observation and feedback and more opportunities for peer exchanges.

More recent studies add weight to these early findings of the High/Scope Educational Research Foundation, particularly Harvard University's Project Zero, which studied the schools of Reggio Emilia and developed protocols for U.S. teachers to use in studying children's work. The book based on the project's work, *Making Teaching Visible* (Mardell and Krechevsky 2003), demonstrates that the engaging projects and complex learning for children in the schools of Reggio are directly linked to the conditions provided for the adults in those schools. The organizational culture is centered around attentiveness to children's interest and thinking and opportunities for the staff to engage in collaborative analysis of their observations of children's work. With the support of a *pedagogista*, whose job is to help the teachers understand children's development, teachers are continually hypothesizing, planning, and evaluating. As any visitor to these schools will tell you, the adults benefit greatly from their debates with each other and from the attitude and role of researcher they take with each other and the children. The learning experience for the adults in the schools of Reggio Emilia parallels the learning experience for the children. It seems obvious that if these elements were part of the organizational framework of every early childhood program, you would see more consistent quality in accredited early childhood programs—they would be closer to our vision of a learning community both for the children and the adults.

It is worth noting that this same notion is taking hold in the K–12 school arena with organizations such as the Coalition of Essential Schools and Project Zero. You can search the Internet for inspiring examples and also find a user-friendly description in *The Power of Protocols* (McDonald et al. 2003). In this little volume, the authors describe their efforts to bring lessons from the field of organizational development into school settings based on Peter Senge's idea of a learning organization for the teachers as well as the children (Senge 2006). Using a facilitated process called "the tuning protocol," teachers are immersed in a school culture in which they study students' work with their colleagues, rather than just assess whether or not students are meeting the benchmarks. Teachers learn to describe the details of what they are observing in their students' work without judgment. They collaboratively explore the possible meanings for the student. Teachers discover ways to scaffold their learning and in the process find their own professional growth significantly enhanced.

The success of the schools of Reggio Emilia and these school reform efforts in the United States point to the role of a program director as the creator of a learning community and a coach and mentor for the adults. It's not rocket science to conclude that adults who are engaged in a meaningful learning process for themselves are more likely to provide a higher-quality experience for children and families. Carol Anne Wien (1995, 144–45) leaves us with a wonderful vision of intellectually engaged teachers that translates into intellectually engaged children:

> Those of us who hope to support the work of teachers (administrators, curriculum consultants, practicum supervisors, teacher educators, and so forth) can help in several ways, beyond simply a better understanding of the context of teacher work in early childhood. Like the support given to teachers in Reggio Emilia, we can work to change systemic constraints so that time is opened up for reflection,

for review of practice, for the surfacing of incipient conflicts that the teacher senses but has not had time to address. We can encourage the reflective process by giving teachers opportunities to document children's activity and the development of their curriculum, encourage them to make changes that they themselves generate, to try out solutions to self-set problems of teaching. Rather than appearing merely as experts with authoritative knowledge, we can encourage their sense of mastery over their work, their sense of agency. Ultimately we must trust teachers to develop the worlds of teaching in which they work, recognizing that their negotiations through two common frameworks for action, teacher dominion and developmental appropriateness, are conflicted, frequently contradictory, stressful, exciting, and challenging and that the agency that they can develop in taking action in early childhood settings is ultimately a preferred way to model for children the process of coming to life, of living in a shared social world of responsibility, of care for others and love of life itself.

The Golden Rule Revisited: Treat Adults as You Want Them to Treat Children

Whether or not you have studied adult learning theory, a director's knowledge of best practices for children can be translated into appropriate practices for educating teachers. How could you justify anything contradictory? Is it fair to require them to attend trainings, ask them to sit and pay attention on small chairs in a cramped hallway, fill their lives with checklists and forms, and then be critical of stagnant and unattractive room arrangements, teachers' use of photocopies, and their insistence on teacher-directed activities? The idea of creating an environment and educational activities for adults that parallel what you want them to do with children is not only an ethical issue but also a pedagogical one. Adults who have never experienced, or who have forgotten, the positive elements of childhood and living as part of a community can hardly be expected to offer them in your program. They need vivid reminders of what these things feel like in order to understand their value. Giving your staff a mission statement, a philosophical lecture, or even the criteria for NAEYC accreditation will hardly put a taste of childhood or community in their mouths.

When people get a taste of something they like, they usually long for more. They are motivated to try to find or create it again. When most of your waking hours are spent in programs with groups of children, this actively influences the quality of your life. Providing adults with experiences that parallel what you want for children should be at the center of a director's thinking.

I believe that professional development works best when it is ongoing and directly connected to what is happening daily in the classroom. It must be free from anxiety. The most consistent time this happens in our program is naptime. While children sleep, teachers talk. This is not a time for announcements, workshops, or other business. We discuss children, their needs, their strengths, strategies for handling difficult behaviors, parents, classroom environments and activities, administrative styles and issues. We also get into personal, political, and social issues. It is a daily processing session. Most certainly we have more formal workshops and staff meetings, but these "professional development seminars" happen almost every day during naptime, informally and without anxiety.

—Margo

As a lab school we have the gift of resources that are not often available to other early childhood programs. I see this gift as a responsibility—not just to model best practice but to inform that practice. We have focused on three areas in the past several years to try to honor that responsibility. The first is our mentoring approach. We have moved beyond orientation manuals with regulations and policies to mentoring for teacher qualities that are integral to our philosophy and beliefs. The second is holding true to our homegrown emergent curriculum approach against all the pressure to buy the current package and to cross walk in a certain way to the new standards. The third is our move to mixed-age grouping despite the lack of support for this in the regulations.

—Linda

Principle

Give Thoughtful Attention to the Environment

If directors want caregivers to offer well-designed and pleasing learning environments for children, directors need to design an environment like that for their staff. If teachers are to give children choices and opportunities for self-initiated learning, then teachers deserve the same from their director. The comparisons of quality learning environments and experiences for children and adults could go on and on.

Strategy *Plan a nurturing environment for the adults*

Take a look at the chart on the next page, which offers some examples of what parallel elements in environments for children and adults might look like. Then choose a couple that you could fairly easily adapt and a couple that could be longer-term goals for your program. You might also present this chart at a meeting to see how your staff would prioritize their goals for improvement. Comparing what you and they come up with is another way to assess how closely you understand your staff's view of their needs and work environment.

Environments for Children	Environments for Adults
Children should be surrounded by softness, art, beauty, natural materials, and living things (fabric paintings, water, rocks, trees, plants, woven baskets, sand, dirt, flowers, animals).	*Strategy:* Put things such as plants, flowers, birds, and aquariums in the office area, staff room, and adult restrooms. Arrange displays of rocks, shells, and other collections from nature and the seasons in areas where adults can look at, touch, and play with them. *Strategy:* Hang attractive photos, paintings, and textures on the walls. Cover hard surfaces with fabric. Provide magazines and books on a variety of topics (nature, science, art, architecture, design) in the office area, staff lounge, and adult bathrooms.
Children need opportunities to be outdoors and to experience changes in the seasons, light and shadows, weather, animals, plants, and gardens.	*Strategy:* Arrange opportunities for staff to be outdoors when they are not supervising children; encourage walks during breaks; organize staff outings to local nature attractions, art galleries, zoos, and botanical gardens. *Strategy:* Hold staff meetings, retreats, and trainings in beautiful environments reflecting nature, natural elements, design, art, and beauty.
Children need to see their lives, families, cultures, and interests reflected in images, materials, and activities around them.	*Strategy:* Have places for adults to display family pictures, collections, or special objects. *Strategy:* Set up a rotating schedule in which staff members share special skills, hobbies, or interests—knitting, appliance repair, computer skills, or book discussions.
Children need time and materials to explore, invent, represent, and make-believe.	*Strategy:* Provide adult-oriented, open-ended materials, games, and puzzles in the staff lounge and office area, during meetings, and at gatherings.
Children need a place for their personal things and a place to be away from the group.	*Strategy:* Give each staff member the equivalent of a cubby; create quiet corners with stuffed chairs, soft lighting, and plants.
Children need physical challenges—using muscles, going fast, and finding balance and coordination.	*Strategy:* Put exercise equipment for staff use somewhere in the building—stationary bike, treadmill, chin-up bar, or yoga mat. *Strategy:* Arrange for staff use of a nearby health club or gym.
Children need opportunities to work alone and with others.	*Strategy:* Use staff meeting time for teachers to work on individual goals, have collaborative discussions, or create documentation displays of recent events.

Strategy Provide time and resources

If you look over the sample Model Work Standards (see appendix 3) developed by teachers and providers across the country, you will see that a key ingredient is input on how they spend their time with and away from children. Providing the time for thinking and planning is in and of itself a coaching strategy. It creates room for reflection, for gathering thoughts, and for collaborating with coworkers. This is valuable staff development time and should not be equated with a break, which teachers also need.

Without adequate resources, your staff is likely to experience more frustration than refinement of their skills, more lethargy than learning from their teaching. Stimulate your caregivers' thinking with catalogs outside the typical early childhood resources. Take a look at ones from garden and landscaping stores, display and craft suppliers, and environmental and other groups supporting crafts from developing nations.

As a mentor, make sure to offer tips on time management and organizing the tools teachers need for efficiently using their time away from children. Keep abreast of how their curriculum is evolving, and surprise them with resources you have located from around the center or community.

How you allocate time for you and your staff is a key element in reaching your vision. We're not suggesting you add more work to your packed schedule, but rather that you examine your priorities, organize your work, and develop your skills in the service of creating a learning community. Keeping clear about the difference between your managing role and your coaching role will strengthen your ability to genuinely contribute to growing understanding and expanded skills in your teachers. In chapter 5 we discuss getting yourself organized with systems and resources that enhance your coaching and community-building roles.

Principle

View Teachers as Competent Thinkers and Learners

How you see teachers and the scope of their work is critical to your success in helping them develop. If you view your staff as people with problems, only noticing their lack of skills and knowledge to manage behavior or plan lessons for learning, you will most likely approach your coaching with quick fixes, one-size-fits-all techniques, and impatience rather than engage with them in the dynamics of the teaching and learning process. Most current approaches to professional development reinforce remediation, emphasizing techniques rather than reflective practice. In contrast, if you acknowledge the complexities of working with children and regard your teachers as competent human beings with rich life experiences, important perspectives, and the potential to rise to their best selves, you will invest the time, resources, and enthusiasm to engage with them in their work.

Our large, multisite program has embarked on a new journey where we see teachers as the key drivers in determining their own developmental needs in a supportive learning community. At our recent virtual Appreciative Inquiry Summits, all of the teachers completed a questionnaire to discover what "gives life" to their best work. We asked provoking questions that moved us from individual thinking to group thinking. For example, we asked, "What is the core role of the teacher?" Once we had the role of the teacher defined, we created a summary statement of our work together. We spent time looking at our destiny, seeing how we can bridge our current reality with our future vision. There were great results achieved. We formed deeper partnerships, and our mutual respect has changed the way administrators work with the teachers. Our next step is to create a strategic program plan that will bring our future vision into reality. New roles will evolve as our teachers help determine their responsibilities and the support that will get them there.

—Susan

Strategy Reflect on a teacher

To help you assess your current view of your staff, start by identifying a teacher you work with who puzzles you. Think of a specific example of a behavior that has you wondering. Reflect on this behavior, and then write some words below that reflect your view of this person.

Words That Describe My View of This Teacher
1.
2.
3.
4.
5.

Now reflect on the words you choose to describe this teacher. Do they reflect curiosity about the teacher? Or do they show negative judgments focused on problems and conflicts? Think of the times a teacher has approached you with complaints about a child. Perhaps you have longed for her to show a little empathy or curiosity about the child's behavior. Perhaps you were dismayed by his certainty that he understood the child completely, by his lack of questions. Just as you want teachers to approach children with curiosity and understanding, you must do the same with staff members. When you enter a coaching relationship, it is important to do so with curiosity and empathy, to look beneath difficult or puzzling behavior in order to meet up with the mind and heart of the teacher you are coaching. Take the time to assess your view of all of your staff in this way, and work to transform your mind-set to curiosity, understanding, and respect in relation to each of them.

Strategy Expand your focus for coaching

When you view your teachers as competent, eager learners, you expand the possibilities for what you believe they can and should be learning. Think again about the teacher you identified above, and make a list of at least five things you think she or he needs to learn to improve.

Five Things This Teacher Needs to Learn

1.
2.
3.
4.
5.

Professional development often focuses on techniques for meeting standards. Study the following categories of goals for mentoring. What categories do items in your list fit under? In light of these categories, do you have any new thinking about how to focus your mentoring for the teacher you identified? What new resources or knowledge do you need to pursue in order to support your teacher?

- clarifying values, philosophy, and theoretical frameworks
- strengthening useful dispositions
- holding a view of children as capable and deserving
- defining the role of the caregiver or teacher
- taking action based on reflection
- learning techniques and skills
- understanding standards and learning domains

Strategy *Compare your view with their view*

To approach a coaching relationship with curiosity, seeking understanding, it is helpful to assess your views of the teaching and learning process alongside your teacher's view. Use the following chart to see where you have shared understandings and differences.

	Reflect on Yourself	Reflect on a Teacher
	Consider yourself as a mentor or supervisor.	*Consider a teacher you mentor or supervise.*
What view of children influences typical planning and responses to behaviors?	I see children as • • •	S/he sees children as • • •
What ideas about the teacher's role influence planning and responses to behavior?	I see the teacher's role as • • •	S/he see the teacher's role as • • •
How is the teaching and learning process viewed?	Teaching and learning work together when • • • •	Teaching and learning work together when • • • •
How are pressures, challenges, and innovative ideas responded to?	When faced with pressures or challenges, I • • When introduced to innovative ideas, I • •	When faced with pressures or challenges, s/he • • When introduced to innovative ideas, s/he • •

With your staff, reflect on the similarities and differences between your views and theirs. Does this comparison give you insight into how you might expand your coaching with them? Promote conversation among your staff members by giving them a chance to fill this chart out for themselves. Lead a discussion asking people to share their responses, giving examples and naming the reasons why they think this way. The goal here is not to get everyone to agree or have the "correct" answers, but to encourage self-knowledge and practice negotiating diverse perspectives on their work with children.

Principle

Emphasize Dispositions as Much as Skills and Knowledge

Dispositions are as critical to teacher effectiveness as are skills and knowledge. We first began to think about the idea of teacher dispositions from reading the work of Lilian Katz (1995). She defines disposition as the habit of mind or tendency to respond to situations in certain ways. Katz stresses that teacher educators should be trying to strengthen worthwhile dispositions for their work with children and families and weaken those that are unhelpful.

This idea proved so useful in our work that in our first book, *Training Teachers: A Harvest of Theory and Practice* (Carter and Curtis 1994), we devoted an entire section to our evolving thinking about the importance of coaching for dispositions. We identified the dispositions we have seen in masterful teachers and reviewed them for teachers to consider in our third book, *Reflecting Children's Lives: A Handbook for Planning Child-Centered Curriculum* (Curtis and Carter 1996). We believe these dispositions are so central to effective teaching that they are worth restating again here, especially in the context of coaching teachers for reflective practices. As you read through the following list, consider how your approach to in-service training supports or undermines these dispositions.

Reflective teachers:

- have delight and curiosity about children's development
- value children's play
- expect continuous change and challenge
- are willing to take risks and make mistakes
- take regular time for reflection and self-examination

- seek collaboration and peer support
- serve as visionary watchdogs and whistle-blowers

Too often directors say and do things with staff that may unintentionally undermine some of these dispositions. If you keep the staff focused on paperwork rather than on children, it will be difficult for teachers to take delight in the play that is unfolding. Requiring teachers to regularly use checklists and assessment tools can quickly take the joy out of observation and documenting children's development. Teachers who are frequently reminded about rules and regulations are unlikely to trust their own thinking or risk trying new things in their work. Like most people, teachers have difficulty sustaining a vision for change if they don't experience support for the risks they take in their daily lives.

On the other hand, some directors behave in ways that support constructive dispositions in their staff. For example, when you set up peer mentoring relationships, you encourage collaboration and peer support. If you regularly share observations and hypotheses about children's activities, you model a disposition you want teachers to acquire—curiosity. As you devote time in staff meetings to uncovering the elements of childhood and community that you want as the foundation for your program, you strengthen your staff's mind-set to resist pressures for an inappropriate, shallow academic curriculum.

If your goal is to strengthen self-confidence, reflection, and independence and to weaken passivity and dependence in your staff, you will encourage and validate staff ideas in all your coaching work. Giving caregivers opportunities to analyze video footage of children in their room will probably promote more self-examination than most verbal feedback you give them. Suggesting that coworkers observe some children at play while you handle their classroom responsibilities has the potential to pique their excitement about child development more than giving them an article to read.

As you develop individual training goals for teachers, consider the dispositions you would like to reinforce in each teacher. Then think through your coaching strategies and consider the underlying dispositions each strategy could strengthen or undermine.

Strategy *Identify how dispositions look in practice*

The concept of dispositions can be nothing but an abstract word or personal inference unless you develop shared understandings of how this looks in day-to-day work life. In *Reflecting Children's Lives*, we translated each of the dispositions listed above into general behaviors described on an assessment continuum. Involving teachers in defining the dispositions most helpful for your program's vision is a powerful staff development tool. You can then formulate concrete descriptions of what these dispositions might look like in practice.

Here's an example from a series of discussions on dispositions toward mess, risk taking, and schedules.

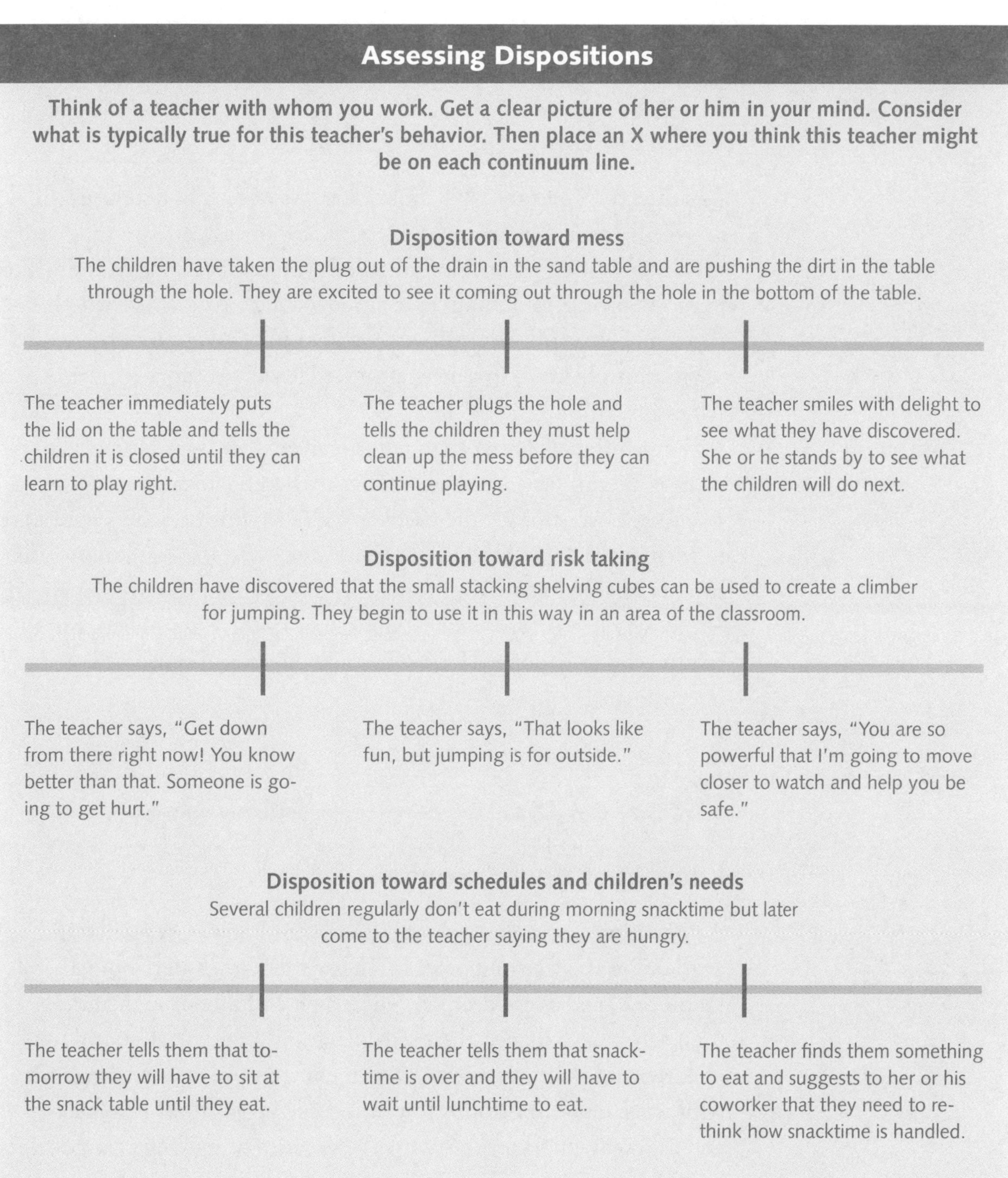

Assessing Dispositions

Think of a teacher with whom you work. Get a clear picture of her or him in your mind. Consider what is typically true for this teacher's behavior. Then place an X where you think this teacher might be on each continuum line.

Disposition toward mess

The children have taken the plug out of the drain in the sand table and are pushing the dirt in the table through the hole. They are excited to see it coming out through the hole in the bottom of the table.

The teacher immediately puts the lid on the table and tells the children it is closed until they can learn to play right.

The teacher plugs the hole and tells the children they must help clean up the mess before they can continue playing.

The teacher smiles with delight to see what they have discovered. She or he stands by to see what the children will do next.

Disposition toward risk taking

The children have discovered that the small stacking shelving cubes can be used to create a climber for jumping. They begin to use it in this way in an area of the classroom.

The teacher says, "Get down from there right now! You know better than that. Someone is going to get hurt."

The teacher says, "That looks like fun, but jumping is for outside."

The teacher says, "You are so powerful that I'm going to move closer to watch and help you be safe."

Disposition toward schedules and children's needs

Several children regularly don't eat during morning snacktime but later come to the teacher saying they are hungry.

The teacher tells them that tomorrow they will have to sit at the snack table until they eat.

The teacher tells them that snacktime is over and they will have to wait until lunchtime to eat.

The teacher finds them something to eat and suggests to her or his coworker that they need to rethink how snacktime is handled.

To connect dispositions with behaviors under discussion, you can create a continuum across the floor and ask teachers to stand next to the response that best represents what they would do. This usually uncovers differences that can lead to tension and conflict among the staff. Another effective approach is to show photos of children at play in messy or risky situations. Have the staff discuss their initial responses to the photo and how their reactions reflect their dispositions. A coaching process that helps teachers collaboratively identify their underlying habits of mind in typical early childhood situations will lead to more self-reflection and fewer knee-jerk reactions.

Strategy Discover with dots

As a director, you may have more expertise and child development knowledge than a given caregiver, so it's often easy for you to identify problems in their practices. Sometimes you can walk into a room and immediately see something that needs "fixing." As a coach who is focused on cultivating dispositions, resist the urge to immediately offer suggestions. Instead, invent strategies that will promote reflection and self-examination.

For instance, rather than tell caregivers that their room arrangement is a setup for continual conflicts between children, give them a way to discover this for themselves. We've supplied teachers with dots to stick in the area of the room where and when they see conflict disrupting engaged play. At the end of the week, they discover a pattern. An activity like this may take a bit longer to solve a problem, but the results tend to be longer lasting because effective dispositions are being cultivated.

Principle

Know Your Adult Learners

Adults bring a complex web of experiences, knowledge, skills, and attitudes to the learning process. They experience a developmental process, just as children do. Their own childhoods and cultural framework have shaped their self-image and how they respond to children and their coworkers. Staff members come to our programs with particular dispositions toward people in positions of authority and different emotional responses to the idea of making changes. To be effective in staff development, you must take time to discover who your staff members are and, in Carol Anne Wien's words, what their "scripts for action" (1995, 116)—or responses teachers typically use without thinking—look like. You must recognize what they already know and what their interests are, and plan training that is relevant and meaningful to their lives. Isn't this just what you hope they will do with the children in their care?

In describing what teachers bring to their work with children, Wien says that "the notion of practical knowledge includes all that the teacher brings of herself to the moment of teaching—beliefs, attitudes, feelings, reflection, gestures, temperament, personal history" (1995, 10). She says practical knowledge tends to override what may have been learned in any course work, especially when education has been lacking in specific training to become a reflective teacher. Wien describes teachers as needing an adult pedagogy that assists them to think in terms of the power dynamics or developmental process involved in situations they encounter. They benefit from coaching, which helps them analyze their own scripts and those of teachers around them.

Rather than waiting and reacting to issues when they arise, we suggest you periodically devote portions of your staff meetings to uncovering and appreciating the personal and cultural differences that influence teachers' practical knowledge. An activity such as True Confessions in Four Corners (see the next page for discussion of this strategy) is good not only for team building but for shaping your approach to coaching each staff member.

If I am to individualize with my staff the way I want them to individualize with children, I have to invest the time to get to know them personally. This is a big job with nineteen people, plus the children and their families. But what could be more important? My view of mentoring is to be as flexible as possible. I coached one teacher to not be so dedicated, to stop giving her all to the center and start having a life. I coached a very reliable but mediocre worker with the children to leave the field. Those who need direction from me get it, while others assume full responsibility for their ongoing development.

—Laura

Strategy Play True Confessions in Four Corners

To help people talk about their experiences and points of view, tell them it's time for some playful "true confessions." Have people get up and move for this activity. Tell the group you are going to ask a question and then designate each corner of the room with a possible answer to choose from. There is no right answer, and everyone gets to determine their own meaning for going to a particular corner. Here are some ideas to get you started.

Learning something new
When it comes to learning something new, I usually:

- read a book or a manual
- seek out advice
- look for a model
- jump in and try it

Once people get to a corner, ask them to explain why they are there. They will usually be forthcoming about what works best for them and often have stories that offer an example of why they or their coworkers are standing in a particular spot. This is an easy, playful way to acknowledge differences among your staff. Remind everyone to make a mental note of how each of their coworkers needs to be supported in their learning process.

Follow this first round of "four corners" with one that acknowledges another potential area of difference among staff members. To keep things playful while encouraging deeper thinking, make use of metaphors. For example, try a category like the one that follows:

Relating to authority figures
My family or my cultural values have taught me to respond to authority figures like one of the following animals:

- a German shepherd
- a giraffe
- a parrot
- an ostrich

The initial response to metaphors is often puzzlement; however, some people immediately identify with one and rush to a corner. Again, you may need to stress that there is no right answer and that their task is to make their own meaning. If they still stand with a confused look, suggest they first think about what their family or culture has taught them about responding to people in authority. Then consider which of these animals might remind them of this way of being.

Ask people to explain why they have chosen a particular animal. If the group is large and your time is limited, you can have them do this in pairs and then ask for highlights to be shared with the whole group. The issue of how people approach someone in a position of authority is relevant to the relationship you as a supervisor will build with them, even if you don't want to be seen as an authority figure. In the debriefing of this round you will likely discover who has loyalty as a primary value and who has been taught to question, obey, or ignore authority figures. This will give you insight into behaviors you might witness and hopefully spark more self-awareness on the part of staff members themselves.

Finally, try exploring people's dispositions toward change. Again, tell them to make their own meaning and go to the corner that represents what's typically true for them, as you read the choices.

Responding to requests to change
When I'm asked to make a change, this is the song you'll hear me singing:

- "Hi ho, hi ho, it's off to work I go"
- "Nobody knows the trouble I've seen"
- "The itsy-bitsy spider went up the water spout"
- "If I had a hammer, I'd hammer in the morning, I'd hammer in the evening, all over this land"

The debriefing of this final round can bring insight as well as laughter. In any given group there is usually a wide range of how people respond to someone who is bringing about change. Some find it easy to roll with things, while others have to be dragged kicking and screaming. Many people like the change process to be slow and drawn out, whereas others want to quickly get on with it. You may discover that some staff members feel you haven't given them the tools with which to make the changes you want. Consider all the responses as valuable information for your coaching relationships.

The use of metaphors in this activity makes it clear that you aren't looking for a "right" answer. There is no fixed truth to how someone interprets the meaning of an animal's behavior or song lyrics, for instance. People often have different reasons why they choose a particular metaphor corner. In the case of the animals we listed, some may choose the German shepherd because, for them, it stands for obedience and loyalty, following an authority figure out of respect for the role. Others may choose the German shepherd thinking it represents strong and fierce barking to challenge authority figures trying to control their behavior. Metaphors help us examine beliefs, values, and behaviors that are not always easy to bring to the surface for discussion.

Reread the questions for each round of "four corners," and choose an answer for yourself. This will help you learn more about yourself and prepare you for the kinds of discussions you can have with this activity. Answers to these questions often reflect the concept of "scripts for action." They are instinctive responses that are embedded below our consciousness. The metaphors help us examine views and behaviors that are often unconsciously shaped by our childhoods. Most work settings don't acknowledge these scripts in a way that helps us reflect on our behaviors and interactions. Doing so in early childhood settings not only helps us understand the impact adults have on children, but clarifies where adults' behaviors come from. Attitudes and behaviors that reflect our instinctive reaction to authority figures or to being asked to make changes often come from unexamined emotions or beliefs that can block our ability to learn and work collaboratively.

A major part of a director's job is to coach staff to examine what changes are needed. In these efforts it's helpful for everyone to understand how they tend to respond to change. When coworkers discover themselves singing different songs in different corners, they can recognize possible sources of tension and gain more empathy for each other. Activities such as these create an acknowledgment and respect for differences, laying a foundation for more productive mentoring relationships.

Principle

Provide Choices for Different Needs and Interests

Take the time to remember something important you intentionally learned in your adult life, and consider what motivated you to pursue this learning. Most likely you had a compelling need or particular interest that led you to and sustained your learning. How can you translate this to your coaching of caregivers and staff? They must have an interest or feel a need for the knowledge or skill you are asking them to learn. If your policies or regulations lack meaning for teachers, they are less likely to be consistent in adhering to them.

Some of the behaviors you coach for are related to policies and regulations that neither you nor your staff had a hand in shaping. They come from an outside regulatory agency or administrative arm of your organization. Most compliance issues are based on behaviors that support your vision, while a few might inhibit it. Each time you find a need to reinforce a regulation, coach teachers to see how it connects to your vision. You may periodically need to return to some of the vision-building activities discussed in chapter 1.

For example, explore how your health and safety policies are tied to creating a neighborhood feeling in your program. Ask why tardiness undermines your ability to function as a learning community. Sometimes you must be creative in meeting requirements if they are to truly uphold your vision. For example, consider how you can keep kids safe while encouraging them to take the risks they need for growth and development. Discuss how you can start with your vision and connect that to the official standards and criteria, rather than defining your program by the standards. Conversations on topics like these are significantly more meaningful than running down a list of regulations. Only after efforts at coaching for these behaviors have failed should you shift to the managing-and-overseeing side of the triangle framework and seek corrective measures.

Most of your coaching and mentoring needs to be individualized for each staff member. You may still have staff meetings focused on a training topic, but these should evolve out of collaborative staff input, needs assessments, and interests. Choosing a focus over time, as the High/Scope research highlights (Epstein 1993), doesn't mean repeating the same training a number of times. Rather, you can come at a topic with a variety of strategies and address goals for different staff members in the same way they are asked to create curriculum that is individualized for children.

Strategy Think of something you have learned as an adult

To rethink your approach to staff development, identify something new you have learned in your adult life. Take a minute to remember how that happened:

- How did you go about learning it?
- What motivated you, and what barriers did you overcome?
- Did anyone else have a role in your learning? If so, how did that relationship work?
- If you learned on your own, what strategies did you use?

Now compare the memory below to the typical in-service training you offer in your program. How is it similar or different?

When I moved to Germany to work for the U.S. Army child development programs, I really didn't know how to do my job. I soon found out that it wouldn't work to just tell the teachers what they should be doing. I began to examine my own education to see how I had come to understand things like DAP [developmentally appropriate practice]. What had my mentors done to spark my interest and turn on my "lightbulb"? Thinking about these questions helped to form my vision of how to work with the teachers at my center.

I tried adapting what I understand about Piaget's theory to my work with teachers. As I began discussions with staff, I tried to find out their prior knowledge before giving them new information or challenging what I was seeing. I did this with storytelling or concrete examples of children's work. I prompted them with questions so that they would come up with their own answers.

—Cathy

Most people's mental image of teacher training is a workshop setting where the director or trainer is in front of the room explaining something to the group. Was this what you remembered in the above activity? Most people say that sitting and listening to someone describe information plays a small role in their learning. Our guess is that the learning process you described above was more involved than that. It probably included such things as experimenting, reading, observing, talking things over with someone, trying out new ideas, making mistakes, and perhaps practicing over and over again. Possibly you were an apprentice to a coach or role model.

Remembering the variety of ways that adults go about learning should help you assess your work with your staff. If your approach to training is limited to "telling" sessions or workshop formats, you might be missing the boat.

Strategy Train with multiple intelligences in mind

Howard Gardner first brought us the term *multiple intelligences*, now frequently shortened to MI. In general, keeping the concepts of MI in mind will enhance our teacher development efforts.

Gardner initially outlined seven kinds of intelligence: spatial, logical-mathematical, interpersonal, intrapersonal, musical, kinesthetic, and verbal-linguistic (1993). Gardner has added to these over the years as his research has continued. Finding or creating an MI self-assessment checklist for staff to complete alerts them to these different learning modes for children, themselves, and their coworkers. You can find examples of these checklists on the Internet. You can simultaneously focus on an early childhood topic and explore the concept of multiple intelligences by having teachers share their understanding using the different modes of MI. Consider how you might adapt the following example for a training topic your staff wants to have as a focus for a period of time.

To investigate the concept of the book *The Good Preschool Teacher* (Ayers 1989), set up MI learning stations where staff share what they understand.

- For spatial intelligence, ask them to draw or paint a representation of the qualities of a good teacher.
- For logical-mathematical intelligence, give them the task of creating a step-by-step diagram or description of the qualities of a good teacher.
- For interpersonal intelligence, have them explore working with a partner or small group to brainstorm a list of the qualities of a good teacher.
- For intrapersonal intelligence, have staff work alone to reflect on a good teacher they have had, considering the qualities that made this teacher so effective.

- For kinesthetic intelligence, give them materials to build a 3–D model that represents the qualities of a good teacher.
- For musical intelligence, have teachers create a rap or song about the qualities.
- For verbal-linguistic intelligence, suggest staff write a short story or poem about a good teacher, and then read it aloud.

Whatever your training focus, you can adapt this activity and use it over time to deepen staff's understanding. You can combine it with other professional resources such as checklists, articles, videos, or books. For instance, set up MI learning stations to explore toddler social-emotional, sensory, or motor needs in conjunction with resources such as the video *Time with Toddlers* (Carter and Reed 1991), the Toddlers series from Teaching Strategies, or the infant and toddler videos and training modules from WestEd's Program for Infant/Toddler Care (PITC). Good books to use on this topic include *Multicultural Issues in Child Care* by Janet Gonzalez-Mena (2000); *Prime Times* by Jim Greenman, Anne Stonehouse, and Gigi Schweikert (2008); and children's books such as *The Runaway Bunny* by Margaret Wise Brown (1972) and *Mama, Do You Love Me?* by Barbara Joosse (1991).

As you move among these resources, don't be concerned about repetition or duplication. As long as you keep things lively and meaningful, you will provide a variety of opportunities for staff to construct their understanding in the way that works best for their learning style. Sometimes do the learning stations first, followed by a section from one of the recommended videos. On other occasions, summarize part of a reading as it relates to the video or something uncovered at one of the MI stations. Space permitting, you could even leave the learning stations set up in your staff room with ongoing opportunities for self-directed learning.

Strategy *Uncover and cultivate passions*

Most directors are inclined to spend precious training dollars on identified weaknesses in staff. But if you heed the theories of adult learning and our principle of providing for different needs and interests, it's important to offer staff opportunities to select training they would like to receive. Directors tend to worry they will choose things different from their assessment of staff training needs, and, indeed, this might sometimes happen. But if you want the adults in your program to be excited about and committed to learning, you need to respect the different directions their interests might take them.

The operative words here are *excited* and *committed*. When emotions get connected to motivation, significant change is more likely to occur. If a staff member really wants to hone expertise in puppetry but her child guidance skills are lacking, how might learning about puppets improve her guidance of children? It's important to go beyond considerations of how puppets might play a role in her guidance strategies. Assess the potential of how the learning process might influence her work in other arenas. What does it take to really master puppetry? Those who have expertise in this area will tell you that good observation skills and empathy are needed for character development in puppets. If puppets are to go beyond entertainment and address the social, emotional, and learning needs of children, puppeteers need to understand children's issues and ways of thinking.

Create opportunities for each of your staff members to identify passions they want to pursue. Sometimes this requires activities of values clarification, storytelling, and sharing of favorite objects. You might ask teachers to each bring samples of something they are collecting—spoons, shells, buttons, pipes, postcards, antique tools, objects with a frog motif. Discuss what got them interested in this and any stories associated with the collection. On another occasion, have them bring a photograph or object that represents a triumph in their life. Spend time in a staff meeting having each person identify one thing they'd really like to understand or be able to do before they die. Your coaching can continue to stimulate this interest that will enliven you, your staff, and the experiences they offer the children.

For instance, as you learn about a strong interest a staff member has, keep your eye out for related literature or workshops you can offer them. Remind staff members of their individual interests as you engage in other discussion. If someone has a strong attachment to animals, periodically ask them to share an understanding they have from this interest that might offer insights into reading cues from children or their family members. Perhaps there are staff members who like to garden, go biking, quilt, or collect rocks. Find ways for these interests to be brought into discussions and the classroom.

For any of these ideas to work, you must be a suitable model. Spend time with your staff showing them the passion you have about something. Bring in photographs or a poem, story, or article. It might be a volunteer project that has nothing to do with children, something you are collecting, information you are trying to acquire, or a skill you want to master. Work together as a staff to find ways to explore what you care deeply about. Have a space in your staff room where you rotate special things staff members bring from home to share. Don't underestimate this as effective coaching and staff development.

Our budget allows up to forty hours a year for each staff member to receive some kind of training. Because we recognize that not everybody learns in the same way, most of this money goes to individual training plans, rather than center-wide workshops. We have some teachers who have used the money to improve their literacy skills, while others have attended science or art programs that aren't specifically related to early childhood. My theory is that if you strengthen a passion, you strengthen the teacher.

—**Laura**

Principle

Promote Collaboration and Mentoring

A learning community has a different feel from that of a typical school setting, where people are expected to learn and master things for themselves. The organizational culture of early childhood programs must counter the dominant culture's messages of "survival of the fittest" and "everyone for themselves." Most early childhood teachers and directors agree that rivalry, jealousy, victim thinking, and passive-aggressive behaviors are self-destructive to individuals and organizations. But that doesn't mean people know how to behave differently. They need coaching and structures that make it clear that together they're better and that any weak link in the program deserves all the collective support they can muster.

Listening skills are also central to developing a learning community. Active listening skills don't come naturally to most of us. On the contrary, most adults need coaching to develop the consistent habit of paraphrasing and acknowledging what they hear in order to build trust and identify misunderstandings. Likewise, adults need to give equally careful attention to what children say, restating and affirming what they are hearing to garner a feeling of respect as well as language development.

Strategy Practice active listening, informally and formally

When your regular communications include active listening skills, you are providing experiential learning for others in your program. People feel heard and respected and come to recognize the value of natural paraphrasing as a way of acknowledging that they understand what is being said. It's useful to take time in staff meetings to specifically outline and practice active listening skills. Have people practice in pairs with role plays or topics you know to be full of emotion for the staff. As a coach, your job is to remind people to first paraphrase what they are hearing before offering a response. Paraphrasing may not be a natural way for most people to conduct conversations, but it's a useful skill to call on when faced with tension, conflict, or miscommunication with a coworker or parent.

Strategy Set up a peer-coaching system

Ideally you will work to get a peer-coaching process in place, one that works well for your program. It should also then contribute to other programs in your early childhood community. This involves identifying staff members who want to make a career of working with children and who show signs of mastering the needed dispositions, skills, and knowledge to do so. You can offer them opportunities to nurture new teachers in your program as well as explore adult learning and human development theories.

As a director, start with yourself, enhancing your own understanding of adult pedagogy and empowerment. Practice your mentoring skills with your most able staff members so that, before long, you can have a peer-coaching system in place. From there, you could join with other directors or training institutions in your area to set up a wider exchange of mentor teachers who receive training and compensation for coaching staff members in other programs. These kinds of mentoring programs are emerging across the country and are helping both to improve the quality of programs and stabilize the workforce.

I learned from one of my board members who lived in the corporate world that I should think of myself as a CEO and mentor my lead teachers as my vice presidents. Strange as that sounded at first, it became a good strategy. I directed most of my mentoring energy to them and told them to do likewise with the staff in their rooms. I brought them current research, ideas, articles, and information from the community. We went as a group together to conferences and to Worthy Wage Day activities. And we continually talked about what we were learning and what we still needed to know. I was responsive to their ideas and issues while continually requiring them to take one more step to grow.

—Julie

Strategy *Build collaborative and mentoring relationships*

As a group, take time to identify the strengths of each staff member and each room. For each, probe to discover what might be called the "signature feature," a particular attribute or skill that contributes something unique to your program. Begin an inquiry as to who wants to be known for what expertise. Whether you develop a formal or informal peer-mentoring system, this recognition will strengthen your learning community. Pairing people for collaborative tasks that cross rooms and age groups can keep the learning mutual. The following list of tips will help you move toward these mentoring relationships in your program.

- Choose a mutual focus for learning, and set individual goals.
- Visit each other's rooms and rooms in other programs.
- Read and discuss relevant literature together.
- Tell stories of things you've observed related to your focus.
- Observe a child together, and share notes.
- Examine children's portfolio collections together.
- Facilitate a staff meeting together on your topic.
- Submit a workshop proposal together for a conference.
- Write articles together for your program newsletter and Web site and other professional journals or blogs.

We are a group of diverse individuals in our program who have learned to collaborate, sustain momentum, and flourish over time. Here are the key elements that have been instrumental in our continued progress.

Passion
Our passion for what we do goes way beyond our commitment to the work. Commitments seem to drain us, but our passion continues to fuel us. We are a group of individuals who came together already passionate about our work with children. Joining together with others who share this level of devotion offers us an unstoppable degree of momentum.

Shared Vision
We want our mission statement to be more than words on paper. It serves to keep our group's energy focused. Our shared vision of purpose and philosophy is a continual resource to reaffirm our individual contributions and actions. Over time it has helped us turn our individual differences into strengths.

Self-Reflection/Lifelong Learning
Our team has access to our fullest potential because each of us possesses a willingness to self-reflect on personal strengths and challenges. Looking inward provides us opportunities to continually discover our emerging talents and growing edges. We all believe that learning is a lifelong process and we are all works in progress along this continuum.

Creative Energy
Our team thrives because we create an atmosphere that values free-flowing exchanges, fosters vision, and limits judgment. Our members share a spirit of creative thought, feeding off each other's ideas and building on our own ideas. This environment provides a scaffold for learning, originality, and energy.

Risk Taking
The challenges of our work have presented a different degree of risk for each of us. The willingness to take on these risks and others has been crucial to our longevity. To help us succeed as individuals, our group has offered us the support and security that encourages our risk taking. Our members feel comfortable with the connections in the trusting environment that we co-create.

I've noticed that when we are all out together, we've developed a unique way of walking. We tend to have a constant flow in and out of smaller conversations—a sort of drifting and shifting from group to group as we all move in the same direction. You have your choice of discussions about different ideas, projects, and visions. You can put your ten cents in one exchange and then just speed up or slow down your walking pace to join another group. It's really pretty amazing.

—Wendy

Every so often I use staff meetings to practice sharing our different views. I choose topics that may initially seem unrelated to our work with children, but they help us sharpen analytic skills and clarify our values. For instance, I brought in copies of a newspaper article about a strike at a nursing home where some of our parents work. We discussed the issues that were raised in the article and shared our own opinions. As the discussion became heated, we had great practice in sharing different perspectives and learning how to disagree. The experience of examining the social, political, and economic interests behind events in our community ultimately enhances our ability to be an antibias program.

—Ellen

Principle

Cultivate Observation as a Skill and an Art

Most teachers come to your program with no formal training in observation skills. Some have taken course work that made the process tedious and boring. The professional emphasis in these courses is usually on objectivity, discouraging the teacher's thinking and voice in the teaching and learning process. Coaching must certainly help teachers acquire the ability to gather objective data. But overall, coaching should promote a mind-set of curiosity and delight, encouraging teachers to use the objective data to reflect on the many possibilities for interpretation and possible responses. When observation skills are refined, teachers can learn more about child development as they cultivate the art of interpretation of what they are seeing.

Provide ongoing opportunities in meetings for your staff to practice their observation skills. Our book *The Art of Awareness* (Curtis and Carter 2000) offers many strategies you can use with your staff to enhance their observation skills, including using photographs and video clips with the following questions to guide your discussions. As the staff share their observations and analyses, you can point out the expanded set of possibilities to consider when the process is a collaborative one.

Questions for observing children:

- What, specifically, did I see?
- What do I think is most significant about this experience for the child? Why?
- What does my data reveal about what the child knows and can do?
- What can I say about how this child feels about herself or himself?

Strategy Learn to observe in many ways

Teachers will grow in their observation skills when you coach them to look closely at the world around them. As they learn to stop and smell the flowers, their eyes get sharper, their hearts become softer, and they begin to see the world as children do. The following activities are playful and useful examples from *The Art of Awareness:*

- Try putting pictures or relevant books in the staff room and restrooms—"spot the difference," "find the hidden object," or Magic Eye 3D books are great tools for building observation skills.
- Offer magnifying glasses, telescopes, color paddles, kaleidoscopes, and other optical "toys" for teachers to play with in the staff room. Bring them to staff meetings, and have teachers use them and talk about the new ways they are seeing the world.
- Include books in your staff library, and signs around the building with quotes from naturalists and artists using beautiful, detailed descriptions of nature and animals.

- Display engaging descriptive observations and quotes about children written by some of our profession's best observers and writers, such as Vivian Paley, Jim Greenman, Elizabeth Jones, and Loris Malaguzzi. These further expose staff to the power of the skill and art of descriptive observation.
- Do your own observations and storytelling about children's activities, sharing your excitement, delight, and curiosity with staff and families. Model the value of visual documentation stories by sharing written notes, photographs, and children's work samples on bulletin boards and in homemade books.

These activitites can be part of a coaching system to enhance your staff's observation skills and their ability to analyze and use descriptive language.

Strategy *Become a community of observers*

As a director, you have a unique opportunity to help teachers become more acute and discriminating observers of children's work and play and of each other. With each visit to a room, you have opportunities to coach caregivers and teachers by describing even a brief conversation or activity you have witnessed. You can informally share detailed descriptions in quick conversations in the hallways and in staff meetings. This modeling shows staff that you value stories that come from listening and observing and it gives them a sense of how to do it themselves.

One of my best coaching strategies is to personally get to know every child so that I have stories to bring to our conversations. When I share stories about individual children with my staff, it puts us on the same side of the table. It alerts them to what I value, and they start gathering stories to share with me.

—Laura

Principle

Create a Culture of Curiosity, Research, and Storytelling

Rather than portraying staff development as a process in which teachers learn techniques and learning games from books or "experts," support teachers in their self-development by cultivating a disposition of inquisitiveness and a desire to analyze activities. When they are encouraged to ask detailed questions about what they are seeing and hearing, teachers become participatory researchers. The stories of their discoveries can generate learning and excitement in others.

Reflecting on the significance of children's activities encourages teachers to see children's play and their own work as more valuable. Using a protocol for thinking through the complexities of ordinary moments and participating in informal research projects strengthens observation, documentation, and collaboration skills. Giving significant attention to the seemingly everyday events of the classroom helps teachers see things in a new light. They are motivated to reflect on their previously unexamined responses to children and continually engage in their own development and learning.

Strategy *Cultivate deep listening*

Vital to a culture of curiosity, deep thinking, and research is supporting your staff to reflect on the idea of listening to children and each other deeply. This is different from active listening or even listening politely. It is the practice of pausing and letting go of your own thoughts and agenda to truly hear the deeper messages and meaning for what is unfolding around you. Carlina Rinaldi from the schools of Reggio Emilia describes this as the "pedagogy of listening" (2005, 15). To help your staff understand this concept, use staff meetings to read and study each of the quotations below and discuss what the quotations mean to each teacher. Ask them to identify specific examples from their work with children in which they used deep listening and what occurred as a result.

> A nun I know who's worked for years with families in poor neighborhoods speaks of a certain mood of "unexamined receptivity," which does not mean, she says, merely the willingness to listen carefully or patiently. "It has to do

with quieting your state of mind as you *prepare* to listen. It means not pressing on too fast to get to something that you think you 'need to get to' as the 'purpose' or 'objective' of the conversation. . . ."

There's something about silence and not being in a hurry . . . that seem to give a message about receptivity. I also think that children need some reason to believe that what they say will not be heard too clinically, or journalistically, or put "to use" too rapidly, and that the gift they give us will be taken into hands that will not seize too fast upon their confidence, or grasp too firmly, or attempt to push an idea to completion when it needs to be left open, incomplete, and tentative a while.

—Jonathan Kozol (2000, 76–78)

When someone deeply listens to you
it is like holding out a dented cup
you've had since childhood
and watching it fill up with
cold, fresh water.
When it balances on the top of the brim,
you are understood.
When it overflows and touches your skin
you are loved.

When someone deeply listens to you,
the room where you stay
starts a new life
and the place where you wrote
your first poem
begins to glow in the mind's eye.
It is as if gold had been discovered.

When someone deeply listens to you,
your bare feet are on the earth
and a beloved land that seemed distant
is now at home within you.

—John Fox (1995)

Strategy Use a Thinking Lens for reflection

The daily reality of working with children presents so many demands that it can be difficult for teachers to take time for deep listening or thinking through their work. Offering teachers a protocol that they regularly use to reflect on the details of their time with children can help them develop a focused and thoughtful approach to the teaching and learning process. The Thinking Lens, which we developed in collaboration with Ann Pelo following the publication of our book *Learning Together with Young Children* (Curtis and Carter 2008), leads teachers to continually clarify their values and beliefs about the teaching and learning process and to plan and respond to children with purpose and intention. Regular discussion with the Thinking Lens will help teachers bring more discipline to the analysis of their work, encourage collaboration, and strengthen their confidence and competence as reflective practitioners.

A Thinking Lens for Reflection

Know Yourself

How am I reacting to this situation, and why? What in my background and values is influencing my response to this situation, and why?

What adult perspectives (i.e., standards, health and safety, time) are on my mind?

What values, philosophy, and goals do I want to influence my response?

What captures my attention as the children explore and follow their pursuits?

What delights me as I watch and listen to the children's ideas?

What irritates or challenges me about their work?

Examine the Physical/Social/Emotional Environment

How are the organization and use of the physical space and materials affecting this situation?

In what ways are the routines, adult behaviors, and language undermining or strengthening the children's ability to demonstrate their competence?

How could we strengthen relationships here?

What child development themes do I see in their play?

How can I take the child's point of view?

What might the child be trying to accomplish?

What ideas or theories might the child be exploring or communicating?

As they play, what are the children experiencing? Why are they moving their hands in that particular way? Why are they turning their heads at that specific angle? Why are they standing up instead of sitting in a chair? Why might they be interacting with others this way?

A Thinking Lens for Reflection *(continued)*

Notice the Details That Engage Your Heart and Mind

What touches my heart and engages my mind as I watch and listen?

As I notice the children work, what are they drawn to and excited about? What do I notice in their faces and the quality of their voices as they talk?

What details do I want to make visible that heighten the value of this experience?

Where do I see examples of children's strengths and competencies?

Collaborate with Others to Expand Perspectives

What might the children be learning from this play and exploration?

How might issues of culture, family background, or popular media be influencing this situation?

What questions do I have for the children's families?

What do I want to talk about with my coteachers?

What theoretical perspectives, standards, and child development principles could inform my understandings and actions?

Consider Opportunities and Possibilities for Action

What values, philosophy, and goals do I want to influence my response?

How can I build on previous experiences of individuals and the group?

Which learning goals could be focused on here?

What new or existing relationships could be strengthened?

What should we do next and think about for the future?

Strategy *Launch a research project*

The idea of teachers as researchers has taken root in the early childhood profession over the past ten years. Programs can learn how to take up informal research in their work with children from models like the schools of Reggio Emilia and those found in the Voices of Practicioners section on the Web site of NAEYC (www.naeyc.org/publications/vop). Launching a research project in your program can be exciting for teachers and help them see the larger significance of their work. Participating in research can help teachers bring early childhood theory to life and real life to theories.

You can begin a research project by identifying a topic related to children's behavior that seems to generate a lot of teacher attention or by focusing on something that teachers value or delight in with children and want to learn more about. Formulate a question related to the topic to help focus teachers' observations. Perhaps provide some simple observation forms for them to document each instance when they notice something related to the question. You may need to coach teachers initially to recognize the details of children's conversation and play. Help them collaborate in analyzing and hypothesizing the significance of the documentation they gather. You can use the Thinking Lens to encourage deeper discussions. Here's an example of how one research project evolved, excerpted from the teacher's documentation display.

In the fall of this year, our program was growing an emergent curriculum project around children's interests in firefighters. As we discussed our observations we became fascinated with the variety of sounds children used in their firefighter play. There were sounds of sirens, water squirting, fire burning, and rescue efforts. As teachers, we kept wanting the children to use their "inside voices" to keep the noise down. But the more we listened and watched we noticed the children seemed to use sounds very purposefully, not just to represent the sounds of firefighting. These were intense and repetitive sounds. It was as if these sounds helped them more fully experience the emotions of their drama and helped them feel more powerful and in control of their fear of fire.

On the way to work on one of these firefighting days, I happened to hear a gospel singer interviewed on the radio. He said his favorite songs were the old African American spirituals that slaves sang as they worked in the fields. He described the sounds used to sing the music as even more powerful than the words. They resonated throughout his body, filling him with an understanding of the meaning of the words and the experiences they described. As I heard him singing the deep, earthy sounds, I was reminded of the children's play. His description matched our hypothesis about the meaning of the sounds the children had been making.

As I shared this interview and my insight with the other teachers, our curiosity surged and we wanted to know more about the role of sounds in children's play. We decided to launch an informal research project to collect data on the noise in our room. We kept observation notes for a month and then met to discuss the significance of what we observed.

The purpose of our study was not to create curriculum or intervene in children's activities, but to deepen our own understandings and ability to respond appropriately. Our observations, collaboration, and analysis of the children's play offered us an opportunity for intellectual stimulation and added meaning to our work. We began to notice things about children that we never paid attention to before. Before starting this little research project we would often stop noisy play without realizing its significance. Our research helped us develop a different relationship to the "noise" in our room. Rather than always getting annoyed, we now try to watch and listen to decide on its meaning and the best response.

—Deborah

Principle

Approach Coaching with Inquiry

Teachers need more than annual evaluations to get a sense of how you see their work at the center. A manager conducts performance evaluations, but a coach consistently invites dialogue and offers encouragement and descriptive feedback. As the ship's captain, you can use your leadership to keep on course. Invite each staff member to identify an aspect of their work in which they would like to engage in collaborative inquiry through coaching and feedback from you. On the managing-and-overseeing side of your triangle framework, schedule time to do this and treat it with the same importance as the other mandates on your calendar. Then on the coaching side, devise some observation and feedback strategies that are specific and supportive, encourage inquiry, and promote reflective practice and collaboration. The following strategies will send a strong message to your staff that you are not there to judge or correct them, but instead available to engage with them around their interests and the concerns and responsibilities they have.

Strategy Develop questions to guide your own observations

It's helpful to have a set of questions in mind to guide your observations of teachers so you don't just react and judge their behavior. These questions can parallel those you want caregivers to be using with their observations of children. They will help you clarify your own filters or biases as you engage with the teachers around their ideas and interests.

Ask yourself the following questions:

- What specifically am I seeing?
- What is my first reaction or judgment?
- How would I name the essence of this experience for this teacher?
- How can I account for what I am seeing? Why might she or he be behaving in this way?
- What strengths do I see in this teacher?
- What could she or he do differently to be more successful?
- What understanding about child development would be helpful?
- What disposition do I want to strengthen or weaken?

I get energy around my work on interpersonal relationships with people. It's especially challenging for me to stick with relationships when people are not pulling their weight. I get annoyed, believing I am letting these people hang on when they really should leave. What I have realized is that the first place I need to start is with my own attitude. When I take the viewpoint that we are a community trying to make this work together, then one person's difficulties impact us all. Rather than always seeing what's wrong about a staff person, I work to promote their growth and create a climate where each person is recognized for the contribution they make to the larger group. I've found that the investment this takes is well worth it because we learn how to get through the rough times together and come out a stronger team in the long run.

—Ellen

Strategy Practice responding to Cassandra

Consider this scene and the possible responses you might make. Then bring the scenario to your staff meeting and ask how each response would be received. You will get valuable information for developing yourself as a coach.

Cassandra is a new teacher in your young three-year-olds' room. She recently graduated with a two-year degree in early childhood education and has lots of enthusiasm and good ideas, especially for curriculum activities. Her good ideas often end up in chaos, however, with you having to go in and help her gain control of the kids and the classroom activities. During small-group time today, the activity she has planned is fingerpainting on the tabletops. As you enter, you see her pleading with a couple of kids to stay in time-out chairs as she chases others to keep them from getting paint on the walls and toys.

How would you respond?

1. You say, "Cassandra, remember we don't use time-out in this program."
2. You jump in, saying, "What a mess! Things are out of control. You get these three kids to the sink to wash up, and I'll get the paint cleaned off the table."
3. You say, "Wow, Cassandra. What a wonderful sensory activity you've planned. The children really like getting into paint, but you look frazzled. How can I help?"
4. You say, "Oh, you look too busy to talk. I'll come back later," and you leave immediately.

Consider how each response might make Cassandra feel. What disposition might be strengthened or weakened by each response? Are there other responses you might make?

Strategy Use questions to promote inquiry

Reflect again on the story of Cassandra. Imagine if you used the following questions to have a conversation with her about the unfolding events in her classroom. These questions suggest you start with the teacher's point of view and her intentions and struggles. The feedback you offer consists of the details you observed and your own genuine questions and curiosity rather than judgments or advice. Take note of the questions for summary and conclusion, which suggest many possibilities for thinking about the situation while still holding the teacher accountable to her own learning process and the steps she will try next. To advance inquiry and reflection throughout your program, consider how you might use some version of these questions in all your feedback and interactions with your staff.

Questions for Coaching with Inquiry

- Tell me your thinking about this activity.
- What engaged your involvement in this activity?
- What did you struggle with?
- Let me tell you the details of what I saw . . .
- Tell me more about . . .
- I'm curious about . . .
- Here's what this activity makes me think of . . .
- Are there any other perspectives we should consider?

Questions to Use for Summary and Conclusion

- Do you have any new thinking resulting from our conversation?
- What are the opportunities and possibilities available here?
- What are next steps for us in working with these ideas?

Strategy Practice with stories

As a final strategy for this side of the triangle framework, read the following stories about two directors, Becky Brown and Yolanda Young. Analyze the nuances of their approaches with the questions that follow the stories. Then review the comparative charts we offer, which highlight the difference between a manager and a coach.

Becky's Story

Director Becky Brown is having her regular meeting with one of her teachers, Juanita, to go over curriculum plans and individualizing for children of concern. She has brought along the performance standard checklist to review that all requirements are being met.

Juanita knows how to complete all her paperwork, and each week dutifully fills in all the boxes on the planning form. As she and Becky talk, Juanita feels a bit guilty when Becky compliments her for the variety of fingerplays included for her circle times. The truth is that Juanita never got to those fingerplays because during circle time this week the kids were all excited to tell new baby stories after Jami told everybody he had a new sister. They just didn't seem interested in doing what she had planned for circle time. Juanita wonders if she's really a good teacher.

Becky asks Juanita how this month's weekly themes around transportation went. She compliments Juanita on all the transportation activities her plans indicate. Again, Juanita doesn't know what to say. The truth is, the kids weren't very interested in most of the transportation projects she offered. She put boats in the water table and trucks in the block area, and each day she introduced a new art project with the transportation theme. Many of the kids stayed in the house area, feeding doll babies, burping them, and putting them to bed. Juanita wishes she had more dolls because there's a lot of competition for them.

Becky reminds Juanita that she doesn't have much documentation of her individual planning, which is a requirement. Juanita says this is something she has a hard time with. Should she admit that she really doesn't get why this is such a big deal and she can't find time to write all this stuff? She keeps quiet. Becky reminds Juanita that this requirement is very important, and she'll review again how to do it. She tells Juanita to get out one child's assessment record, find an area of weakness, and plan an activity around it to do with the child. Juanita dutifully complies by writing down that she will work with Jami on his colors. She smiles to communicate she now understands, but this paperwork still doesn't have much meaning for her teaching. She thinks it will be hard to get Jami interested in colors when all he wants to do is put the doll babies to sleep.

Finally, Becky pulls out the list of this year's curriculum themes and gives Juanita the suggested activities for the upcoming month. She reminds her to get a list of any supplies she needs turned in by the fifteenth. Becky suggests Juanita talk with the other teachers about what they're planning to see if materials can be shared. As she leaves, Becky reminds Juanita about next week's required training on "Math Their Way" and also to get her parent newsletter article turned in on time.

Yolanda's Story

Director Yolanda Young is looking forward to dropping in on the teachers in the Rainbow Room during their planning time today. She's excited to show them the photos and observation notes from her visit to their classroom this week. The children used tape and string to invent an amazing crane to lift the blocks as they played in the block area.

During the meeting, they read and delight in the things they heard the children say during the play. Yolanda asks what learning and development they think was involved. They report complex problem solving, classification, math, spatial relations, and fabulous social skills, to name a few. She asks if they have any ideas about individual planning from watching the play. They make notes to build on Amanda and Ryan's interest in the cranes and to address Amanda's language needs and Ryan's small-motor skills.

Yolanda shares the news that two families are leaving the center next month. She suggests the moving theme might be linked to the children's emerging interests in moving blocks. The group brainstorms a list of books, props, pictures, and songs and hypothesizes how the children might respond to them. Yolanda offers to find a couple of luggage carts and boxes and suggests they watch what unfolds and share more at their next meeting. The teachers eagerly agree.

Yolanda asks to see documentation of this month's curriculum activities and notes on individual children. She looks at their photographs and samples of children's work. Teacher Jane has created a handmade book telling the story of play in the dress-up area. There is also a set of anecdotal notes on Eric's emerging writing skills. Yolanda loves to look at these collections. She feels they help her learn so much about the children's development as well as the teachers' thinking.

Jane expresses some concerns about how much instruction to give around writing skills. Yolanda and the teachers talk for a few minutes, uncovering some differing opinions. One teacher thinks that children gain self-esteem and confidence when they know they are writing letters adults can read. Another thinks that when children's invented printing is respected, confidence and positive self-image grow naturally. Yolanda inserts clarifying questions into the discussion to discover how specific observations of Eric can lead them to the answers they are seeking. "What clues does Eric give you about his confidence or frustration with writing? Does he seek help or seem concerned about adult approval? How is he involving others in his literacy play?" Yolanda offers to look for helpful resources in her files and any training opportunities in the community. She suggests they focus on this area by watching the children and comparing notes to see if they can get more insight.

The team shows Yolanda a curriculum web of activities they may offer around a bicycle race happening in their community. Yolanda says she knows that teacher Phyllis is an avid biker, and she'll be sharing her interest with the children. She thinks a number of parents will also be involved. The teachers ask Yolanda if they need to transfer all of their ideas onto the standard curriculum form or if they can just use the web as their plan. Yolanda is cautious, reminding them of the elements needed in a plan:

- There should be attention to arranging the learning environment so that children's curiosity is stimulated.
- Props should be added to sustain individual and group interests the teachers have noticed.
- Different materials should be made available for children to represent their ideas.
- Provision should be made for all the developmental tasks and learning domains children need to pursue (such as social, emotional, large- and small-motor, math, science, and literacy skills).

Yolanda says if the teachers can invent something that addresses these elements but better meets their needs, she'll advocate for its use.

Compare the Approach of These Two Directors

- What goals do Becky and Yolanda seem to have for their programs (for curriculum, for children and families, for staff development)?
- What strategies and approaches are they each using to reach their goals?
- How do Becky and Yolanda's approaches encourage or undermine reflective practice and teacher dispositions needed for a caring, learning community?

Consider Your Approach in Light of Becky and Yolanda

As you spent time examining the approaches Becky and Yolanda take in directing their programs, did you see yourself in one of them?

Becky is a highly organized, efficient director who has developed and mastered systems to guide her program. She operates primarily from the managing-and-overseeing side of the triangle. As she meets with Juanita, we see her using techniques that are taught in management courses—using checklists, giving descriptive feedback, offering praise and concrete assistance in addressing a weakness. But how effective has she been in coaching a promising teacher like Juanita?

In some ways, Becky's approach actually undermines her goal of supporting Juanita. She reinforces the dispositions of distrusting one's own ideas and intuition and instead relying on authority outside oneself. Her approach encourages Juanita to focus more attention on the rules and regulations than on the children.

Yolanda, on the other hand, operates more clearly from the coaching-and-mentoring side of the triangle framework. She keeps herself attuned to the real happenings of her program and builds her coaching activities and interactions around meaningful events taking place. In fact, the unfolding events and daily lives of the people in her program are the foundation for her guidance. We see a glimpse of her thinking about managing and overseeing in her response to the teachers about requirements in documenting curriculum plans. She is clear about standards and elements for quality but flexible in giving teachers autonomy in how they meet these. Yolanda mentors with genuine interests, ideas, and resources rather than rules and regulations.

If you were to do a comparative analysis of Becky's and Yolanda's approach to directing, here's how it might look. As you read the items in each column, put check marks beside items closest to your thinking and behavior. Then decide if you are satisfied with the balance in the roles you play in the triangle.

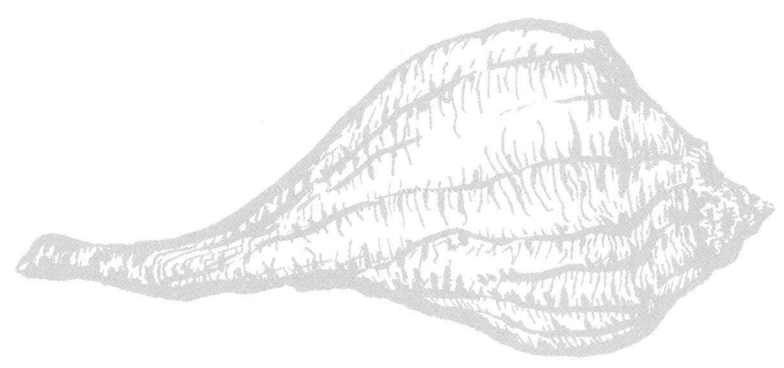

Becky	Yolanda
Goals	
• Meeting standards through compliance and conformity. Relies on checklists and paperwork to demonstrate goals are being met. • Weekly preplanned curriculum activities coordinated around yearly themes. • Having parents see their children participating in posted activities. Keeping parents informed with a newsletter. • Assessing and individualizing focused on children's deficiencies. • Requiring all staff to attend training on information she deems important.	• Creating a learning community through active involvement of children, families, and staff. • Evaluating progress toward goals based on people's relationships and self-initiated involvement. • Teacher-initiated curriculum planning based on observation, unfolding events, and knowledge of children and families. • Reflecting the lives and events of children and their families in the curriculum. Parents are central to the evolution of what is planned for the curriculum and environment. • Assessing and plans for individualizing done in the context of emerging interests. • Autonomous, self-reflective thinkers collaborating in self-identified staff development activities to improve their practice.
Specific Approaches and Strategies	
• Reviews plans with teachers, reminding them and looking for evidence of compliance. • Requires standardized planning forms and a list of supplies turned in by a specific date. • Gives feedback and praise based on forms; little knowledge or inquiry as to what really occurred or how the teacher felt about it.	• Observes in classrooms and contributes to planning with ideas and resources. • Encourages teacher collaboration to invent planning forms that reflect the quality elements and their teacher needs. • Engages in dialogue with teachers based on what she saw and heard; coaches by seeking their ideas and encouraging deeper understanding.

Adopting the Mind-Set of a Coach

Your personal style of directing might be different from either Becky's or Yolanda's. The issue here is not one of style, but of a mind-set that translates into effective coaching strategies. When you are working with caregivers to enhance their understanding and nurture certain dispositions and skills, you will be most effective if you take off your manager's hat. If you invest in cultivating mentoring skills, you set the stage for staff members to become more autonomous, self-initiated learners.

Whether she is aware of it or not, Becky's behavior reveals a strong goal to have a staff that is in compliance and adhering to standard practices. Yolanda goes beyond that with the goal of having a staff that is reflective and creative in responding to the ever-changing demands of their work. She knows that teachers who are able to analyze, hypothesize, and consider diverse points of view will individualize more appropriately for children. Yolanda is coaching her staff to be reflective thinkers, not rule followers.

Setting goals and wanting teachers to be reflective doesn't automatically translate into coaching behavior. Yolanda employs specific strategies to model and nurture this goal along. Her approach is to coach through inquiry. She takes notes and photographs and brings them as concrete data to launch staff reflection. Her contributions in staff meetings set the tone for a reflective planning process, one that generates excitement and engagement on the part of others. She offers not only current information relevant to the children's lives but specific resources to help the staff grow curriculum from that information.

Notice the listening and communication strategies that are part of Yolanda's interactions. She restates what she hears and identifies potential conflicts, expecting there will be discussion and learning from them. When a teacher expresses a learning need, she takes it seriously and commits herself to follow through with specific resources. She encourages her staff not just to see and do things her way, but to see themselves as researchers, self-evaluators, and inventors. Yolanda communicates respect and support as she mentors her staff in upholding her high standards for quality.

Practice Assessing Your Approach

As you consider the approaches of Becky and Yolanda, are there any new insights for your own work? Make a two-column chart for yourself. On the left, write the heading "Current Approach," and on the right, "New Things to Try." As you fill in the chart, refer to your weekly calendar, agendas for staff meetings, and conferences with individual teachers. Be specific and honest, setting aside any excuses or hesitations. After you have filled your paper, go down the right column and set some priorities for yourself.

Working as a coach can be as rewarding for you as it is for your staff. When you encounter bouts of discouragement, remember the tenacity of the midwife and of the coach who brings a team to the Olympics.

Chapter 5

Your Role of Managing and Overseeing

Director Phyllis is very responsive to staff, parents, and children. She can often be found sharing a story of delight about a child or the vision she has of her program as one big happy family. Wanting to always be available to staff and parents, Phyllis has an open-door policy. When people come to her office, she waves them in, whether she's on the phone or at the computer. Phyllis always says she's eager to hear what's on someone's mind, but she frequently shuffles through papers or continues to answer the phone as they set out to tell her why they've come.

The staff really likes Phyllis, appreciating her warmth and genuine praise of their work. She often tells them, "You teachers know what you are doing, and it's my job to back you up with the parents." Phyllis doesn't want to impose on her teachers' time and avoids scheduling meetings if there isn't some important decision pending. Teachers are glad Phyllis has trust in them, but you can't help but notice that they don't feel supported by her management style. They don't feel that they have time to talk with each other because of the way Phyllis sets up their schedules. Privately, staff members reveal their discouragement about Phyllis's lack of follow-through on ideas or needs they have brought her—"She always has a good excuse, but she is continually forgetting things or misplacing papers. I'm not really sure I can count on her to do what she says."

And on top of everything, there's this third-party quality endorsement thing. Despite the excitement Phyllis has created about working with the new NAEYC accreditation system, there is also disgruntlement brewing over the feeling that some teachers don't seem to pull their weight. Some of the teachers are using their home computers and printers and a lot of their own, unpaid planning time to get the required documentation into binders, while others aren't willing to do the extra work. There is talk of "special treatment" and "favoritism" and "unrealistic expectations for such a ridiculous salary." One teacher was recently overhead saying, "Miss Phyllis always makes me feel like I have a lot to contribute here, and I like taking leadership. But I think she should expect everyone to work on this accreditation, not just a couple of us. I'm starting to feel like she's taking unfair advantage of me just because I'm loyal."

Managing to Make Your Vision a Reality

Phyllis, the director in the above story, is well liked by those in her program. Her good intentions and convincing talk paint a picture of a quality workplace. She has the notion of staff empowerment and the desire for a family feeling in her program, but ultimately the leadership and structures required to make this a reality are missing. It's not even clear if there is a competent manager at the helm. Phyllis would do well to heed the words of Thoreau when he said, "If you have built castles in the air, your work need not be lost; that is where they should be. Now put the foundations under them."

Throughout this book we've encouraged you to think of your work as going beyond mere management tasks. This is key if you are trying to lead your program with a vision. When you function *only* as a manager, then you are not engaged in the coaching and community-building process so essential to your vision. But if you neglect the managing-and-overseeing side of your job and operate primarily with good intentions and intuition, you soon create a credibility gap between the vision you espouse and your ability to follow through in creating it. Failing to be clear about standards and policies or neglecting to organize all your tasks into workable systems will surely jeopardize the survival of your program, not to mention your sanity.

Take another look at the triangle framework.

If any side is not strong, the imbalance created can easily lead to a collapse of quality. Perhaps you are creative in developing strategies for coaching and mentoring, or you excel in building and sustaining community. Yet for every strategy on those sides of the triangle, you need to be clear about compatible policies, expectations, support systems, and resources on the management side. Without these, your good ideas are not likely to bear fruit.

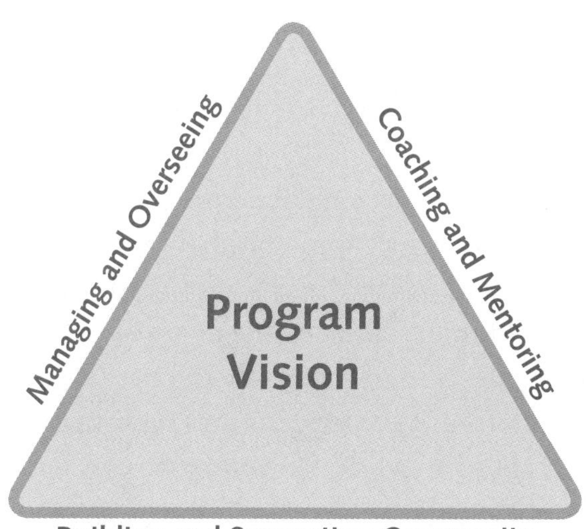

The Internet, the library, and many management certification programs offer a substantial body of resources to help you with the day-to-day tasks of managing your program. You can find articles, books, Web sites, blogs, classes, and seminars to help you with such things as fund-raising, budget development, software and technology, time management, and human resources. Our intent is not to duplicate those resources here, but rather to offer a way of thinking about your managing responsibilities so that your policies and systems support, not undermine, the vision of your program as a caring, learning community. This chapter offers some principles and strategies to consider in developing your policies and systems. It is not intended to be comprehensive in any way, but we hope it will give you a taste of possibility. A list of valuable management resources can be found at the back of this book (see Resources).

Cultivating the Organizational Culture You Want

Begin your managing-and-overseeing work by looking at the current climate in your program. Examine how you approach your tasks, and determine the values and priorities that your behaviors and management systems convey to staff and families. In *A Great Place to Work*, Paula Jorde Bloom discusses her research on how the interplay between people and the environment and between work attitudes and group dynamics supports the professionalism of an organization. In discussing the concept of organizational climate, she says, “Although it is not clear whether climate or satisfaction comes first, job satisfaction seems to be higher in schools with relatively open climates. These climates are characterized by a sense of belonging, many opportunities to interact, autonomy, and upward influence" (1997, 2).

With our vision of early childhood programs as places for thriving childhoods and learning communities for adults and children alike, we might expand on the dimensions she has identified as influencing an organization's climate. The term *organizational culture* describes how people live and express themselves together in that setting, whereas the term *climate* suggests the conditions that influence our feelings and ability to work. Obviously the concepts are interrelated, and both Paula Jorde Bloom and Jim Greenman have made important contributions in adding these components to the assessment of early childhood settings.

There are five ingredients I want in my organizational culture.

Passion/intense curiosity
Someone called kids carnivores of information. They are passionate about learning. Adults can get back to that.

Questioning
Kids question everything, even things they know about, just to see if the answer is the same or maybe to see if the question has changed. We should too. Ask each other "why," and keep asking until we get an answer other than "because," or "I said so," or "because we've always done it that way."

Reflecting
Kids do this when adults shut up long enough for them to think. Adults tend to be afraid of silence. We act like we believe that without a physical product, there is no "work." I wonder if many of us believe that thinking is not working, especially when people we supervise say that's what they are doing. We just focus on the output.

Celebration
We have to celebrate our successes. We gloss over these too lightly and too often.

Provocation

We ask teachers to offer kids provocations, but what provocations are we offering them? For instance, we are 150 years from "official" slavery. Where do we want to be 150 years from now? What does that mean for helping children learn? Native people believe in planning for the seventh generation. What do we want our children to carry forward in behalf of babies of the twenty-second and twenty-third centuries? Our organizational culture should be provoking that kind of thinking.

—**Michael**

In the late 1990s, through the efforts of the Center for the Child Care Workforce, early childhood program staff developed an assessment tool, the Model Work Standards, that highlights the components of work environments linked to quality for children in child care. This tool is a welcome addition to our work and substantiates Bloom's point:

> One valuable insight gained during an assessment of employee attitudes about their work environment is a sharper understanding of where perceptions differ between administrators and employees. One of the more common findings, for example, is that directors often believe they give far more feedback to their staff than the teachers perceive they get. Another common difference is found in directors' and staff's perceptions regarding staff involvement in decisions about different organizational policies and practices. . . . Directors typically rate the organizational climate of their programs more favorably than do their teachers. (1997, 19–20)

Bloom goes on to describe the benefits of having a systematic method to measure staff perceptions of the organizational climate. Sometimes directors are reluctant to do this because they fear that staff will complain about things there are no resources to fix. Nevertheless, when you welcome staff feedback on how the work environment feels, you unlock the potential for creative problem solving. A tool such as the Model Work Standards or the Program Administration Scale (PAS) helps directors see clearly where they should be headed. As with accreditation criteria, it can serve as a weather gauge and concrete reference point for budgeting and/or grant writing.

Your organizational climate is created by a number of factors that fall on the managing-and-overseeing side of the triangle, and it is affected by your work on the other two sides. In your role as a manager, you formulate long-range goals that guide the development of your program toward your vision over time. You are responsible for creating and upholding standards and policies that support your long-range goals. You establish the systems that ensure and document a quality program, embodied in the daily procedures, routines, and schedules through which everyone involved in the program experiences its values. You create structures to support teachers with time, tools, and resources to do the work expected of them.

You can see these tasks as a burden and as a distraction from the work of building community, or you can develop policies, systems, and routines that are aligned with your vision. When you consider principles to guide this side of the triangle, your goal is to have them reflect your values of embracing diversity, empowerment, and participatory democracy, as well as your vision of early childhood programs as caring, learning communities.

To develop your thinking and help you move into action, we recommend further study of related resources recommended at the end of this book (see Resources). In the meantime, here are some guiding principles and a sampling of strategies to move those principles into practice. Many strategies require you to dive in boldly, while others allow you to dabble, just getting your toes wet. All encourage you to color outside the lines, to see yourself as an able player, not helpless in the face of barriers before you. These principles and strategies suggest a new way of seeing and acting, a reinventing of your own power on behalf of a vision for children, families, teachers, and caregivers.

FORMULATING LONG-RANGE GOALS TO SUPPORT YOUR VISION

Most significant changes desired for a program require a strategic planning process. Forge a commitment with staff, parents, and the community, and call on a consultant or agency such as United Way to help design the process. Strategic plans often involve a three- to five-year timeline, and such a commitment can seem daunting for a transient early childhood program. Consider entering into collaboration with other early childhood or related programs in your community to mobilize a critical mass of colleagues to share resources and support each other. When you adopt a strategic plan, you have specific goals, timelines, and people responsible for action plans. This moves your managing-and-overseeing role to a new level of professionalism and your vision within closer reach.

Principle

Create a Continuous Cycle of Evaluating and Planning

Evaluating and planning go together like salt and pepper or peanut butter and jelly. In between is the everyday work of acting on your plans. Far too often, directors act without planning or evaluating, or they make elaborate plans that they never act on. Here are some basic strategies to keep in mind.

Because I had served on so many monitor and review teams for Head Start, I had insight into the process. When it came time for my own program review, I decided to take an active approach. Rather than sitting back and waiting for the review team to tell us about how we were doing, I wanted us to take the lead.

I began to meet regularly with the staff to determine the areas we would like feedback on. We choose those areas that we saw as our strengths and those that we wanted to improve upon. This was a powerful process because we felt more invested in the review than ever before. It meant we were requesting specific help that would be meaningful to us rather than waiting defensively for the bad news.

This process changed the way we thought about evaluation. We became less defensive about our weaknesses and more able to really utilize the feedback we received to create changes in our program. Our staff now actually looks forward to review time.

—Louise

Strategy *Conduct regular program evaluations*

Each year your managing-and-overseeing work should include a rubric for evaluating your program. You can design your own form, survey, or interview questions, or you can use one of the standard program review assessment tools such as the NAEYC Accreditation Criteria, the Environmental Rating Scales (ITERS, ECERS-R), or the Program Administration Scale (PAS). These evaluations deserve more than a passing glance. Tally the responses and look for patterns—identify both your program's strengths and its weaknesses. Then use your strategic planning process to address the weaknesses. The annual evaluation and planning processes should complement each other, with the evaluation giving you the information to help guide strategic planning and providing milestones to let you know how far toward your goals you've come.

Strategy Develop a clear understanding of the planning process

Most libraries and bookstores have resources that outline the strategic planning process for a business, and many communities have organizational development consultants who can be hired to get you started, if not guide you through the entire process. Typically a strategic plan involves these components:

- clarity on values and vision
- assessment of current needs and operations
- identification of specific goals
- analysis of barriers to overcome
- measurable objectives with a time frame
- action steps that include the designated people responsible
- evaluation and adjustments (see our prior discussion about the annual program evaluation)

There are both elaborate and simple strategic planning forms you can use to document your plans, decisions, and accomplishments. A simple one that works for most small- to moderate-sized early childhood programs looks something like the chart on the following page. It is an example of a how a program can discover whether their systems, policies, and allocation of resources align with their vision and values. (See appendix 7 for a blank form.)

We started last summer revising our vision. We compared lots of other vision statements; made lists of what children, families, and staff deserve; and then began working on clarifying the values we wanted reflected in our systems and policies for staff. We began with staff first to boost morale and to emphasize how important we believe they are to our program. I think once we finish the planning and implementation work of aligning our systems and policies with our values for staff, children, and families, we will have a solid foundation to build upon in years to come.

—**Becky**

Vision	Children and families in our program come from a range of cultures and economic groups.		
Goals	**Barriers and Issues**	**Specific Objectives**	**Action Steps (Who and When)**
Diversify our population.	Current staff is homogenous.	Hire staff of color for next three openings. Recruit bilingual staff.	Contact community organizations. (John and Elise by March board meeting) Attend meetings like Black Child Development and Asian Refugee Alliance. (Director and two lead teachers) Send notices to college classes. (Director)
Revamp any policies that may be barriers.	Environment only reflects Euro-American culture.	One in-service workshop will be held each month.	Research training options. (Director and two leads; June 2010)
Yearlong staff training on antibias, cultually relevant programming.	Materials are all in English.	Target relevant workshops at conferences.	Write grant for additional training funds. (August 2010)

Strategy Take time to plan the planning process

For a strategic planning process to be effective, it has to be thought out carefully. The planning begins long before the first meeting is held. Here are some steps to consider:

- Decide how to make the planning process as inclusive as possible.
- Identify key groups to have represented.
- Outline elements of process.
- List needed resources and tools.
- Project the possible timeline and estimate the frequency of meetings.
- Review helpful facilitation and group-process skills.
- Create folders or notebooks for each planning member to organize related notes and resources.
- Begin the process with a purpose statement and review of history.
- Build into initial meetings activities for the planning group to get to know each other's strengths, assumptions, and hopes.
- Give as much attention to the process as to the end goals.

When I came to direct our program, I felt it had the basis to be much more than it was. The day-in, day-out tasks of directing are a treadmill that is difficult to get off. I knew that if we didn't formalize a plan for big changes, it would never happen. We formed a strategic planning committee of parents and staff who began to ask "Who do you think we are?" in a series of focus group discussions to assess our strengths and weaknesses, our opportunities and threats. We included the kids in this. We set some priorities for our facilities, financial health, staff compensation, and strengthening our antibias practices. Our plan has clear goals, action steps, and a timeline, so I am confident we are on the road to greatness.

—Laura

Principle

Refuse to Adopt a Scarcity Mentality

We can address both short- and long-term program needs by refusing to have a scarcity mentality, a mind-set that there will never be enough. Most current resources for our programs don't match our needs, let alone our dreams. Yet the attitude we develop toward resources can become a self-fulfilling prophecy. If we confine our vision to the current limitations of our budget, we put policies and systems in place that can actually lower our standards, erode the quality of our programs, and lead us farther from our vision of a learning community.

As a director, you will find that your greatest challenge is to let your vision, not your current resources, drive your decision-making process. Our intent in this book is to awaken in you an active commitment to a vision that goes beyond how things are. To keep this vision alive, you must regularly stir up the soil, add fertilizer, and plant new seeds. Otherwise you will find yourself drifting down the path to accommodation, adopting a scarcity mentality, and accepting the limitations of your current situation.

Carl Sussman puts it well: "Providers need to cultivate the cognitive dissonance of living with inadequate facilities while harboring an ambitious vision that could sustain a greatly enhanced program" (1998, 15). He writes about Sandy Waddell, an inspiring director, in his article "Out of the Basement: Discovering the Value of Child Care Facilities." Waddell decided to break out of the classic scarcity mentality of an early childhood program director and undertake an ambitious renovation of her facility.

The drive and determination necessary for such an undertaking usually leave some disgruntled souls in its wake. When you step outside the passive, nurturing, and accommodating roles typically assigned to females and to those in the early childhood field, some may criticize and label you. But if your vision and principles propel you, your efforts will not only serve your program well but also uplift the profession as a whole. Each time a program breaks through the barriers placed in its path, there is another model to emulate, and momentum grows toward refusing to accept the limited vision and resources you've been given.

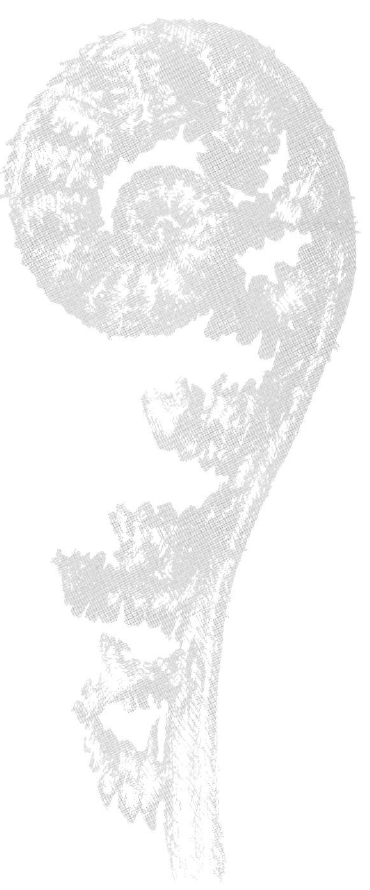

Having worked together for several years, the teachers in my program interact in a fine orchestration. In the writing center, a teacher is working with a group of children interested in China and introducing them to Chinese symbol writing. A second teacher is working with three students on an elaborate block structure, while the third teacher is observing and photographing a group of children in the dramatic play area who are having a picnic. It was not long ago that this level of interaction could not have been achieved. Just three years ago our board of directors decided that small-group instruction was what our school believed in, so they funded a third teacher for each classroom. Funding this change seemed like a huge barrier at first. It was not possible to raise tuition to cover the cost of the third teacher, as we wanted our program to be affordable to all members of the community. The answer came with the creation of our extended day program. We are a part-time preschool program ending each day at noon. Our new extended day program now offers children classes until two PM, five days a week. The program has about fifteen classes each week with topics such as karate, ballet, yoga, cooking, and tumbling. The fees we charge for these optional classes fully fund the third teachers and also allow us to participate in additional staff development opportunities. By having a strong vision, carefully planning, and executing, we have been able to transform our classrooms and learning environment to fully benefit the children entrusted to our care.

—Sabrina

Perhaps you are unsure where this kind of determination will come from. Directors typically say they want to be realistic as they consider policies and resources for their program. "It costs too much" comes from our lips too easily in response to visionary ideas. Consider again these concepts of being realistic and costing too much. What's the real picture of quality in your program? Is it close to your vision? What is being sacrificed? Are you or any of your staff members reaching burnout?

In his poem "Harlem," Langston Hughes asks, "What happens to a dream deferred?" What are the costs—to your energy and your physical and emotional well-being and to those of the children, families, and staff in your program—of deferring your dreams? Have you considered that this cost might be too much? We have a growing body of research and literature that is confirming this point. Until we shift how we think about the full costs of providing quality child care, we will continue to incapacitate ourselves. In the introductory chapter to *Reaching the Full Cost of Quality in Early Childhood Programs*, Barbara Willer says, "The full cost of quality therefore holds a dual meaning. It refers to the costs of program provision while fully meeting professional recommendations for high quality, while also implying the social costs that are incurred when quality is lacking" (1990, vii).

Strategy Move your budget toward the full cost of care

In 1990 NAEYC published Willer's *Reaching the Full Cost of Quality in Early Childhood Programs*, a handbook that added information and tools to their accreditation criteria to help directors compute what providing quality child care *really* costs. Though this valuable handbook is currently out of print, you can use the worksheets in appendix 8 of this book to help you build your budget around your quality needs, not your parent fees. Once you have a realistic picture of what it really costs to provide a quality program, you can use this data to challenge your own scarcity mentality.

Next, use your full-cost-of-care data to determine how your budget priorities and policies need to be refocused. To begin developing a strategic plan to address the changes you want to make, use the form offered in appendix 7.

Make use of all the communication systems you have in place to educate parents, board members, the general public, and policymakers about the actual dollars required to provide quality child care. Put displays on bulletin boards, include information in e-mails, put articles in your parent newsletters, and send letters to newspapers and legislators. Post information on Web sites and blogs. In appendix 8 of this book you will find an example used in years past by many programs on the annual Worthy Wage Day for child care workers—a mock invoice given to parents showing how low teacher wages are making up the balance between parent fees and the full cost of providing quality child care. Consider how you could adapt something like this to raise awareness and advocate for an adequate funding system for child care programs everywhere.

A previous director in our center realized that we would never get parent involvement in the Worthy Wage Campaign until they knew the hard, cold facts of what our teachers made. Families were absolutely shocked. As a result, we began to get a wage scale in place, immediately invested in our lead teachers with a 50 percent pay increase each year. We then began to step up our assistants and part-time staff. This created a much stronger commitment on the part of both families and our staff and took away some of the initial antagonism that came from the huge disparity in their economic circumstances.

—Julie

Strategy Invest in your staff

A centerpiece of your short- and long-term goals must be investing in teachers and other caregivers. Consider ways you can move your program along the following lines:

- Create policies and budget line items to pay for and reward staff for ongoing training.
- Transfer some of the time and money you spend each year on continually recruiting and training new staff directly into the existing staff who want to make early childhood a career.
- Build your budget with a salary scale that goes beyond the high end of what is typically paid in your community.
- Design a career-path system to help you stabilize a core of excellent teachers who are paid well to mentor others.
- Create supportive working conditions with staffing patterns to allow off-the-floor paid time for staff to meet in teams to reflect on their work, study documentation and create learning stories for portfolios, meet with parents, and mentor other teachers.
- Enhance your new staff orientation and ongoing professional development budget with funds that steadily increase each year. Include funds to enhance skills of your administrative team as well.

Over my fifteen years as a director, I have worked through many issues with many teachers. Some teachers leave while others stay as contributing members of our learning community. What I have found most effective is to apply my understandings of working with children and families to my work with teachers. If I follow and reinforce the teachers' interests, they will learn and develop to their highest potential and in turn contribute more to our program. For example, a teacher who had been working with infants and toddlers expressed an interest in returning to work with preschool age children. An opportunity for her to do this presented itself, but she was initially hesitant about taking on the bigger leadership responsibilities the job required. I assured her we would support her as much as necessary and immediately included her with a group of preschool teachers attending a multiple-day conference so she could feel connected and supported. Another teacher expressed a desire to teach kindergarten, despite the fact that we didn't serve that age group. To respond to her passion, I wrote a grant, and we worked together to design a very successful integrated arts kindergarten. My philosophy is to find my teachers' passions and support them as much as I can, even if it means changing or adding to what we do. The results are that I get to keep good teachers who help me expand and enhance the program. What could be better?

—Wendy

James Hunter in *The Servant* says "employees will spend roughly half their waking hours working and living in the environment you create as the leader" (1998, 27). That passage struck me to my core. I always feel that I am very cognizant of the sort of workplace I set out to create. When we moved into our new building, I called staff together to have a "funeral." I told them we had to bury all our negative feelings and start anew. We each wrote on slips of paper things we needed to bury. Then we put them in a pot. We took it outside and burned them all. As the smoke rose, it burned our eyes and reminded us of how negative energy can blur our vision.

—Michael

Strategy Be generous with your nickels and dimes

A scarcity mentality often leads directors to rationing basic tools, supplies, and the paid time staff members need to do their job well. Generosity in this department will build staff morale as well as competency. It will save you money in the long run, not to mention heartache.

- Put money into carving out some kind of staff room with comfortable chairs, lighting, and a workspace. Furnish it with tools teachers need—a telephone, computer, Wi-Fi Internet access, e-mail, copy machine, digital cameras, printer and paper, etc.
- Make it a policy to pay staff for time spent thinking, planning, organizing, and collaborating.
- Nourish caregivers and teachers with plants, flowers, and healthy treats on a regular basis.
- Give teachers autonomy and concrete assistance in getting the supplies they need for their work. Long delays in purchase orders for a project can undermine their best efforts.
- Set up efficient purchasing and petty-cash systems to accompany each room's budget so that caregivers can have the things they need in a timely fashion. Along with the standard early care and education vendors, be sure to include other resources to allow for more creative purchases.

Strategy Involve others in expanding your nickels and dimes

All centers need a budgeting system that goes beyond the families you serve for the big dollars you need. Nonprofit programs tend to write grants and hold fund-raisers, while large for-profit programs can now be found seeking investors on Wall Street. Whatever your larger plan for financing your center, don't overlook the sources for your nickel-and-dime items right in your own community.

- Ask families to donate technology and related supplies. When they consistently see and read documentation stories of how their children are spending time in your center, most families will gladly donate digital cameras, laptops, printers, or ink cartridges.

- Develop a system to solicit families for contributions of time, resources, and services. This could include donating food for staff meetings, helping with documentation displays, doing laundry, and shopping.
- Contact local businesses in your community. They are often glad to donate space or refreshments for events; scrap lumber for children's carpentry; and remnant fabric, paper, mat board, or foam core for documentation displays.
- The secret to soliciting these donations is to build relationships and have ongoing conversations with people about your needs. It is also important to put a system in place for retrieving and storing material donations. Families and members of the business community are often more than willing to make a contribution to a program or director they know firsthand.

Strategy *Adopt a business mind-set when big funds are needed*

This advice comes from Carl Sussman, who reminds us to adopt the core strategy of business when funds for a major project are needed—use other people's money (Sussman 1998). Traditionally, nonprofit early childhood programs have been reluctant to take out bank loans, something their counterparts in the for-profit sector do all the time. When you consider the tangible, indirect, and marketing payoffs of a major capital improvement, taking out a loan may be one of the most effective strategies for improving the learning and working environment of your program. Find someone with experience in business finance to help you. Consider the same approach to keep your technology and related support systems up to date.

CREATING THE EXPERIENCE OF COMMUNITY WITH YOUR SYSTEMS

People's experience working with an organization's systems can either alienate them or give them a sense of belonging. This is especially true when it comes to upholding standards and regulations. Take, for example, the practice of grouping children in age groups and constantly moving them to a new room when they have a birthday or there is an opening to fill. Licensing and budget constraints often suggest directors should favor this system, which continually disrupts relationships. Your vision of a learning community can be significantly undermined by management systems that are rule-oriented rather than people-oriented and that fail to involve others in a democratic process or take into account the value of consistent relationships.

Many organizations proudly display antidiscrimination statements and claim to embrace an antibias approach. But a closer look at their policies and procedures reveals cultural blinders and practices that limit the people who will feel at home in the program. In your efforts to simultaneously comply with standards and regulations and grow a healthy community for your organization, consider these principles and strategies.

Principle

Use Relationships and Continuity of Care to Guide Your Decisions

If your vision is to grow your center as a learning community for adults and children, then relationships need to be at the center of your thinking. The work you do on the building-and-supporting-community side of the triangle must be backed up with policies and practices on the managing-and-overseeing side. Do your enrollment practices and staffing patterns reflect the value of sustaining relationships, or do they just meet budget goals? The early childhood field has built a strong case for continuity of care informed by theories of attachment (Bowlby 1973), emotional competency (Brazelton and Greenspan 2000), and brain development (Siegel 1999). Continuity of care refers to the policy of assigning a primary caregiver or teacher at the time of enrollment and ideally continuing this relationship for multiple years.

One of the strongest voices for continuity of care is J. Ronald Lally of the Program for Infant/Toddler Care (PITC) at WestEd. He has challenged those who question the wisdom of keeping children and teachers together for multiple years for fear of the negative impact of a bad teacher. "We should root out bad teachers rather than use them as a justification for endorsing questionable practice," he writes (2007, 7). Citing extensive research, Lally makes the case for attachment relationships strengthening a child's sense of confidence, emotional well-being, and language and cognitive development: "We have thirty years of social emotional research that show us what infants and toddlers are looking for in relationship. We know, without question, that the supportive presence of a caregiver allows a child to learn to persist in the face of a challenge" (7). The task for directors is how to translate this knowledge into the challenging task of enrollment and staffing practices to achieve continuity of care. (See appendix 9 for examples of overcoming barriers.)

Strategy Design rooms that work for infants and toddlers

A combination of licensing requirements and enrollment and budget issues often compel directors to move infants into a toddler room, thereby disrupting all the relationships that developed among the caregivers, children and their families, and the children themselves. Infants and toddlers have different play habits once the babies begin to walk and increase the speed and expansive reach of their mobility. As toileting begins, there are still more needs to consider for the toddler environment. As you undertake caregiving for infants and toddlers, consider redesigning your rooms to accommodate infants and toddlers together, eliminating the need for a smaller, specialized infant room. Create a room that will meet the needs of an expanded age group of children under three. You may need to do this in stages, but continue to keep the primary relationship of the child, family, and caregiver in the forefront. Alice Rose, the Family Member Programs flight chief at McGuire Air Force Base, suggests you plan infant/toddler rooms using your state's licensing square-footage regulations based on the toddler age group, but initially enroll it with up to eight infants in a ratio of 1 to 4. Then, as the group ages up, you can add toddlers from your waiting list, up to fourteen children with a 1 to 7 ratio.

Getting rooms ready for continuity of care is a lot of work, but the payoff is definitely worth it. We didn't have the luxury of designing a building from scratch but rather had the task of taking an existing building and making the space work. The task was to designate rooms that had the flexibility to start as an infant room with a ratio of 1 to 4 for a total of eight babies and then grow to accommodate fourteen toddlers with a 1 to 7 ratio. Our rooms already had diaper changing tables, but infant rooms did not have child-sized toilets or low hand-washing sinks. We slowly converted space. In two rooms we added two toddler-sized toilets in a side area with transparent walls with low sinks. With careful thinking about storage to accommodate the changing needs of the children, we purchased some collapsible cribs, nap cots, and low chairs with removable trays in lieu of high chairs. Eventually we added some glass patio doors between rooms so that we can share staff and space at the beginning and end of the day to keep our budget manageable. Ultimately we found continuity of care is a big support to parents because they love having their children with the same caregiver for several years.

—Alice

Strategy *Expand the age group for preschool rooms*

Instead of having separate rooms for children ages three, four, and five, consider enrolling children with a combination of those age groups for each of your preschool rooms. This will keep children, families, and teachers together for multiple years and eliminate most of the transition difficulties as children have birthdays. Older and younger children each have things to learn by being together. As part of the group moves on to kindergarten at the end of each year, the previously younger children assume the senior role and help acculturate the new group of younger children into the classroom routines.

Strategy *Have teachers loop with the children*

Another term used for continuity of care is *looping,* whereby teachers "move up" with children as they age, and then return to work with the younger children when their group graduates. Some teachers are initially reluctant to work with a group of children of a different age, but you can work to create the organizational culture and peer mentoring to help all your staff gain the needed confidence and skills to do so.

Principle

Involve Staff and Families in Active Exploration of Standards

Within the reach of every director is an array of carefully thought-out and field-tested materials promoting professional performance standards, best practices, quality criteria, and assessment tools. The early childhood profession has clarified the components of quality experiences for children, and with the initial efforts of the Model Work Standards and later the Program Administration Scale (PAS), we have a comparable set of component standards for the staff work environment. Keeping these quality components in front of everyone is a major part of your managing-and-overseeing work. What systems can you put in place to involve everyone in that task and make them active players and keepers of the standards?

Strategy *Form task groups*

As you undertake introducing your program to assessment tools such as an accreditation self-study or one part of your state's Quality Rating System (QRS), call for volunteers from your staff and families to take on different sections to study, assess, and oversee quality improvements. This will engage them far more than being told or given all the components to read. If you present these as tools for data collecting, discussion, and decision making, the process itself will be a pedagogical strategy to help others internalize the standards of our profession. Here are some tips to help the task groups run smoothly:

- Ask the task groups to discover what is working and what is really needed, rather than who is in compliance and who isn't.
- Ask each task group to be the eyes, ears, and mouth of its component area. Guide them to take pride in becoming an advocate for this aspect of quality, rather than adopting a complaining or policing mentality.
- Make it known that, as the director, you count on them to keep needed improvements or praise for this component area in the limelight.
- Have the task groups examine how the program policies and procedures related to their component area are affecting your

organizational culture. For example, ask them to consider questions such as:

- Does the paperwork system for tracking individual children support teachers' work with children or detract from it?
- Are the daily staffing patterns and schedules meeting the need for consistency and communication among children, families, and staff?
- Are efforts underway to reduce staff turnover and appropriately reward teachers and caregivers?

The key that I am looking for is to bring joy into the classroom. I really am not worried about what label we put on what we are doing. But I am very concerned about the children experiencing joy and wonderment on a daily, if not moment-by-moment, basis. Sometimes this requires that we work on our adult relationships. During the pre-service training, we worked on communication styles, conflict resolution, and collectively setting a vision for the center. We explored what the staff needed from me, the director, and what they would offer me, and what I needed from the staff and what I would offer them. It was personal and meaningful.

The teachers then worked on their classroom environments. I suggested that they work as a team, going from room to room creating the environments together. Part of this activity was intended to encourage the teachers to get to know one another better. There is a different relationship that evolves as you do manual labor together and make selections in decor. They saw each other's strengths and weaknesses and began to build stronger relationships. The other part of my decision was to help them visualize the center as a whole, belonging to the children and families and staff all together. I was trying to avoid the territorial attitude about rooms that sometimes occurs. They also saw the limits of each classroom, so they understood the challenges of the teachers working in each room. Because the teachers had had this experience and this time together, when the real work of caring for children began, they knew how to approach one another, how to support one another, and when to avoid one another.

—Kathryn

Strategy Create games to enliven discussions of standards

If your goal is to solidify understanding among teachers and families about quality learning and work environments, try turning the standards into games.

Redefine the ABCs and the Three Rs

Periodically work to expand aspects of quality standards in the playful vernacular of our early childhood culture. For instance, have teachers or family groups create a new ABC book, delineating what they see as the deeper components of quality care and education. Or ask them to try redefining the three Rs by describing what they see as the rights of children, families, and teachers. Remember that if it is to be sustainable, hard work must be laced with play and a joyful spirit. Anything worth doing is worth having fun with.

Sorting and Matching Games

This type of game works especially well with tools formatted into comparative columns such as NAEYC's Developmentally Appropriate Practices or accreditation standards, the book *Essentials for Child Development Associates Working with Young Children* (Day 2004) from the Council for Professional Recognition, or the Caring For or Creative Curriculum series from Teaching Strategies. Use the following general approach:

- Photo-enlarge and cut up slips of paper with the different standards.
- Give small groups one or two slips each, and have them all go on a scavenger hunt in your center to find examples of the standards.
- Ask them to bring back to the whole group concrete examples of what the standard looks like in practice. They could share photographs, concrete objects, or drawings.

Drawing Games

A version of the popular drawing game Pictionary can be another fun way for staff and families to internalize certain quality components or procedures required in your program. The following strategy works well for visual learners and offers everyone a new memory tag for important regulations in your program (you can also turn this game into "sculptionary" by using modeling clay or playdough to represent the concepts):

- Make up slips of paper or file cards, each with a different concept or quality element written on it.
- Divide the group into two teams.
- Ask one person on each team to pick a piece of paper or file card and then draw the concept on easel paper or a white board, while the other team tries to guess what they are representing.
- Have a discussion about the concept or quality component after the answer has been guessed.

You can also play a variation of this game using a charades format, where team members act out the concepts.

We used *The Visionary Director* for our Strengths-Based Coaching (Francis Institute for Child and Youth Development) and created a game to explore the triangle framework. We provide three different colors of craft sticks—red for Managing and Overseeing (administration), green for Coaching and Mentoring, and blue for Building Community. We ask directors to write down three things that consume most of their time in their job and then to choose a colored stick for each of the three—depending on which side of the triangle it fits—and write a few words on each stick summarizing the task. Then in small groups we have directors organize their collective red, blue, and green sticks by color, and line them up to form a triangle. Most often the red administration line is the longest, and that opens up a discussion about the need for balance in our work. Finally we ask directors to write down three things they really wish they could do in their work and choose the appropriate color stick for each of these three dreams. They then add this to their group triangle or create a new one together. This usually results in a more balanced triangle and sets the stage for some concrete goal setting.

–Joy

Principle

Seek to Counter Inequities of Power and Privilege

Whether you are developing your personnel and enrollment policies or setting up systems for communication, tuition collection, or health and nutrition, this principle can guide your thinking. Ask yourself questions such as:

- If I create a policy that all tuition must be paid by the fifth of the month, whom might I be excluding from our community?
- When our communication systems are primarily based on handbooks, memos, e-mails, and notices, are we putting anyone at a disadvantage in our program?
- What assumptions in our health and nutrition systems might be biased? For example, some foods are taboo for a particular ethnic group. Different cultural values and practices may dictate how food groups can be combined, served, or eaten.
- If we extend benefits to spouses or families, how does it affect gay or lesbian staff, if they are not allowed to legally marry?

It will never be possible to address all the possible variables that diversity might bring to your program, but this principle will keep you alert to unintended bias and perpetuation of injustices that you don't want as part of your program. In many cases it will provoke discussions that need to take place in a democracy and unearth new awareness and creativity.

It's not enough to just believe in something. I've learned over the years as a director that I have to create management systems to support the philosophy we have of being inclusive of many different types of families. One way I have done this is to have a flexible tuition payment system. For example, I've developed a sort of barter system where an adult family member works for us in the office or the classroom evenings or weekends to accomplish something I would have had to pay someone else to do. I first set up these nontraditional payment plans when I saw someone getting behind in their tuition. I want to ensure that we serve a variety of families, so I need to keep thinking of formal yet flexible ways respond to different families' needs.

—Paul

Strategy *Seek feedback from all stakeholders in your community*

Who is a part of your community? Identify all the different groups of people who might potentially be involved in your center as families, staff members, volunteers, or board members. At the very least, consider diversity along the following lines: culture and race, class, disability, gender, religion, and sexual orientation. Ask individuals from each of the communities you identify to review your personnel, enrollment, health, and nutrition policies and your procedures and forms.

Strategy *Expand your approach to communication*

To make program information and functions accessible to as wide a variety of people as possible, use a broad array of communication systems. Consider some or all of the following alternatives:

- one-on-one conversations
- buddy systems
- e-mail
- blogs
- a program Web site
- phone trees
- group meetings
- written notices
- visual displays such as posters or bulletin boards

In addition, take the initiative to translate key written materials into one or more languages as a way to reach out to other potential staff and families for your program. Consider simultaneous translation for parent meetings if a number of your families speak languages other than English.

Strategy *Make diversity and antibias work part of your orientations*

When you do interviews or orientations for new families and staff, walk them through visual examples of how your antibias policies look in practice: have a variety of images on the walls; show them documentation notebooks of past curriculum projects; let them look over books, dolls, and materials to get a flavor of how you approach diversity. Also, ask prospective new families and staff what diversity they might bring to your program and how you might actively support that.

Strategy *Formulate personnel policies and systems to encourage diversity among staff*

When developing personnel policies and systems, consider the needs not only of current staff but of the potential staff members in your community. Develop flexible policies, benefit packages, and floating holidays to accommodate the diversity of staff needs.

DESIGNING SYSTEMS TO PROVIDE TIME FOR REFLECTION AND PROBLEM SOLVING

If your policies provide the structure to support your vision of community, the systems that grow from those policies directly control people's experience of community in your program. Systems organize the many responsibilities you have as a director and shape the way staff members feel about the workplace and about themselves. Indirectly, they are a pedagogical tool that accompanies the specific coaching and mentoring strategies you employ. For instance, you can create procedures, paperwork, and accountability systems that foster reflection, collaboration, and active participation, rather than ones that emphasize meeting the requirements, checking-off boxes, and not asking why. Inherent in this approach is the notion that people should participate in developing systems they will be responsible for following.

Directors deal with mounds of paperwork. Some trees are sacrificed for regulatory bodies outside their programs, while others are sacrificed to meet their own requirements for documentation and accountability. The paperwork systems you develop and require also have a big impact on how staff members see the priorities of their work. No one likes or genuinely benefits from meaningless paperwork.

The goal of record keeping and documentation should be to support and provide evidence of progress toward your vision. You can design accountability systems that encourage particular dispositions in staff and families and enhance everyone's experience of the community you dream of creating. Make a commitment to yourself and your vision that all documentation systems you put in place encourage people to think, assess, and offer solutions to problems they encounter.

After attending a Visionary Director seminar with Margie and Deb, our directors were all abuzz, but also full of "yeah, buts" and "I wish I could do thats." I wondered out loud to my directors, "What's keeping you from doing this kind of work?" Overwhelmingly, "time and paperwork" was the resounding reply. "Oh, is that all?" I replied with a smile and a twinkle. I then challenged the directors to really do what they learned in the workshop—spend time in the classrooms, engage in meaningful conversations with staff, and make the time to reflect on their programs. I immediately told the home office staff not to ask for reports or other paperwork for a week and for the management staff to refrain from calling the directors with corporate business. Imagine a week with no paperwork! I wanted the directors to engage in intentional application of the presentation they had heard without the excuse of paperwork.

I remember a mentor director questioned how to begin her training with a new director without reviewing the paperwork. I challenged her to begin with the vision and how to make that visible and to focus on how to relate with new staff and families. In retrospect, some directors made incredible changes. One had time to think more clearly about her outdoor space and by spring of that year made big changes. Another brought her staff together to think concretely about the vision and mission of the program, and together they created a collage for families. A few other directors began the process of investigating mixed-age groupings for preschool and toddlers, and that has now been instituted in five of the centers. Still another reevaluated her environment beyond the ECERS and has since created an entryway where family information is found on a beautiful mirrored dresser wreathed by garland. Families feel welcomed by a Victorian couch and small table and chairs.

During their annual performance appraisals, almost all of the directors shared that the most meaningful professional development of the year had been the ideas from *The Visionary Director*, and the challenges that followed.

—Bill

Principle

Use Child Assessment Systems That Enlist Teachers' Excitement

Across the country, supervisors, special education staff, and teachers in pre-K, Head Start, and other early intervention programs express frustration over the time required to meet assessment and individual planning regulations. Many admit the systems they're using have little real meaning for them or the children. The joy of observing and following the amazing process of child development has been replaced by an accountability system that teachers bemoan. In contrast, when teachers are actively involved in creative and useful ways to observe, record, assess, and plan for children, it is one of the most affirming parts of their job.

If your attention is primarily on whether your staff have their paperwork done, teachers will come to dread rather than treasure this aspect of their work. As you model and offer feedback around assessments of children, encourage your staff members' curiosity about and delight in the children's development by emphasizing your own experience. Share your observations, notes, and questions about children's play. Arrange for teachers to observe children as they engage in self-chosen activities (often called "play-based assessment") rather than activities directed by teachers. This encourages teachers to see that attention to children's daily activities is critical to knowing their developmental progress.

Strategy *Design forms that encourage curiosity and delight*

When teachers have minimal skills in observing and individualizing for children, systems that require them to check boxes and answer yes-or-no questions hinder their professional development. Instead, they need assessment systems that foster thinking and analysis and include reflective questions, problem posing, hypothesizing, interviewing, and personal reflection. Here are some examples of questions you might put on an assessment form:

- What specifically did you see the child doing?
- What is your reaction, and what might be influencing it?

- What is the child trying to figure out in this situation?
- What experience, knowledge, or skill is the child building?
- What questions, inventions, or problems is the child encountering?
- What does this child find meaningful? challenging? frustrating?

Strategy *Use Learning Stories as an approach to assessment*

One of the most inspiring approaches to assessment can be found in the narrative Learning Story conventions developed in New Zealand. This system involves teachers using their documentation skills to write a detailed description of a significant endeavor a child has engaged in, along with an analysis of what the teacher thinks this means for the child and the opportunities and possibilities for what might be offered next. The Learning Story also invites the child's family to share their perspective on the observation. Many teachers in New Zealand consciously speak to the child as they write the story, even as they include reference to how the story specifically illustrates some aspect of the five strands of their national curriculum, Te Whāriki. (See appendix 15 for more information on Learning Stories conventions and how these can be integrated with our recommended Thinking Lens protocols to help teachers analyze their stories and uncover opportunities and possibilities.)

Strategy *Provide time for collaborative discussion among teachers*

If collaboration is central to your formal system of assessment, teachers will learn to analyze, hypothesize, and plan next steps together. When systems encourage teachers to see themselves as researchers engaged in the process of learning about each child, staff members are more alive in their work and appropriate in their planning for children. Use some or all of the following suggestions to make room for collaboration:

- Rotate teacher and/or substitute schedules to give teachers a regular time to meet together.

- Include time in routine staff meetings for sharing highlights of an observation and for collaborative hypothesizing.
- Post or circulate examples of collaborative discussions for teachers to learn from each other.

I am always looking for ways to access grant money to open up some more possibilities for staff development. Oftentimes there is grant money available for particular topics or issues. When I write the proposal, I try to frame our specific interests and needs around the grant requirements. My goal is to use extra funds from grants to free up staff time for planning and meeting, as well as to help us acquire new resources. I know that whatever the topic or focus, the process of thinking and planning together builds a collaborative, supportive climate for all of the work we do.

We titled one of our most successful projects "Culture, Conflict Resolution, and Kids." The funds we got for this project enabled us to strengthen our basic philosophical approach to professional development and designing curriculum. The extra money helped pay for staff to document real-life conflicts for discussion and problem solving, as well as training on cross-cultural communications and conflict resolution. We had extra paid staff time to develop case studies with accompanying narratives, to work with children's stories and plays about settling disputes, and to set up a workshop series on cross-cultural communications and negotiating conflicts from different perspectives.

—Lisa

Principle

Involve Staff in All Phases of Evaluating Their Job Performance

In addition to the coaching and mentoring roles so important to directing work, your managing and overseeing responsibilities call for you to conduct a performance evaluation of each staff member at least once but preferably twice a year. You should view these functions as separate and distinct and provide that clarity for your staff. Some directors are quite comfortable with doing performance evaluations, whereas others feel awkward and avoid its formality. Evaluations are important not just for marginal or mediocre staff members. Without evaluations, the ongoing development of experienced and master teachers can languish or stagnate.

All evaluations should include self-assessment—a focus on strengths and the development process—and clear goals and action plans for the next area of growth identified. Evaluations should be based on observable evidence gathered over time, not just the week before you schedule the conference with a caregiver. This means you must devise a system for observing along with evaluation forms that cover the data that is important for your discussion and goal setting. (Samples of forms we've developed are in appendix 5.)

Strategy Supplement checklists with observational narratives

Most approaches to staff evaluations involve using a standard form with a checklist as a quick way to rate how well the staff member is performing. This can make performance reviews efficient and fair but quite often renders them meaningless when it comes to genuine growth and development. Checklists help make things that feel intangible more solid, but if they aren't accompanied by some narrative comments or specific observations, they become subjective. You might include anecdotal notes in your performance evaluation files or use video or photos as tools for discussing specific considerations. These techniques capture the flavor and tone of a caregiver's performance, which are lacking in a checklist.

Strategy Plan the cycle of supervision and evaluation

Particularly with a large staff, it's easier for you to keep track of evaluations if they fall within a regular cycle. It's also less anxiety-producing for staff if they know when they can expect to be evaluated. Consider designating certain times of the year for evaluative observation sessions, as opposed to coaching. Establish a clear cycle of supervision in which you observe, document, discuss, set goals, practice, observe again, document, and so forth. This practice keeps evaluation in its proper context as just one point in an ongoing cycle of growth and discovery.

Strategy Experiment with different forms

No standard evaluation form will meet your specific needs as effectively as a form you've designed yourself. In addition, it's important to see forms as flexible, able to change for different purposes and situations. Try developing evaluation forms together with your entire staff to ensure you've taken into account cultural differences and other issues that are important to staff members. Develop different observation forms and strategies to cover different areas of focus. Create separate evaluation forms for each position on your career ladder, acknowledging different levels of knowing and growing. Finally, experiment with different methods for staff to regularly evaluate your performance—anonymous feedback, direct feedback, forms from books, forms created by you and staff. (See appendix 5 for examples.)

Strategy Acknowledge the power differential in the evaluation process

Performance evaluations always reflect issues of power relationships in a workplace. You should not pretend these relationships don't exist, but rather see your role as providing a mirror or snapshot so that staff members can see themselves more clearly. From this side of the triangle, your responsibility with staff is to uphold professional standards. But as with your mentoring-and-coaching role, your ultimate goal for performance evaluations is to enhance teachers' power to develop.

Meet together one-on-one to compare an individual's self-assessment with your assessment of her or his performance; then discuss possible goals for the coming period based on your discussion. Together, create action steps toward those goals, and make sure you have systems in place to follow through with these plans. On your form, designate a place for the staff member to sign her or his agreement or disagreement with your evaluation, date it, and make sure that the staff member gets a copy and a copy stays in her or his personnel file.

One of the toddler teachers came to us with a background in family child care as opposed to center-based child care. When I became the director, she had been with the center two years and was a highly dependable, valued employee, the kind who stays extra hours to set up or clean up, sweeps the playground, takes care of the library books, and so on. But as the head teacher, the stress of responsibility for guidance and discipline with toddlers was getting to her. During her evaluation she told me she really didn't want to be the head teacher and asked several times for a less stressful position. I gave her the option of becoming an assistant in our kindergarten program, and she worked there for a year with moderate success, still having difficulty with guidance and group management.

We discussed these continuing concerns, and I offered her the position as our cook. She dived into the job and was the best cook we ever had, rounding out our philosophy perfectly. Menus began to reflect what was happening in the program as well as in the larger community. The kindergarten children began writing her letters requesting specific menu items. She wrote back and told them when they could expect their requests to appear at lunch or breakfast. One of the toddlers who was fascinated with trucks of any kind was invited to the kitchen every Wednesday to "help unload" the food delivery truck. He always managed to carry something off the truck, often the large containers of spices.

One morning I arrived to find a two-year-old sitting on the prep table stirring a large bowl of eggs. She had a difficult separation that morning and had been invited to the kitchen to help make French toast for breakfast. This wonderful cook kept a corner of the kitchen readied for any child who needed special attention to get through the day. She knew all of the children by name, and they all knew her. She readily left the kitchen to give a helping hand to any teacher or administrator who needed it.

But alas, as budgets tend to do, ours became tight. The only way to give the teachers a raise was to do away with the lunch program and have the children bring their own lunches. As these budgetary discussions were underway, I talked to the cook and reassured her that her job was not in jeopardy, but it would likely change. She asked me if she could return to the classroom. She thought she was ready. I thought she was ready too. As we start a new year, our center cook is once again a classroom teacher. She is doing a wonderful job, even with guidance and discipline.

—Margo

Principle

Plan Training to Reflect Your Vision of a Learning Community

Along with a budget line item for in-service training, you need a careful plan for how you will spend your precious training dollars. As consultants often called upon to provide training to programs, we're discouraged by the lack of thought that goes into many of the training requests we receive. Directors sometimes ask what topics we'd like to focus on, rather than addressing a particular training need in their program. Even those who call with a specific focus in mind seldom view our training as part of an overall plan.

To develop an effective in-service training program, it's helpful to have a focus for each individual staff member and also the program as a whole. The focus should be drawn from conducting training needs assessments and using individual performance evaluations and program tools such as those mentioned above. Mandates generated from outside agencies requiring staff training in such things as first aid, CPR, sexual abuse, and blood-borne illness prevention training should be integrated into individual plans so that staff members are not required to attend these mandated trainings more often than necessary.

Ongoing professional development should be a requirement for everyone working in early childhood education, with a specified minimum number of hours per year that the program budget covers. Nevertheless, caregivers should choose the training they want to attend within the agreed-on focus and goals.

Make mandatory attendance at a given training the exception rather than the rule. Isn't this the approach we want teachers to take with children? On the whole, we've seen a significant difference in the eagerness to learn of teachers who *choose* our training, compared with those required to attend. What a waste of limited resources to mandate attendance without ever asking what teachers need or want!

Strategy *Develop individualized training plans*

In order to provide meaningful training, have staff conduct self-assessments to determine their needs and interests. Then develop individual training plans with a specific focus. For each staff member, identify goals, a timeline, and an evaluation process. Keep track of local professional development opportunities, and notify teachers of ones that are relevant to their training focus. Research specific resources for them as well. Be sure to formalize some time spent observing in other rooms, reflecting, problem solving, and collaborating with a mentor as legitimate in-service training. Consider designing a portfolio system for teachers to document and show evidence of their growing understanding and skills within their training focus. Finally, don't forget to celebrate and reward achievements.

Strategy Expand your approach to program-wide training

With individual training plans underway, it is also important to establish a focus for program-wide training to enhance your entire learning community. Involve families and staff in choosing a focus for a year, using information from program evaluation tools, group interests, or problems encountered. Perhaps you want to create more opportunities for children to feel powerful in your program, and thus decide to pursue training relevant to that goal. If a child in your program is deaf, that might be an opportunity for everyone to learn American Sign Language. Maybe there are persistent conflicts between children or some of the adults, and everyone could benefit from training to improve listening, paraphrasing, and conflict negotiation skills. If families repeatedly express concerns about school readiness skills, you could explore how children learn to read and write and focus on developmentally appropriate ways to foster literacy skills.

Launching a center-wide research project is another valuable professional development tool. For instance, rather than more workshops on child guidance, consider having teachers gather detailed observations of how children are making efforts to form relationships with their peers. Studying those observations together as a staff, perhaps using the Thinking Lens protocol, will uncover more ways teachers can affirm, support, and scaffold social and emotional intelligence in the children. Our profession has a growing body of resources focused on teacher research, including an overview and examples in the Voices of Practitioners section on NAEYC's *Beyond the Journal* Web site. (See Resources for related literature and Web sites.)

Learning happens when you focus on a topic over a period of time using a variety of strategies. Once the program-wide focus is determined, your role is to schedule the time, acquire the resources, and design the delivery systems.

I was so excited to learn about emergent curriculum approaches that I couldn't wait to help my staff learn how to do this. My excitement led me to try many things and thus tend to overlook the small steps the staff was making toward my main goal. When one of the teachers accused me of wanting to have "little Adinas" running around, I thought about that statement and realized that I didn't want clones of myself. What I did want, however, was my teaching staff to be the most creative teachers they could be.

I began to realize how important it is to find out from the teachers what areas they feel they need training in. As I began to involve them in the training process and in our work toward accreditation, I saw much more sharing between classrooms and individuals. During the accreditation process, I saw staff members become more comfortable speaking out in the group and even delivering presentations to others. From these experiences I realized the most important piece to working with adults in child care is to help them feel they are important in so many ways—from actually caring for the children to working as a team. Most of all, my job is to help them to realize their own special talents in working with young children.

—Adina

Strategy *Provide many ways for achieving training goals*

Think of a good early childhood classroom, where the teacher provides many ways of exploring the same concepts. Adults, too, need diverse opportunities to play and experiment with new thinking. Consider some or all of the following:

- Arrange for classes to be held on-site or locate offerings in the wider community.
- Hire a consultant to offer a training series on the topic, with periodic visits to observe and coach.
- Attend relevant conference sessions as a group and schedule follow-up discussions (see the sample conference attendance planning form in appendix 10).
- Arrange for group visits to other programs known for strength in your area of focus (see appendix 11 for an example of an observation form designed for this purpose).

- Identify in-house staff members to acquire expertise in an area and then mentor others.
- Focus a portion of each staff meeting on storytelling related to the topic of the meeting.
- Have a parent and teacher lead a book discussion group together.
- Collect and display related resources, books, and articles in the staff lounge, bathrooms, and office areas and on bulletin boards.

Strategy Acknowledge and celebrate progress toward your training goals

One of the manager's critical tasks is to make the program's growth visible to staff members and families (who may be so deeply involved in the program that progress is invisible to them) and to the community at large (who may be completely ignorant of the strengths of the program). Consider some of these techniques:

- Create visual displays with photos and observation notes to document progress and make it visible to all.
- Invite visitors from the community to see what you are doing.
- Solicit recognition in the media.
- Celebrate accomplishments with social events and a significant purchase for the center.

Principle

View Time as a Building Block

How we think about time in our programs is directly related to the growth available for the people there. Consider time a worthy investment, not something to rush through. In *The Fifth Discipline*, writer and business consultant Peter Senge asks (1990), "If a meeting takes only fifteen minutes, are we really going to learn anything?" In *Negotiating Standards in the Primary Classroom*, Carol Anne Wien writes of the dangers of structuring our child care centers around a school-like time schedule for activities and routines (2004):

> Time in schools [is] conceived as a moving train, and one catches or loses it. . . . (101)
>
> This production schedule organization of time is, to me, the most taken-for-granted aspect of Western schooling—that is, the assumption that what is normal is the organizing of events in a linear line, one after the other through days, weeks, months, and years. We have lost the conception that there are other ways to use time in learning. It does not occur to us unless we experience powerful exemplars of different handlings of time, such as aboriginal views of time as circular, or agrarian views of time as cyclical, such as in the approach of the early childhood educators of Reggio Emilia. Until we experience other models of organizing time, we don't grasp that organizations of time are cultural inventions. . . . (88)
>
> Breaking the vise of production-schedule uses of time is perhaps the most helpful practice an administrator can offer to open up the range of possibilities for teachers. (53)

Bringing these two voices together leads us to question the way we structure time both for the children and the adults in our programs. If our systems require the adults to chop their time into little blocks, what will this do for their thinking process and the way they behave with children and families? If we organize staff meetings as a series of disjointed announcements and trainings, is it realistic to call this staff development? Wien strongly recommends allocating resources for professional development to help teachers cope with the political demands of teaching standardized curriculum, the trend of the fragmentation and mechanization of education, and the industrialization of classroom life, which overrides the deep theoretical, practical, and historical knowledge of the early care and education field.

Viewing time as an investment will help you guard against the "fast food" or "artificial flower" mentality. Time invested in relationships and in sowing and growing new seeds doesn't always show immediate results or bring relief to your bottom line. But with time on their side, teachers and children in your program get more nourishment and opportunities to bloom. Jim Greenman reminds us, "Avoiding rigid and narrow schedules that choke or loose schedules that frighten or intoxicate generally requires a thoughtful and complete analysis of how all the program structural elements interact—time, space, goals, organization, and people—and creative problem solving to minimize negative side effects" (2007, 114).

The time schedules established for children and adults have a huge effect on their experience of quality. When it comes to allocating time in our programs, it is far too easy to fall into habitual patterns and neglect our values as we design our schedules and use of time. In fact, when directors look to increasing ratios or group sizes and altering staffing patterns as cost-cutting or profit-margin enhancement strategies, they are putting consistency and continuity for children on the chopping block. If we expect staff to use their break time for planning, or require them to plan, do paperwork, have family conferences, and attend meetings on their own time, we will never stem the turnover crisis. Staff members need paid time to think, evaluate, and plan. These tasks are a prerequisite for doing their job well. They need time to be together for discussions and trainings of interest, and they need time for visiting each other's classrooms and other environments for children out in the community. These are the building blocks of quality.

How you organize time in your program grows or defeats the vision you hold. Here are some strategies to consider.

Strategy *Use colored dots for analyzing how time is spent in your program*

As a director, first do your own analysis of the balance of your time that is spent working on each side of the triangle framework. Take your calendar from the last couple of weeks and add to it anything you did that isn't noted for each day. Then use a package of colored adhesive dots or different colored pens to code each item as follows:

- Put a red dot in front of activities that are about managing and overseeing.
- Place a green dot next to each item that involves coaching or mentoring.
- Place a blue dot next to the times you were intentionally working to build or support an experience of community in your program.

Now count the number of red, green, and blue dots you have. Are you satisfied with the balance in how you are spending your time? If there are changes you would like to make, stop here and develop some priorities and plans for yourself.

Have your staff members do a similar assessment of how time is spent in their classrooms. Ask them to write out their daily schedule, including all the things between the lines that they do with the children. Suggest they do the following:

- Put a red dot beside each time block where they are making the choices or directing the children in what to do.
- Place yellow dots for times when children are in a transition, a holding pattern, getting ready, or waiting for the next activity.
- Place green dots for times when children are free to make their own choices and initiate their own play activities.

As you did in evaluating your own time, ask teachers to look at the overall balance of dots. Encourage them to find ways to reduce the number of red and yellow dots in order to expand the blocks of time children have to engage in self-chosen activities.

> What I have found works best in building a sense of community in my program is to make sure I do the simple things like saying hello and good-bye to everyone, every day. Simple things matter, such as spending at least a few minutes in each room every day, responding to complaints and difficulties quickly, and making sure we rarely cancel or postpone regular staff meetings. When I let paperwork take precedence over human contact, the whole program suffers.
>
> **—Ellen**

Strategy *Reclaim time on behalf of your vision*

We have never met a director who didn't fret over having too little time to get everything done. The question is who's running the show, you or your unfinished tasks? You have the opportunity to create systems and organize time to lead your program in the direction of your vision. Here are some ideas to help keep time in line with where you want to be:

- Organize your schedule so as to have regular contact with all families and staff.

- Create specific time blocks for you to be in rooms coaching teachers.
- Designate a portion of your schedule each week for reading and thinking.
- Hold regular all-staff meetings, alternately used for training, problem solving, and community building.
- Use a floating teacher for weekly team meetings, mentoring, and parent conferences.
- Schedule quarterly professional development days and annual retreats for all staff, preferably on weekdays with the center closed.

Principle

Design Meetings around Community Building and Staff Development

With busy lives and tired bodies, there's nothing worse than sitting in a boring meeting at the end of a long workday. Whatever frequency and time frame you use to schedule staff meetings, make them consistent, reliable, and something people can look forward to. Staff meetings should be an engaging, important part of the satisfaction staff members get from their work. This means holding meetings in a comfortable setting, having refreshments, allowing time for community building, and following a clear agenda.

Some people find it helpful to hold several shorter meetings in a month, whereas others prefer a monthly three-hour evening meeting. Whatever format you use, designate some time for staff development and other time for problem solving and decision making. Limit announcements and information sharing that can be more efficiently handled through written notes or other means that don't eat into precious time together.

For the problem-solving and decision-making portion of your meeting, provide a way for staff members to have input into these agenda items, and design a process for addressing these issues from meeting to meeting. This will provide consistency and an opportunity to experience and learn effective communication, facilitation, and problem-solving skills. Chapters 3 and 4 have additional specific strategies that can be used in staff meetings.

I decided to do a couple of presentations and show slides of Reggio Emilia at our staff meetings. I knew it wouldn't work to try to require the staff to move in this direction. In fact, that would defeat my whole purpose and undermine the real meaning of what the Reggio approach has to offer. My excitement about Reggio did spark an interest among a couple of staff members, who approached me saying they wanted to try it. This got us on the road and forced me to make a commitment to support their growth in exploring Reggio. To me, this is an example of how an important sense of direction for our program comes from the staff. That year seven teams of teachers voluntarily joined in a commitment to explore the Reggio approach. As others saw their changes, ten more teams joined.

We chose areas of focus for exploration, using discussions, planning and evaluation, and some hands-on activities to provoke our thinking. For instance, we actually explored different art media to discover how they can be used by the children to represent ideas. We also explored what skills, strategies, and support are needed to use them effectively. When a new idea or activity seemed risky to pursue, I asked for volunteers to be our pioneers to go out and explore, experiment, and come back to the rest of us to share their discoveries. For example, we realized we needed to do something different in our relationships with families. Our pioneers tried a new approach with home visits, asking the families to tell them about their hopes and dreams for their children and what kinds of adults they wanted them to be. What we heard totally changed our views of our parents and families.

—Karen

Strategy Devote staff meetings to enhancing teacher development

You can provide effective professional development during staff meetings if your primary goal is to provide a *learning process* for your staff rather than trying to convey information. Time devoted to active learning in staff meetings conveys the importance you place on thinking and growing, and it helps your program develop as a learning community for adults as well as children.

In our book *Training Teachers: A Harvest of Theory and Practice* (Carter and Curtis 1994), we discuss the components of adult learning at length and offer our approach to planning professional development meetings and workshops. Here's an overview of the process we recommend, followed by an example of a pedagogical agenda for a one-hour staff meeting, using the sample one-hour format from the High/Scope Training of Teacher Trainers model (Epstein 1993):

- Start your planning process for a training session by brainstorming an overview of the core ideas on the topic.
- Prioritize and narrow the ideas you want to work with so that they fit the particular goals and time frame you have.
- Design an opening activity to spark initial thinking on the topic. This is similar to what some call an icebreaker, but it is designed specifically to give the group a common experience around the ideas to be taken up.
- Debrief this activity with a mini-lecture connecting the ideas to the reflections teachers have on the experience they just had.
- Design or choose one or more activities for practice in applying the core ideas to be explored.
- Conclude with a brief discussion of next steps, a summary, and an evaluation. Next steps might call for further training, taking up other ideas from your brainstorming, or practical things caregivers want to begin doing.

Here's a sample workshop agenda that follows the points above:

1. Training Overview (5 minutes)
2. Opening Activity to Reflect on Topic (10 minutes)
3. Debriefing and Discussion of Core Ideas (15 to 20 minutes)
4. Practice Applying Ideas (15 to 20 minutes)
5. Next Steps and Follow-Up (5 minutes)
6. Summary and Evaluation (5 minutes)

For example, if you want to spend an hour exploring sources of emergent curriculum for teachers to consider in their planning, an hour's workshop might look like this:

1. **Training Overview** (5 minutes)
Using an emergent approach to curriculum doesn't mean just standing around waiting for something to happen. Teachers can create what the Italians call a "provocation," arranging for a discovery or activity that might spark children's interests.

2. **Opening Activity to Reflect on Topic** (10 minutes)
Display a selection of interesting boxes or bags, each with a different object or picture that isn't immediately identifiable as to what it is—things like dried seed pods or other items from nature, diagrams or x-rays, kitchen gadgets, hardware, or Styrofoam packing shapes from shipping boxes. Ask people to form pairs or small groups around one item that intrigues them. They should generate a list of questions or ideas they might have about the picture or object.

3. **Debriefing and Discussion of Core Ideas** (15 to 20 minutes)
Initial questions might include:

- What intrigued you about the picture or object?
- What would make it possible for you to pursue this interest?

Points to cover in discussion:

- Emergent curriculum can come from something in the lives of children, their families, the wider community, or your own interest.
- If you want to introduce something as a possible topic to explore, initiate interest by arranging for a discovery or an engaging way for children to explore what they might be drawn to.
- Observe with attention to children's interests and ideas, rather than something you want to teach them about the topic.
- Based on what you discover about what seems engaging to the children, plan further opportunities for their exploration.
- Consider a number of ways children might represent their ideas about this topic with different media.

4. **Practice Applying Ideas** (15 to 20 minutes)
Pass out a few short scenarios for teachers to discuss in small groups, considering the following questions:

- How could you provide a provocation to capture the children's attention?
- What are possible questions, ideas, or misinformation children might have?
- How might you provide different opportunities for children to explore and represent their thinking?

5. Next Steps and Follow-Up (5 minutes)
Ask each teaching team to identify something of excitement in their own life, the children's lives, or the families' lives that might be a source of curriculum. Tell them to make this the focus of their next team planning meeting, going through the same questions just used in the practice session.

6. Summary and Evaluation (5 minutes)

- Ask if there were any new insights from today's discussion.
- Ask if there are any outstanding questions that need to be taken up in the next meeting.
- Ask if there are any suggestions for how time could have been better used in exploring the topic.

Staff members become motivated to learn when their appetite has been whetted through active engagement with ideas that relate to their real-life experience. Thus, even for an hour-long training, we recommend devoting at least half of the time to exercises that have participants actively involved. In longer workshops the sample time frames can be expanded, but the bulk of the additional time should still be spent in the practice of applying the workshop ideas.

Paid time for the adults to gather away from children to pursue their own problem solving and learning is a precious commodity. It is foolish—not to mention unethical—for us to waste it out of carelessness, poor planning, or weak facilitation skills. If you feel you need more skills in facilitating meetings, managing group dynamics, or conducting workshops, make that a professional development goal for yourself. You can draw on numerous print resources, workshops, and classes. You can also begin to study those who you think have good skills in this area. Be systematic about learning this important management skill.

Strategy Choose a focus for your professional development for the school year

While it's tempting to cover a variety of topics during your valuable professional development days, consider an alternative approach of choosing a focus and approaching it in a number of ways, thereby deepening rather than scattering the learning experience. A series of disconnected staff meetings throughout the year may get some content covered, but it doesn't help teachers develop their craft. Rather, staff members need a carefully designed and sequenced set of experiences to practice applying theory to practice, akin to learning to play a musical instrument, mastering a sport, or becoming a writer, astronaut, surgeon, or woodworker.

Time and money for in-service professional development is never adequate, so you should plan to use it to grow your organizational culture and community as well as to enhance theory and practice. One approach is to choose a topic, such as learning environments, and then center each in-service day around particular questions related to that topic. For instance, "How do learning environments foster relationships and create a sense of belonging and group identity while honoring children's individuality and family culture?" "How can our indoor environments more intentionally invite active bodies, rather than trying to squelch or control them, thereby conveying that movement and activity aren't of value to us?"

Another approach could be to have a protocol for self-reflection to serve as a Thinking Lens for each topic you take up during professional development days.

Inspired by the questions used for professional development at Chicago Commons [see Afterword], we develop a research question each year to give us a shared point of reference for observation and study. Our research question is linked to our yearlong professional development focus. Several years ago, for example, our yearlong focus centered on the intersections between anti-bias curriculum and the Reggio-inspired practice of pedagogical documentation. During our monthly staff meetings, quarterly professional development days, and our annual staff retreat, we explored this intersection from a range of perspectives, with the intention of strengthening our antibias work with children, families, and each other. Our research question at the beginning of the year was: "How do children explore and express their cultural identities in their dramatic play?" Later in the year we added a second question: "When do children call attention to difference, and when do they ignore it? How do they use difference in their relationship with each other?"

—Ann

Strategy *Reallocate your professional development dollars for a mentor teacher*

As you steadily build a budget for professional development in your center, you are likely using the money to send teachers to conferences and invite speakers to do presentations for your staff. Consider a possible pilot project to use these dollars differently. Pool all your professional development money together to hire a part-time mentor teacher to provide a systematic yearlong protocol to help your staff learn and grow together. The programs that we've seen stretch themselves to experiment with this model have found the desired outcomes far greater than any other use of professional development money. Even if you only try this for a year, you will have grown an organizational culture that is more intentional in its practice of learning together. (See Afterword for some examples.)

Making Good Use of Your Power and Influence

Because there are so many forces that seem out of our control, it's common for directors to see themselves as having very little power and influence to make change. The truth is, through the organizational climate you create, you have far more influence than you may imagine. The approach you take in developing your policies and systems makes an enormous impact on how things unfold in your program. Unless you work under the umbrella of a larger organization, you have direct decision-making power over these areas and can use them in the service of your vision. We've found that even directors who are bound by larger agency policies can creatively work around most constraints. You can access a powerful resource when you approach your work with a "can do" rather than a "no way" attitude. Supporting this attitude with additional skill development and know-how will enhance your leadership in ways that spread beyond your program.

Thus, we end this chapter where we began, stressing the importance of cultivating the kind of organizational culture that supports your vision. These pages have offered you a number of principles and strategies to build on for the managing-and-overseeing side of your work. But before you jump in and make use of them in an arbitrary fashion that may appeal to you, we suggest you first get some honest input from those you work with.

Practice Assessing Your Organizational Climate

Wise managers periodically play the role of meteorologist. Check out any possible clouds or storms brewing with staff, children, and families in your program. You can easily turn Bloom's "Ten Dimensions of Organizational Climate" (2005, 190) or the Model Work Standards (Center for the Child Care Workforce 1999) into a weather report of your program (see appendixes 2 and 3). Consider including additional dimensions that reflect an experience of community.

To use the "Ten Dimensions of Organizational Climate" as a quick assessment tool, create a large graph on chart paper listing each of the dimensions (collegiality, professional growth, supervisor support, clarity, reward system, decision making, goal consensus, task orientation, physical setting, innovativeness) vertically along the side of the paper and three possible ratings. For instance, sunny/no sign of clouds, partly cloudy, and dark clouds, across the top of the paper, so that it looks something like the chart on the next page.

Ten Dimensions of Organizational Climate			

collegiality			
professional growth			
supervisor support			
clarity			
reward system			
decision making			
goal consensus			
task orientation			
physical setting			
innovativeness			

- Ask each person to plot a rating for each of the dimensions, using a colored adhesive dot or marker corresponding to their rating for each category.
- Have each person connect their dots with a single line.
- Leave the completed chart posted in your lounge for a week, and see what kind of climate you have.

Sometimes there are surprises, such as finding yourself in the eye of the storm. This suggests you may need to pursue a more formal, in-depth assessment of your organizational climate, perhaps with the aid of a consultant. On other occasions, the results are an affirmation of the good things about your organizational culture. We recommend you hone your skills as a meteorologist rather than avoiding or denying the possibility of bad weather.

Chapter 6

Bringing Your Vision to Life

Imagine a program

Where children are respected for their feelings and their desire to belong
Where they are supported in their desire to explore, their eagerness to take on new challenges, and their urges to feel powerful and competent in many ways
Where they discover the magic and wonder of the world
Where they can connect with others, younger and older, alike and different

Imagine a program

Where children and adults indulge in having fun
Where they abandon themselves to joy and serious intellectual pursuits
Where they use a variety of materials to represent what they understand

Imagine a program

Where teachers are emotionally and intellectually engaged in their work
Where they work closely together to explore their questions and theories
Where they eagerly voice and engage with a variety of opinions

Imagine a program

Where teachers form close partnerships with families
Where families are welcomed, encouraged, and supported to contribute to the life of the classroom

Imagine a program

Where teachers have the resources they need
Where they receive the time and materials to nourish their hearts and minds

*Can you imagine this as **your** program?*

We bring this book to a close by inviting you to imagine yourself having made significant progress in bringing your vision to life. Close your eyes and imagine what your center might look like if it were refocused on a value that is truly important to you. Get some pictures in your mind. Imagine some conversations that might be going on among the children, between the teachers and children, between the teachers and families, between families and their children, and among families in your center. What would they be excited about? Proud of? Eager to offer a helping hand toward? What specific things would they be thanking you for?

Bringing a vision to life is a process, a journey; it is not a fixed destination. Once you identify a value you hold dear and imagine how it could be reflected throughout a program, you have already taken some important steps. Now consider one small thing that you could begin doing in a new way, one specific change you could make when you walk into your center tomorrow morning that would better represent this value that is important to you. Choose something else you would like to concentrate on as a goal for the start of the next school year. Then think about something that is going to take considerably more time, perhaps five years to have firmly in place. Consider these three time markers—a change that can be made tomorrow, a change that can be in place next year, and a change that might take several years—as the seeds of a strategic plan you will take more time to flesh out with the involvement of others.

This book has offered you a management framework to support your work in the form of an equilateral triangle, with each side called out to understand the distinct roles that must be fulfilled in your job as a director.

For each side of the triangle, we've offered distinct principles with strategies that highlight actions you could take. In reality, the principles and strategies for each side of the triangle work in tandem, often overlapping and so entwined that they don't appear to be separate functions of a director's job. At this point, we feel it would be useful to provide you with some fuller stories of directors who have put their imaginations to work and begun moving forward step by step. Sometimes their experience has had them taking a few steps backward, but their commitment to deeply held progressive values helps them stay the course.

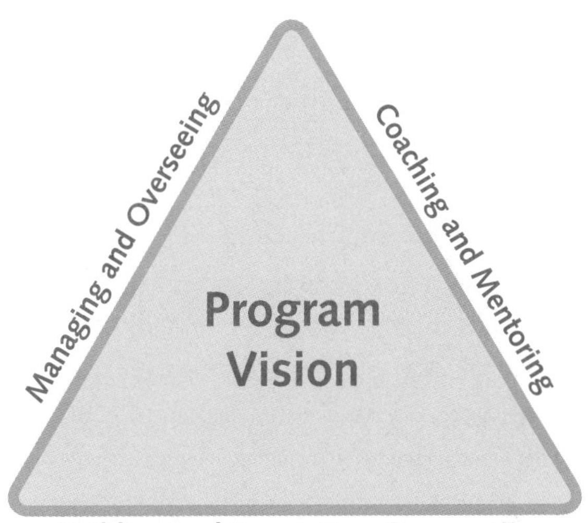

In the stories that follow, you will meet four directors who are diligently pursuing a vision surrounding a value they strongly believe in. Anyone familiar with the daily realities of early childhood programs will recognize the dilemmas these directors regularly encounter. What may be less familiar and more inspiring is their refusal to let these difficult struggles limit their thinking. They refuse to accept mediocrity as a daily definition of acceptable quality. As you study the principles that each director is working with and get a picture of their innovative practices, keep these questions in mind:

- What dispositions or habits of mind does this director exhibit? (For example, where do you see perseverance, efforts to seek other perspectives, an expectation of the continuous change and challenge, a willingness to take risks?)
- How does this director illuminate working with the triangle framework? (For example, how are resources being aligned with values? How are systems being developed to support mentoring and community building?)
- In what ways is this director thinking outside the box or choosing to color outside the lines? (For example, how is he or she trying unconventional approaches, seeking ideas from other communities, or rejecting a scarcity mentality in decision making?)

PUT RELATIONSHIPS CENTER STAGE

Director Lettie was energized with the possibilities for enhancing the quality of her program with the expansion of an infant/toddler wing to the existing center. She invited a group of teachers and families to work with her to define a vision for these new services. Over a six-month period, the group visited model programs, researched current knowledge and best practices, and listened to stories and advice from many people, including other directors, teachers, and parents. They read through various vision statements and policy handbooks, and then began brainstorming their own ideas about what they believed children, staff, and families of their center deserved from this new program. They all agreed that high-quality relationships with these very young children, their families, and their caregivers were the most important value they wanted to reflect in the following vision statement.

Vision Statement for Our Infant/Toddler Program

Focusing on Children

We see each child as unique, with individual preferences, interests, and important family connections. We strive to know each child through careful observation, cultivating strong relationships with families and studying child development theory. At every stage of development, children have a profound desire to connect with others and learn about the world around them. We consider all of these important elements as we form relationships with children and their families and plan our environment and activities.

Cultivating Relationships

Strong connections with family members and significant others are the foundation for the healthy growth and development of young children. We put relationships at the center of everything we do, from cultivating our own meaningful connections with children, helping children stay closely connected to their families, and providing opportunities for relationships among families, to developing strong teaching teams within the staff to ensure a quality program.

Ensuring Partnerships with Families

We believe that families are the experts when it comes to knowing their children. Throughout our program we support and validate all families and ensure they are represented and included in the daily life of the program and the care and education of their children.

Creating a Homelike Environment

To ease the transition between home and school, we design cozy, homelike environments with elements of beauty and softness, ensuring feelings of security and a sense of calm. In our environments, there are places for children to be quiet and alone as well as being active explorers using their bodies and senses. We follow a predictable schedule so children can feel secure, yet we maintain flexibility in order to focus on children's individual needs and rhythms.

Planning Experiences

We see the time that children spend in our program as filled with rich possibilities for development and learning. We regularly plan experiences where children can explore and interact with materials and people to discover things about themselves, others, and the world around them.

As Lettie reviewed their newly defined vision, she was pleased that at the heart of every component of the statement was a commitment to relationships. Lettie had seen a number of beautifully written vision statements during her research, but rarely did she think the programs she visited lived their ideals; they didn't walk the talk. She also knew firsthand the difficulty of running a visionary child care center. Busy lives and rigid schedules, demanding caretaking tasks, and ever-increasing regulations and requirements do little to support connections and a sense of community among the people in a program. Still, with the opportunity presented by this new program, she was committed to moving ahead in a different way. She vowed to devote attention and resources to ensuring that relationships were at the heart of everything they did.

Lettie decided to focus on her role of managing and overseeing. She believed that if she designed management systems and allocated resources—time, money, skills, and knowledge—to encourage and sustain relationships, then the center could make this vision a reality throughout the entire program. Through Lettie's leadership we can identify a number of principles and see the innovative practices her program instituted to make relationships the center of their work.

Principle

Focus on People, Not Paper

Lettie realized that most of her time and resources were primarily focused on meeting budget priorities, licensing requirements, and professional standards. This resulted in mounds of paperwork and a top-down model, emphasizing efficiency and getting things done. The time and infrastructure for deeper connections among people suffered under Lettie's approach. It became obvious to her that her systems favored paper, not people, and those systems weren't very useful for nourishing the real lives of people in the center.

Innovative Practice

Invest in initial encounters

Lettie started to work toward the new vision from the moment a family contacted her center. Rather than just sending them a brochure or offering quick information over the phone, she began to see this initial encounter as the beginning of an important bond with budding new members of the child care community. With this mind-set, she took more time to find out about the child and the family and to reflect a warm, welcoming manner. She followed up by mailing a homemade book titled *We Are Waiting for You*. To enlist the teachers' involvement, she asked them to develop these books, which contained photos and text reflecting the many ways the children, families, and staff in the center work and play together. A blank page was included at the end, suggesting that children and families describe and draw a picture of how they hoped to be involved when they came to the center. She knew she was on the right track when several children came in with their families and pointed to a photo in the book, saying, "Show me where I can do this." Not only did they feel welcome, but they had already imagined themselves a part of the program.

Innovative Practice

Host community-building orientations

Lettie realized that her usual procedure of handing a prospective family a stack of paperwork to fill out and talking at them about the rules and routines of her program wasn't the way to begin a significant relationship. Instead, once a family agreed to enroll in the center, Lettie invited them to bring photos and other mementos to share more meaningful things about their child and family. Rather than meeting with each family individually, she instituted multifamily tours and orientations. She wanted to send a message right from the start that her center was a place to connect with others for support and friendship. She structured these meetings with time for families to learn about the program along with time to fill out required paperwork. And with an eye to the center's new focus on relationships, she purposefully started the meetings with time for the families to share photos and hear each others' stories about their children and family life.

Each family was invited to turn the photos and stories into a page for a family book left at the center, and a photo of the family was framed and placed in the child's room. To reinforce the bond between the child and teachers, a framed photo of the child with his or her teachers was sent home with the family. In addition, the teachers also made homemade books for all of the children to take home, with photos and names of the children and families in that group.

These efforts required time and resources up front but made a significant impact in welcoming new families and helping them form relationships with others right away. Children and their families had concrete experiences and objects to help them recognize faces, learn names, and make meaningful connections. The teachers saw the effect of their efforts firsthand as they observed family members taking time to read about each other in the books. The children reflected the power of these connections, too, when they used their family photos to comfort themselves or offered a friend the photo of his mommy to help him stop crying. These were certainly concrete signs of the vision Lettie and her staff were reaching for.

Principle

Make Communication Meaningful

Lettie began to realize that her top-down procedures for meeting requirements and getting things done spilled into communication with families and teachers. Charts, forms, lesson plans, checklists, and even newsletters were undermining relationships through their institutional and depersonalized tone. Lettie wanted to create ways to invite dialogue and involvement through meaningful interactions and storytelling.

Innovative Practice

Invite families to participate in communication systems

The recommendations and requirements for infant/toddler programs had the potential to lead Lettie down her typical track of focusing on paperwork, but she was determined to try something different. She asked the infant/toddler teachers to record diaper changes using a simple chart and to track sleeping and eating for each child on a second daily form. The form also had a place to record significant moments and activities that the child was a part of that day. Lettie suggested that for a couple of months the teachers notice how many parents read and/or asked about the information on the forms. Filling out these forms took a lot of the teachers' time, hurriedly completed during naptime or during quick moments throughout the day. Lettie wanted to make sure this was meaningful communication for the families. She also wanted to coach the teachers to be more intellectually engaged in their caregiving chores and partnership with the families.

After observing and talking with the families, the staff discovered that the parents of the infants did rely on the specific information offered on the forms to help them know their child's caregiving needs. The families of toddlers were less interested in detailed information, wanting just a general summary of "did she or didn't she eat, sleep, poop," etc. All the families were most interested in the moments and activities that were meaningful during their child's day. Using this information, the teachers and Lettie developed a new communication system. They kept the more detailed tracking form for the infants and created a more general one for the toddlers. Their goal was to reduce the amount of time they spent reporting this kind of information, while still providing families the information they wanted.

To respond to a family's joy in reading about their child's more meaningful experiences, Lettie purchased a beautiful journal for each child. Two or three times a week, the teachers added photos and wrote special notes to the child about what they noticed and delighted in as they spent time together in the program. The journal entries included child development information that Lettie coached the teachers to consider as they wrote, but she encouraged them to write in the tone of a story for a baby book. The journal was sent home at the end of the week for the family to read and then write a response to the child and/or caregiver. At the end of the year the journal was given to the child and family.

It took awhile for the teachers and parents to get into the habit of journaling. People had varying degrees of investment and comfort with this process, particularly when there were language differences and struggles with literacy. Lettie slowly carved more time during the teachers' days for their journal work and built flexibility into the number of entries she expected. She encouraged the addition of many photos to reflect the stories, and made sure to support the teachers and families through these challenges. Over time the journals have become a treasured, shared connection between the families and teachers and will be a powerful gift for the children when they are able to read about their time as a baby.

Innovative Practice

Use interactive technology to enhance communication

Lettie saw how the stories of meaningful moments with children in the journals created wonderful, shared connections among the infant/toddler teachers, individual children, and their families. She wanted to figure out how to extend this atmosphere of collective delight in the children's development to the larger community. To this end, Lettie wrote a grant proposal to Gifts in Kind International (see Resources) to fund cameras and laptops for each classroom and training for her staff, who needed help to learn to use them. With these new resources, Lettie set up a laptop and projector in the entry hall and regularly showed slides featuring the children's activities.

Next she invited interested staff to learn how to create a blog. The teachers were amazed at how easy it was to create blogs. After developing a release form for each family to sign granting permission from families to post their children's pictures, a number of teachers began to upload weekly photos and stories of their group's activities for families to read at their leisure. The teachers posted questions and asked for comments about the blog, and families began to share ideas and struggles. The blog became widely appreciated by the families. Many reported they were pleased to be able to share information about their child's life with grandparents and other family members who lived out of town. For families who didn't have computer access, the teachers printed the weekly blog posts and displayed them on their bulletin boards. The teachers used the blog in place of writing and printing newsletters, and found that they could often use them as entries for the children's individual journals as well.

Many of the teachers were skilled and loved technology. They saw the benefits of using these tools in their work with children and families, so they found time in their schedules or after work to write their blog posts. Other teachers needed more coaching and time to make blogging a regular part of their practice.

Lettie was committed to promoting meaningful communication in her center, so she was gradually finding new ways to carve out more time in teachers' schedules and free up the budget for this kind of work. Her new idea was to figure out how to hire a floating staff member to move around the center throughout the day, giving release time for regular staff to work on their communication with families. Her vision was that eventually sharing the stories of children's lives and learning would be a part of everyone's job description and the entire organizational climate.

Principle

Bring and Keep People Together

The emphasis on family involvement in many child care settings focuses on children and families and their individual relationship with the center. If families come together, it is usually for brief social events, meetings focused on what the center staff thinks is important for families to know, or work requests where families accomplish a predetermined task. Lettie realized this was exactly how she had been thinking about family involvement in her program, and she wanted to make a change. She eagerly began to think about the possibilities for families and staff to develop deeper relationships with each other and together make real contributions to the children and each other's lives. What could she do to help her center truly reflect the concept of a village raising the child?

Innovative Practice

Institute continuity of care

Lettie knew that one of the hallmark components of a relationship-based program in infant/toddler services is continuity of care or looping (see appendix 9). This approach supports the importance of children building and sustaining relationships with the same people throughout their earliest years in child care. Rather than moving children to different rooms with different caregivers based on age and ratio, Lettie did more research on the best ways to keep children, families, and teachers together in the same group until children were three years old. She learned that most programs run into trouble when they design a space just for infants. As children grow older and more mobile, the room is inadequate for active toddler bodies and they have to be moved. Instead of having an infant room and a toddler room, Lettie created spaces that could accommodate a range of ages—birth to three. In this more flexible space, furniture and equipment could be moved around and in and out rather than the children, families, and teachers needing to move to another space to keep them together. As normal attrition occurred, Lettie could add a range of ages from her waiting list. Keeping these groups together over the years was not only valuable for the children's important connection to familiar caregivers but also for the deeper bonds and friendships it encouraged among the adults. In the current busy world of disconnected family life, Lettie found that her program became the new neighborhood for children, staff, and families.

Innovative Practice

Plan family meetings to build relationships

Rather than using family meetings for center business or lectures on parenting, Lettie decided to use her meetings to offer families an experience of community and collaboration. Her agenda always included activities such as having parents make a gift together to leave for the children (including cooking, building, or sewing something), and studying messages or suggestions that the children sent for the teachers to communicate to the parents, discussing the children's points of view, and then sending a message back. For example, at one meeting the families played with toys and materials that the children played with, and then left photos and remnants of their work for the children to see and discuss the next day. Lettie saw how these activities offered shared experiences, encouraged communication, and provided concrete objects that reflected and reinforced community connections. The families and staff had a wonderful time together, and the children showed eager interest as they looked at photos of their own families involved in their activities. She also noticed that there was increased attendance at these meetings.

Innovative Practice

Hold group family conferences

Rather than following a traditional approach of planning teacher-family conferences around individual children's progress, Lettie suggested that the teachers plan group family conferences. This unique idea was initially difficult to promote. Nevertheless, Lettie was dedicated to the vision that relationships are as important as focusing on individuals. What better way to reflect that than in families coming together to get to know all of the children? Lettie suggested that individual conferences could be scheduled for families who wanted them and for staff who had concerns about individual children, but each classroom would also provide opportunities for families to get together to learn about other children than just their own.

The infant and toddler teachers put together a slide show of photos and stories of the children's activities at the center. Teachers offered opportunities for the families to study the children's growth and development through the stories and photos. The focus of the discussion was on the adults' shared amazement at the incredible competence that these very young children displayed and at the delight in the unique personalities and qualities that each child brought to the group. The staff found the families became more invested in and fascinated by all the children, not just their own. Some family members communicated that this interaction helped them stop worrying about and comparing the children. The staff and families had a shared experience of knowing the children, which became a special, strong bond among them.

The preschool teachers invited small groups of family members to come together whose children had close relationships during playtime or who were a part of a longer investigation together. The teachers gathered photos, samples of the children's work, and written documentation of their ideas and discussions with each other. They offered the families opportunities to study the children's work and also to try out some of the activities themselves. Families came to love these group conferences as they made connections with each other and gained deeper understanding of the other children in their child's life. They said that the conferences caused them to take children's ideas more seriously and deepened their relationships with other children and their families away from the program.

Lettie found that planning group conferences took the staff as much time as planning for individual ones, but the group conferences cut down on the time it took to meet with each family individually. And with this shared experience of knowing children, the connections and sense of community among the people in her program exploded!

Principle

Invite Meaningful Contributions to Solve Problems

Lettie realized that her typical way of responding to parent concerns, complaints, or other problems associated with licensing or budget constraints was to take the issue on herself, coming up with solutions on her own and then scrambling to get family or staff volunteers to "fix" the problem. This approach often left things undone, or Lettie would find herself and a few other "regulars" joining her in the burden of getting something accomplished. Lettie's new mind-set of putting relationships at the center of everything motivated her to consider how she might use challenges to grow community.

Innovative Practice

Enlist excitement to build an infant/toddler playground

The playground for infants and toddlers at Lettie's center was very uninviting; it was given little attention when the program was designed. Some of the families began complaining that it also seemed unsafe for their children. Lettie decided that rather than see this as another problem to be fixed, a playground project could be an opportunity to get people excited about the possibilities for building an enchanting place for children to experience the wonders of nature.

She started by creating a bulletin board in the hallway with the theme Share Your Favorite Memories of Being Outdoors. The bulletin board included a brief description of the project and photos reflecting the vision of creating a magical outdoor place for the babies. Lettie offered paper and pens with the following questions for families to answer and pin to the board:

- Where in the outdoors did you love to spend time as a child?
- What did you play with?
- What were the sensory elements you noticed or remember now—light, air, color, sounds, smells, textures?

She also began to briefly interview people when she saw them around the center. Lettie compiled the responses to create a list of the elements, and then invited interested families to come to a meeting to begin designing the area. One of the parents had a landscape business and volunteered to head the project. The group met over time to identify the materials and equipment they wanted and how to find recycled materials and donations. They planned two different Saturday work parties when parents and staff worked to install the beautiful natural play space, with plantings, pathways, and boulders that reflected the natural loose parts, textures, fragrances, and safe challenges that had been on the list of outdoor memories. Lettie was amazed at the involvement of the families in this project. Some of them were drawn to the creative process of designing the space, and others loved getting outdoors, using their bodies and power tools to build the space. The feeling of camaraderie as they worked together on behalf of the children created a sense of pride and ownership as well as built stronger connections between families and the program. Lettie came to understand that making a significant contribution that has interest and meaning for the people involved is a powerful way to build community.

Innovative Practice

Invite the village to raise the children

One of the issues that often flared up in the center was families' reactions to children's conflicts. Certain children developed reputations for their aggressive behavior in the classroom. There were often "parking lot" complaining sessions among families. They directed Lettie to hurry up and "fix" these children. Lettie used her new mindset of focusing on building relationships when a similar problem emerged in one of the infant/toddler classrooms.

Emily, a new two-year-old, entered the room midyear, after the original children and families had formed significant relationships. The only experiences that Emily had with other children was the time she spent jostling with her four-year-old brother. Emily's first few weeks in the program were bumpy for her and the other children because she would push, pinch, and bite in response to not getting what she wanted. When parents started complaining, Lettie decided to invite the staff and families to work together to address the issue. She was up-front about her goals. Lettie explained that she knew that children's behavior was often an issue among families, and she wanted to encourage a cooperative approach to resolving these issues, not anger or blame.

Lettie began the meeting by going around the circle asking each person to name how they saw their children's strengths in forming friendships and working cooperatively. It was heartening to hear in their stories the desire and abilities that these very young children were bringing to cultivating relationships. Next Lettie asked the group to name how the adults could help children work through their conflicts. During this discussion the different perspectives among the staff and families became clear. The teachers explained how they were perceiving and responding to this situation through their understanding of child development, Emily's relationship with her brother, and her lack of experience in a peer group. The teachers were gently intervening to coach Emily to learn to express herself more appropriately. The teachers said that they were focusing on developing a relationship with her and giving her time to learn the ways of the group.

The families felt Emily needed firmer guidance in response to her aggressive behavior. One parent exclaimed, "She never hears the word *no*." One parent admitted she was fiercely protective of her child and couldn't help but feel angry toward Emily when the mother saw her child being hurt. Others felt worried that their children were learning it was okay to use aggressive behavior. The group ultimately understood each other's points of view and came to agreement around pulling together to embrace Emily as a full member of the group while offering clear messages about inappropriate behavior.

Lettie was delighted by how quickly the issue dissolved. She felt that all parties gained new insights. The teachers saw that indeed they could be giving Emily firmer guidance while still being positive and supportive, and the families saw the role they could play to connect with Emily, rather than feel negative about her behavior. Lettie thought this meeting would go a long way in helping families approach behavior issues in a different way. She knew this was just the first of many similar situations they would face as their children spent time with other children throughout their years at the center. These parents would also have an experience to draw on of cooperation rather than blame, and could really become part of the village that helps raise the children.

Bring Your Vision to Life

Take some time to reflect on Lettie's work. Use these questions to help guide your reflections:

- How did Lettie integrate her leadership work from each side of the triangle?
- If you were to put relationships center stage in your management, coaching, and community-building routines, what routine or system might you want to start revamping?
- How would you describe Lettie's disposition?
- What disposition do you want to strengthen in yourself to begin your revamping work?

BUILD REFLECTIVE PRACTICES

Michelle joined a directors' group that met to stay current with policies, professional trends, and current developments in their community. The agenda for each of their monthly meetings was divided into four sections:

- networking and strengthening relationships
- professional and community updates
- helping a member solve a problem
- discussing a shared reading to explore new possibilities for expanding quality in their centers

Sometimes she found it hard to leave her center to get to the meetings, but she knew that the relationships she had formed and the support she had gotten from this group had been a lifeline for her over the years.

Reflecting on the value of the group for her development as a director influenced Michelle to change the organizational culture at her center to better reflect her vision of a learning community. She came to understand that she needed to put structures and policies in place to help her teachers become self-reflective, collaborative planners and problem solvers. This required her to steadily revamp her budget, staffing patterns, and systems for orientation and ongoing professional development of her teachers. Michelle steadily developed a mentoring and coaching approach to help her teachers think together and become more confident planners and decision makers.

Principle

Invest in Your Teachers Right from the Start

Michelle recognized that the continual need to hire new teachers had become her nemesis, so she set out to revamp her approach. She knew her standard approach to interviewing and hiring wasn't uncovering a candidate's disposition toward collaboration and reflection. When she was honest with herself, she realized that she was so eager to fill job openings that she did little more than a hasty review of health, safety, child guidance, and curriculum requirements before putting a teacher in a room to assume responsibilities as a full team member. No wonder so many teachers had a short tenure at the center. Or if they remained, they often became teachers who were never "up to speed" or "on the same page" as Michelle and the rest of her staff. Michelle realized she needed to invest in her teachers right from the start to encourage them to likewise invest in her program.

Innovative Practice

Interview candidates in small groups

Michelle developed a new practice for interviewing candidates. After candidates passed a preliminary screening to determine if they met the job qualifications, Michelle brought candidates together to participate in a group interview modeled after a typical staff meeting. Inviting three candidates together, along with a couple of staff members, she set up an agenda resembling one the staff often used as a group to explore issues, solve problems, and make decisions. She always included some documentation to study together, and she and the other teachers specifically asked the candidates for their ideas on the different aspects of the agenda. Michelle was open with them about the purpose—the idea was not to make candidates uncomfortable or put them on the spot to find the "right" answer, but to get a sense of how they thought about things and how they participated in team discussions and decisions. It was a chance for candidates to assess the program as a potential workplace, as well as for Michelle and her staff to assess whether the candidates would be a good fit. Over time, Michelle created a form to assess how each candidate demonstrated the qualities she was looking for.

Innovative Practice

Create systems for reflection in your orientation process

Michelle began shifting her budget and staffing patterns to support an orientation process that provided new teachers time to engage in reflective practices. She began to understand that staff turnover was rarely the result of teachers not understanding all the regulations and requirements of the job, but quite the opposite. Michelle came to see that she often lost potentially great members of her staff not only because of inadequate wages but because she threw them into a deep, Olympic-sized pool without giving them carefully fitted goggles and a clear life support system. How could they become long-distance swimmers if their orientation and ongoing professional development was focused only on treading water?

Initially she carved out the first day of employment to be one without any direct responsibilities for children, but focused instead on observing in classrooms, seeing a video, and meeting with teammates. She established a three-month probationary period during which she regularly observed and gave feedback to new employees and had them reflect on learning goals for themselves. Over time her orientation system evolved to include three initial days of employment without responsibility for children. During their orientation, new teachers read articles that highlight the center's philosophy and pedagogy, practiced using tools to gather documentation, completed reflective writing assignments, and met with a peer mentor to discuss the program and orientation process. The three-month probationary period was expanded to include an hour a week of release time for new teachers to work with a mentor and to review a series of articles and videos organized into training modules, with continual reflective writing assignments.

Michelle discovered that the supports she put into place and the practice new teachers got with writing assignments strengthened their confidence as well as their disposition to be self-reflective.

Principle

Reconceptualize Professional Development as a Daily Experience

While she continued to work on the managing side of the triangle to improve salaries, Michelle steadily worked to delineate her organizational culture by improving the working conditions that underpin reflective practices. This required some imaginative shifts in her thinking as well as her budget line items. Rather than viewing professional development as training needed to meet licensing and accreditation standards, Michelle came to see that her teachers needed a method of thinking through the daily challenges of their job. They needed encouragement to let joy overtake the feelings of stress in working with children. Rather than sending her teachers to workshops to learn the latest behavior management techniques or assessment tools, she allocated resources to help her teachers become better observers and documenters, more self-assured and collaborative decision makers.

Innovative Practice

Develop teachers as thinkers, not technicians

Michelle moved her own thinking away from compliance issues toward creating a culture of inquiry in her program. The words "ask why, ask why not" hung as a bold banner in her office. Her goal for her teachers was for them to see themselves as contributing to the professional knowledge about child development through their careful study and negotiation of different perspectives on the children in their care. She also learned that they needed to become increasingly self-aware and answer the question Parker Palmer (2007) poses: "Who is the self that teaches?" Without professional knowledge, self-knowledge, and a curiosity about the perspectives of others, Michelle knew her teachers would be less likely to work with intention and more likely to perpetuate unintended bias or cultural blinders.

Drawing on her directors' group discussions of the book *Learning Together with Young Children* (Curtis and Carter 2008), Michelle put in place a protocol or Thinking Lens for her teachers to use in individual reflections and staff discussions (see appendix 14). Asking themselves questions such as the following helped the teachers make reflective thinking a regular part of their routines for responding to children and planning for them.

- How am I reacting to this situation and why?
- What in my background and values is influencing my response to this situation and why?
- How is the organization and use of the physical space and materials impacting this situation?
- In what ways are the routines, adult behaviors, and language undermining or strengthening the children's ability to demonstrate their competence?
- How could we strengthen relationships here?
- What details can I make visible to heighten the value of this experience?
- How do I understand the children's point of view in this situation?
- What other perspectives could enhance my understanding of the meaning of this situation (e.g., perspectives of families, coworkers, colleagues)?

- How might issues of culture, family background, or popular media be influencing this situation?
- What theoretical perspectives and child development principles could inform my understandings and actions?
- What values, philosophy, and goals do I want to influence my response?

As they talked through their observations, Michelle mentored all her teachers to consider their own perspectives; to highlight the details that engaged their hearts and minds; to consider the perspectives of the children, professional resources, families, and their coworkers; and to plan their next steps accordingly. Over time she discovered that these questions become a natural way of thinking, talking, and planning.

Innovative Practice

Design clear accountability systems

Michelle was quite pleased when she got her budget to the point of giving teachers paid planning time. But it wasn't long before she discovered that not all her teachers knew how to use the time productively. To complement the changes she made in her system for orienting new teachers and her regular use of the Thinking Lens protocol in staff meetings, Michelle continually refined her approach of holding teachers accountable for using their planning and meeting time to reflect and take action on agreed-on plans.

As a manager she took three bold steps. The first was to reformulate paid planning time into a per-child figure and then to assign the total time per classroom to the whole team to allocate as needed on a weekly basis. Particular team members negotiated time needed for an extended conversation with a family, resource gathering, updating a child's portfolio, or putting together a documentation display. Individuals then shared the outcome with their team.

Next, she reorganized her staff positions to create more hours for two of her school-age child care teachers. This reduced turnover by adding eligibility for health care and vacation benefits for those two positions. She used the extended hours to provide coverage to schedule weekly meetings for all teaching teams.

Finally, Michelle set a new standard and protocol for team meetings. She mandated that the agendas be divided into two parts. The first part was to be used for discussing observations and documentation using the Thinking Lens, with the clear expectation that each teacher would bring something for the team to consider. Anyone who failed to do so was given the attention of the team to uncover and remedy the source of the problem. They might discover work habits that needed to be improved, insecurities about documentation skills and procedures, or personal circumstances that distracted the teacher from this responsibility. They would attempt to support the teacher in overcoming any barriers, and Michelle stayed alert to whether this became a pattern that needed more intervention.

As teachers moved to the action part of the Thinking Lens protocol, they decided who would take what particular next steps and accordingly distributed the hours allotted their team for planning or off-the-floor hours. They then moved on to the second half of their meeting, which focused on business and scheduling details, housekeeping, and problem solving miscellaneous logistical concerns.

Innovative Practice

Provide side-by-side mentoring

As Michelle continued to grow her center over the years, she experienced the typical ups and downs that most nonprofit early childhood centers go through. During stable times she found herself balancing her responsibilities on each side of the triangle framework. But in the inevitable periods of constant brush fires, Michelle's attention was pulled in so many directions that her mentoring of new teachers fell by the wayside, as did her efforts to keep more seasoned staff challenged to continue their professional development. She recognized that expanding her mentoring leadership team would be a valuable direction to move in.

Michelle proposed to her staff that those who were ready to assume more leadership meet with her one evening a month over dinner to develop a system for more consistent side-by-side mentoring for teachers at the center. Three teachers took up this invitation, and over the course of several months they identified each person's particular strength that could become a focus for side-by-side mentoring. For example, one teacher focused on creating a classroom culture and environment that welcomes children and families, helping new teachers set up the physical environment, routines, and room meetings toward that end. A second teacher focused his work with teachers on learning to observe and use documentation with the Thinking Lens protocol to plan curriculum. And because most teachers seek help with guiding children's behaviors, that became the focus for the third mentor—supporting teachers to use a reflective rather than technique approach.

By again drawing on the Thinking Lens protocol, teachers were mentored to find details that uncovered the children's perspectives, and they were challenged to meet up with the children's hearts, minds, and emotional intelligence, rather than jump on their behaviors.

To manage this new side-by-side mentoring system, Michelle adjusted her staffing patterns to provide coverage for up to six hours a week for different members of the mentor team to work with teachers wanting help in a particular area. Sometimes the mentor went to a teacher's room to coach her as she worked; on other occasions the teacher was released to watch the mentor in action with his or her own group of children. After the first six months of implementing this side-by-side support for teachers, the overall confidence and performance of the teachers were strengthened.

Later there were periods during which mentors and the center's budget had a respite until the next cycle of new hires or areas of need were identified. Michelle discovered that this mentoring system benefited both new and experienced teachers, as it provided professional development opportunities for everyone.

Bring Your Vision to Life

Take a moment or two to reflect on Michelle's efforts to align her systems with her vision of her teachers as self-reflective, collaborative planners and problem solvers. Use these questions to help guide your reflections:

- What dispositions do you see Michelle bringing to leadership?
- How are your dispositions similar to or different from Michelle's?
- What aspects of her vision appeal to you?
- What could you imagine yourself doing that is inspired by this story of Michelle's work?

STRENGTHEN CONNECTIONS TO AND CARE FOR THE NATURAL WORLD

Sarah was the director of an early childhood program located in a beautiful river valley, rich with farmlands, volcanoes, rivers and bays, and a variety of wildlife. Like many other places in the United States, her community was besieged with strip malls, big-box stores, and fast-food chains. Over the years, people had begun to lose touch with nature. The children and their families seemed to share more interests around the latest TV and movie characters and visits to indoor plastic-filled play spaces even when the tulip fields were ablaze with color in the spring or the eagles were soaring above the river looking for salmon to eat. One winter morning it all came home to Sarah. On her drive to work, she was filled with awe by the sunlit mist hovering over a farm field covered with thousands of snow geese. She shared her excitement with a few of the families and children as they arrived, asking if anyone else noticed the geese. Not one of them had noticed, even though they drove by those fields every day. A feeling of despair stayed with Sarah all day.

Sarah thought about her own childhood, full of memories of vivid experiences of the warm air on her skin, the expansiveness of the sky, and the adventures she found among the trees. Her connection with the landscape and weather was an integral part of her identity and the joy she found in living. This bond with the natural world enriched her life, and she deeply wanted the children, staff, and families she spent her days with to share in this great love. As the natural world was more and more compromised, one of Sarah's major fears was that few would care because as children they didn't have experiences where they fell in love with nature. Her worries were fueled by recent studies of the negative effects on children of spending less and less time outdoors and the need for more stewards of the planet in the face of the growing climate crisis. She started to think seriously about playing a more active role with the children and adults in her program to encourage love and care for the natural world. She believed she could do this by finding ways to build a shared identity and sense of place around her program's unique landscape, usurping the role that popular culture, TV, and fast-food restaurants played in the children's and families' lives and relationships at the center. She enthusiastically shared her vision with a few staff members and parents who she knew had similar passions and values in relation to the natural world. Together they set to work to engage the community.

Principle

Use Meaningful Experiences to Build Shared Values

Sarah wanted to provide experiences that would entice the children and adults in her program to fall in love with, enjoy, and protect the unique landscape in which they lived. She knew that talk, books, posters, and pamphlets, or even experts with dire warnings and lists of benefits, only went so far to engage people's bodies or brains. Sarah and her small committee were determined to help everyone immerse themselves in the natural wonders around them, heightening their senses, their spirits, their minds, and their respect for nature.

Innovative Practice

Create a field guide for the center grounds

Sarah began by inviting her staff to go outdoors. During one of her staff meetings, she told everyone she would like to make a field guide of their outdoor area as a reference and study tool for people at the center. She asked each staff member to take a clipboard and pencil and find an area on the grounds of the center where they were drawn to the natural elements. She suggested they sit and look and listen for a long while, feel the textures, and smell the fragrances. When they felt they knew the place well, they could take photos, do some sketching, and write detailed descriptions to document and share their discoveries.

One teacher focused on the details of the bark of one of the cedar trees—its texture, smell, color, and significance. Another studied the sandbox and the tools and natural items there. She described how the area could be used and enjoyed. This activity reinforced Sarah's ongoing approach to coaching her staff around close observation and careful analysis. She believed this activity would help her staff get better at observing children and structuring time for them to slow down and relax in the natural world.

Sarah gathered all their work and put it in a binder that was displayed in the main hallway of the center. Everyone could study the wondrous world right outside their doorway. She challenged the teachers to share what they did and what they discovered with the children and families and to offer ways for their group to participate in adding more to the field guide. Many of the teachers worked with the children to do the very same observation and documentation activity, and the field guide grew. The community came to love the field guide, and they were reminded of the wonders of the natural world right outside their door that the guide represented.

Innovative Practice

Plan family field trips to explore the local natural environment

Sarah and her committee organized monthly Saturday field trips where families and staff were invited to gather to enjoy the seasons together. In the fall they went to the local pumpkin patch. In the winter they participated in the eagle festival. In the spring they met to marvel at the vibrant, colorful tulip fields, and in the summer they took easy hikes in the woods to local swimming holes. Sarah printed photos and created a display in the hallway documenting their time together as well as highlighting the natural wonders. She always made sure she included a small table with rocks, leaves, and other items that reflected the trip and the season for people to explore. The families and staff who attended the trips were able to revisit the experience, and the other families were enticed to think about a trip to take with their families. Sarah knew the community building that occurred as a result of these field trips was an added bonus to her goal for connections with the natural world.

Principle

Call for a Curriculum That Focuses on the Natural World

The field guide and field trip activities generated great excitement among the staff to continue working on strengthening the children's connections to and care for the natural world. Sarah recommended that the staff work together to develop goals for the children to learn about nature. She wanted to ensure that this project worked toward her goals for ongoing professional development while encouraging connections with the natural world. There wasn't money in her budget to pay for extra staff time to work on this, so Sarah carved out time during each of their staff meetings to focus on developing goals. It took several months to brainstorm the elements they wanted to guide their curriculum planning. They drew on resources from the Arbor Day Foundation's Nature Explore program (www.arborday.org/explore) and Barbara Lehn's book *What Is a Scientist?* (see Resources) to come up with a list.

Science and Nature Curriculum Goals

We want our curriculum to support children to:

- Become lifelong learners
- Develop an identity shaped by a sense of place in the natural world
- Expand a sense of wonder and joy in the natural world
- See how they are connected to and affect the natural world
- Desire to care for the earth and other living things
- Learn from their senses
- Observe closely and notice details of the world around them
- Describe, draw, and write what they see and think
- Compare and sort by looking carefully
- Count and measure to make comparisons
- Experiment by trial and error, and test predictions
- Keep trying over and over
- Work together, and have fun!

Innovative Practice

Launch a program-wide science and nature study

With their curriculum guide in place, Sarah and the staff looked to invite family support for their efforts. They launched a school-wide science and nature study through a number of activities. At their annual school auction they shared the science and nature goals with the families and asked them to donate funds to enhance this aspect of their curriculum. Even though the program was small, the thoughtful specificity of their request generated over $5,000 for the project. Before ordering any new materials with the donated money, the teachers launched an informal research project observing and documenting the ways the children demonstrated they were already beginning to accomplish the science and nature curriculum goals. Sarah earmarked some of the donated funds to pay two of the teachers to take the lead on this project.

The lead teachers helped the others to create display boards with stories and photos showing the children "learning like scientists and naturalists." The lead teachers worked with others during their weekly planning time to study their documentation together. The leads encouraged other teachers to invite children to assist in ordering materials that the children thought would help them learn more about science and nature. The leads made sure that other teachers had thoughtfully decided what to order and how they would use the new materials.

Each of the classrooms took up different aspects of studying science and nature throughout the year, from hatching butterflies to conducting experiments with balance and gravity. Not only was the program-wide study of science and nature a powerful tool for offering children important experiences, but the teachers told Sarah how much they had deepened their understanding about how children learn. They said the goals they had generated helped them analyze and understand their observations of the children's play and learning. Sarah's goals for ongoing professional development for her staff were being met through a project everyone was excited about, and the families were big supporters.

Innovative Practice

Become a designated wildlife habitat

Sarah invited the teachers who thought their children would be interested to develop curriculum activities geared toward becoming certified as a Backyard Wildlife Sanctuary (see the listing for the National Wildlife Federation in Resources). The teachers ordered the official packet and worked with the children and families in their rooms to study and implement what it would take for their playground to be certified. One of the groups spent months building beautiful bird houses with the help of a dad who was a builder. The children were very invested in this project and were extremely proud when the program was able to hang the official certificate in the hallway. The study of habitats spread throughout the school, and before long the children were using natural materials throughout the play yard to create habitats for fairies, worms, butterflies, and other living and magical creatures. The children and teachers became more involved, making plans for each habitat, including planting special flowers and building magical twig houses throughout the yard.

Principle

Use Family Interests and Expertise to Grow Your Vision

As the focus on connecting with the natural world spread throughout the center, more and more parents came to Sarah offering ideas for what else could be done. Although many of the ideas were wonderful, Sarah understood that her staff had enough on their plates. More work would overwhelm them. She suggested that the parents form their own committees to lead the new projects themselves.

Innovative Practice

Form a family club with a mascot

One group of families was interested in extending the focus on the natural environment to recycling efforts. They formed the Chester Club, choosing a worm they named Chester as their mascot. They believed the children would identify more with the work if they had a creature to relate to. Chester and his committee began sending weekly notes to the children and families to help them think more about how to care for the earth and the contributions they could make. Over time this group led many projects, including helping the classrooms weigh and sort their garbage. They located a recycling center at the entry to the school so everyone could see how much garbage was generated and how much of it was recyclable. This concrete strategy had a huge impact on the community's view of waste and recycling. The toddler group even got into the act. They developed an ongoing relationship with Lou, the garbage collector, waiting eagerly each week for his arrival in the big garbage truck and toddling out to give him pictures they had drawn. As an extension to the recycling effort, a group of children and adults constructed a worm bin to compost the food waste from the school. The Chester Club was thrilled by the children's eagerness to feed and care for Chester and his other worm friends.

Innovative Practice

Learn about farms and gardens

Another group of families was interested in farming and gardening and wanted to share that aspect of the natural world with the children. They formed a committee that was involved with many projects, including planting a community garden that the children and adults helped care for and harvest, taking family field trips to local farms and farmers markets, and hosting a children's art show to display the children's paintings and drawings of food, farms, and gardens. Sarah was overjoyed with the community-building aspect of all this work, as well as the many different ways that families were enjoying the outdoors with their children.

Principle

Keep Thinking Bigger

Sarah felt she could honestly say that her program's identity was becoming firmly rooted in joy and care for the natural world. In her daily life, she was living her vision of sharing a love of nature with the people around her. So when she learned of a grant from the Arbor Day Foundation to design an outdoor nature classroom, she and her community decided to apply for it. Theirs was just a small rural program. The other programs applying were large organizations like the zoo, but Sarah wanted to keep her thinking big! They would do the work to apply for the grant, and even if they didn't get it, the process would continue to help build the community and keep everyone focused on the natural world.

Innovative Practice

Design an outdoor classroom

To their surprise and excitement, the center received one of the grants to help design a nature classroom. The grant opened up many new possibilities for enhancing and spreading the vision of love and care of the natural world to the people in Sarah's program, as well as new opportunities to reach out to the larger community. A group of interested staff and family members, many from other committees, agreed to work with the Arbor Day Foundation to develop a plan and a landscape design. The staff launched a study with the children to help design the outdoor classroom. The planning and designing process took a number of months, and the design for the nature classroom was a sizable project that would require abundant resources, including money, time, and hard work. Sarah and the group were excited to get started, but they knew it would take patience and dedication to reach this new goal. Sarah believed that the process of working on the nature classroom was in itself a concrete way to immerse the group in the natural world. With a five-year plan and a commitment to the vision, they began their work.

Innovative Practice

Raise funds in ways that reinforce your vision

Funding for the nature classroom project was a huge hurdle to completing the work. Sarah decided to take small steps and think about how she could concretely connect people with the natural world as they worked on fund-raising efforts. They launched a number of projects with this in mind, including producing calendars to sell with the title "Go Outside." A small group of staff and parents did research and designed the calendars to focus on local outdoor activities that families could do with their children. They involved the community by asking for short written descriptions from parents about places they took their children, details of the natural landscape, and what they enjoyed doing while they were there. The calendar's photos featured local flora and fauna, reflecting the seasons, with children from the program immersed in it. The calendar included dates and places of community outdoor events and sweet stories of families' visits to different places. Not only did the calendars raise money for the nature classroom, but the families who developed it and others who used it were absorbed with thinking about the natural world.

The teachers launched another fund-raising project to sell note cards. They had the children go outside with clipboards, pencils, and paints and create art of the natural world. They turned the drawings and paintings of trees, birds, and flowers into note cards that were sold to families and the greater community. Like the calendar, this project offered a way to raise funds but also got the children connecting with nature.

Innovative Practice

Reach out to the community to grow your vision

The Arbor Day Foundation grant gave Sarah's program more visibility and respect in the larger community. It also allowed her to expand her vision of connecting children with the natural world to more children than just those in her program. She and her committee immediately began to take advantage of their new standing by creating a new fund-raising campaign to market their project, but even more importantly to spread the work about the importance of children learning from nature. One of the parents had recently graduated with a degree in marketing and was eager to begin a portfolio. He helped create a brochure and a PowerPoint presentation that could be presented to various groups and businesses in the community. This was also an opportunity for Sarah's staff to gain more skills, as she invited them to be the spokespeople at chamber of commerce and Rotary Club meetings.

The emphasis of their presentations was as much about educating the community about the importance of their vision as it was support and fund-raising for the project. The community stepped up in response to Sarah's leadership, acknowledging the urgency of getting kids back outdoors. People have donated materials, services, and physical labor for the monthly weekend work parties that take place in the program. The community has a long way to go, but while they are on their way, they are spending time outdoors, enjoying each other's company, and taking care of the environment on behalf of their children and themselves.

Bring Your Vision to Life

Whether you work in a rural or urban area, consider aspects of Sarah's values that resonate with you. What evidence do you have that the children in your program have a connection with and feel a sense of responsibility to the natural world?

Consider how you might adapt some of Sarah's innovative practices for your own setting. Experiment with some out-of-the-box thinking!

TAKE CHARGE OF STANDARDS, OUTCOMES, AND ASSESSMENTS

Roberto came to work in an established nonprofit child care center that had a good reputation, seasoned teachers, and a satisfied parent population. As he settled into his director role, he began to discover a number of discrepancies between his view of high-quality child care and the accepted practices of the center. In fact, he was surprised that the center was one of the early programs to receive NAEYC accreditation, because they were using preset curriculum themes cycled through every year and a letter- and number-of-the-week curriculum with worksheets to teach literacy and numeracy. This didn't match his understanding of NAEYC's view of best practices and developmentally appropriate, responsive curriculum. The center's current approach was a far cry from his vision of what children deserved. Roberto learned that parents were concerned about school readiness and had asked the teachers for homework that they could help their children with in the evenings. Wanting to be responsive and thinking this might make their jobs easier, the teachers had gone along with this request, and the previous director hadn't objected.

As he began to get to know the teachers, parents, and board members, Roberto discovered that no one could clearly articulate their view of how children learn. Teachers seemed more focused on satisfying the parents, a disposition he appreciated but one that led to a very limited, if not misplaced, view of school readiness. Along with a focus on play, social skills, and emotional intelligence, Roberto's views about preparing children for success in school included nurturing their dispositions toward learning. He wanted children to be excited and confident in themselves. Roberto's own teaching experience and tracking of professional literature shaped his goals for and ideas about appropriate curriculum for young children. He believed all children are capable of intellectual engagement when the curriculum centers on their interests, offers interesting materials, and provides opportunities for in-depth projects.

During his first meeting with the board of directors, Roberto was presented with a copy of the state's early learning standards and the newly unveiled Quality Rating Improvement System (QRIS) the state was adopting to support and reward programs meeting the quality standards they delineated. Board members, who were mostly parents, wanted the center to begin to align their curriculum with the benchmarks in the standards to ensure that children would be taught lessons that met the desired outcomes. They also wanted the director to begin moving the program toward reaccreditation, the highest tier on the QRIS, which would offer more financial rewards to the center. Roberto took a deep breath to digest how much was already on his plate. He knew he must quickly roll up his sleeves to take charge of putting these standards and rating scales in the service of his greater vision. If he failed to act with clear intention, Roberto realized he could get swept away in meeting requirements and lose track of his dreams for what his center could offer children, families, and teachers.

Principle

View Standards and Rating Systems as Tools, Not Rules

Roberto knew that the revised NAEYC accreditation process now evaluated over four hundred criteria and that the directors he talked with found this totally daunting. He heard stories of directors working into the wee hours of night for months on end trying to get all their documents in order. If he was going to ask his staff to undertake this work, it would have to be done in a meaningful way and actually help his vision grow. After all, the intent of the process was self-study and improvement, not just getting a certificate to hang on the wall.

Roberto wanted to use the standards and accreditation criteria to unleash more potential in the teachers and children in his program. This meant his initial approach to this work had to be undertaken from a coaching and community-building perspective. He decided to start the process with a focus on the children, not the paperwork.

Innovative Practice

Expand the definition of desirable outcomes

Nagging at the back of Roberto's mind was a discomfort with what he saw as trivial learning objectives for children. He had more substantive goals in mind and wanted to expand the thinking of his teachers and parents beyond that list of benchmarks. Inspired by an example he found on a Web site (see the listing for Early Education Advocates in Resources), Roberto designed his first community meeting with parents and staff to explore the outcomes they wanted for their children. To prompt some considerations beyond limited academic notions, Roberto developed a chart with starting phrases for their discussion together. To ensure his Spanish-speaking families could comfortably express the heart of their thinking, he included their first language in the chart.

When they leave our program, we want children to:	Cuando se van de nuestro programa, queremos que los niños:
Trust in . . .	Tengan confianza en . . .
Believe that . . .	Crean que . . .
Know that . . .	Sepan que . . .
Know how to . . .	Sepan como . . .
Question . . .	Pregunten como . . .

To his delight, teachers and families became so engaged in the discussion that they weren't able to get to all the phrases on the chart. They requested another meeting to continue the work. When they met again, Roberto added some additional considerations into the discussion. He chose a few of the state's early learning standards and asked the group to suggest how they might relate to the desired outcomes in their chart. An animated discussion ensued around certain items and why some were indicated as benchmarks. This opened the door for Roberto to make the point that educational choices should overtly acknowledge the values, hopes, and dreams of a community and that this was his intent in leading the program. In the succeeding months, he was able to connect this discussion to an examination of current practices in the center, bringing teachers and parents to the understanding that they needed to invent some new approaches that would better reflect their values. If he had just worn his manager's hat and pressed a new set of mandates on the teachers, they wouldn't have developed these deeper understandings, and parents wouldn't have bought into the changes he began steadily proposing. His gentle coaching with examples of children's eagerness to engage in meaningful explorations began to shift their thinking about curriculum practices. Six months into his work as director, worksheets and preset themes were no longer visible.

Innovative Practice

Form work teams for different accreditation focus areas

Roberto recognized the value of family involvement in the center, along with the teachers' eagerness to please families, but his goal was to provoke more critical thinking. He decided to request teacher participation on work teams to gather documentation for ten sections of accreditation criteria. He started with the sections focused on children, writing the name or topic of each section on slips of paper to be drawn from a hat. These became work teams who studied the criteria for each section and eventually developed the necessary documentation to put in the classroom binders. To launch their work, Roberto provided a demonstration, taking photos of activities currently going on in the classroom and asking how each example did or didn't satisfy the criteria. This helped teachers look more closely at the intent of the criteria and the possible ways it might be expressed.

Through Roberto's work with families and staff, everyone was beginning to buy into his vision that the state standards and NAEYC accreditation criteria were not rigid one-size-fits-all rules to adhere to. Rather, they were valuable tools for reflecting on the center's work with children.

Principle

Develop Systems to Hold Yourself Accountable to Your Values

As he diligently worked at coaching and community building in his center, Roberto recognized the need to strengthen his management systems to reflect the center's values. He particularly wanted to explore some provocative ideas he had been reading about the use of time in shaping an organizational culture. (See Wien and Kirby-Smith 1998; Phillips and Bredekamp 1998.) He copied a quote from Carol Anne Wien's book *Negotiating Standards in the Primary Classroom* and hung it over his desk to ponder: "Breaking the vise of production-schedule uses of time is perhaps the most helpful practice an administrator can offer to open up the range of possibilities for teachers" (2004, 153). If his center valued responding to children's interests and working closely with parents, he knew he needed to structure more time for them to work in this way. Roberto began to set up his staffing patterns with more overlaps in scheduled shifts so that morning and afternoon teaching teams had opportunities to talk in person. This also provided more flexibility for teachers in how they scheduled the children's time, their breaks, and calls to families. Roberto set a management goal for himself to build steadily toward the goal of hiring a permanent floater to also open up more possibilities for teachers.

Innovative Practice

Untiming the curriculum

In thinking about how to coach teachers to open up some new possibilities for children in their classroom schedules, Roberto decided to try the idea that Carol Ann Wien and director Susan Kirby-Smith (1998) wrote about. He asked his toddler teachers to remove clocks and watches from the room and to keep a journal of how this affected them and the children. For the children's security, they agreed to keep the order of routines in the room the same, but to have the changes in activity flow from closely observing the children and their rhythms instead of by the clock. He tracked down some literature on play rhythms in young children to help the teachers interpret children's engagement more accurately. After an initial few days of teacher anxiety about how things would go without a timepiece to guide them, Roberto's teachers acquired some of the same insights as Kirby-Smith's teachers. They had to observe the children and communicate with each other more intentionally than they did in their typical practice. They realized that though they thought of themselves as sensitive and respectful with children, their rigid time schedules were giving children the message that their own activity was less important than what the teacher wanted them to do.

Innovative Practice

Design your own forms and checklists

As the accreditation work teams continued their efforts of documenting how they were meeting different criteria, they alerted Roberto that some forms the center was using didn't reflect their current thinking. For instance, if he wanted his teachers to plan curriculum that was responsive to children's interest, accountability to that should be reflected in the center's curriculum planning forms. He held a series of staff meetings to generate a statement of their curriculum planning approach and to design a new form for teachers to use. They subsequently went on to develop new checklists to track how the values and goals of their center met the intent of other accreditation standards.

This proved invaluable in organizing their documentation and helped teachers become more articulate in explaining why they did what they did and how it met the intent of the standards.

Principle

Expand Your Thinking about Assessment

Toward the end of his second year in his program, Roberto encountered another hurdle he needed to overcome: identifying an assessment system to use in tracking children's progress toward the state benchmarks. This was especially challenging because each of the commercial assessment tools that fit the criteria of being research-based had some aspect that troubled him. Some were clearly focused on children's deficits, while others assessed children outside the context of their everyday play. None of the assessments addressed certain desired outcomes his parents and teachers had so thoughtfully collaborated on defining. Roberto wanted an assessment approach that would have meaning for the teachers and parents and also the children. His teachers had grown tremendously in learning to observe and document, and he wanted to have this be the foundation of their assessment work, not add another required tool that would take their time and attention from the good work they were doing. Teachers already had a binder for each child with documentation stories and work samples. Did they need to add a developmental checklist to this informal portfolio? Where else could he look for an assessment model that was a better fit for his center's developing values?

Innovative Practice

Find resources and inspiration outside your borders

Because he wanted the center's approach to assessment to match their values and be in line with the outcomes they defined as important, Roberto decided it was time to bring families and teachers together again to explore their options. A number of new families in the center, and a few new teachers as well, would benefit from learning about their work on outcomes. After an overview of past work and current concerns, Roberto suggested they make a list of desirable and undesirable attributes in an assessment approach. In the first go-round he discovered that families really didn't have enough experience to think deeply about the task, so he planned another set of meetings to review sample tools, inviting families and teachers to ask around and also search the Web for options. Several people brought examples, and the one that got everyone most excited was from New Zealand. With this example as a striking contrast to the other approaches, Roberto called the group back to the task of defining desirable and undesirable attributes in an assessment approach.

Desirable aspects of assessment approaches	**Undesirable aspects of assessment approaches**
Assets-based approach to describing learning	Deficit-oriented; a medical model
Includes a focus on dispositions or approaches to learning	Focuses only on skill development or limited academic outcomes
Includes a narrative to show how children make sense of experiences and construct knowledge	Measurement- or checklist-oriented
Involves the child and family in revisiting, reflecting, and setting goals	Done out of context with no engagement of child or family
Used to generate individual learning activities and becomes part of the shared culture, history, and literacy experiences of the classroom	May be misused as high-stakes testing to reward or punish programs
Creates a record of child-constructed knowledge and approaches to learning; creates links to the family and community for growing that knowledge	Records only an assessment item, not the process of learning; may not be culturally appropriate
Objectivity is viewed as bringing together multiple perspectives from teachers, family, and the community	Claims to be objective without acknowledging covert biases
Encourages teachers to make their thinking visible as they explore the meaning of the child's learning with coworkers and families	Minimizes the role of the teacher

Called Learning Stories (see appendix 15), the New Zealand model is research-based and seemed most compatible with their center's practices. Roberto resonated with this choice and was especially pleased that it wasn't something he had to purchase. With more Web browsing he found some examples of child care programs in the United States using the Learning Story approach, including a Web site with examples and guidelines (earlylearningstories.info). Next, he needed to put on his coaching hat to help his teachers correlate the New Zealand approach with his state's benchmarks. Roberto was reminded once again of the value of stepping outside your own borders.

Bring Your Vision to Life

As a manager, your role is to keep your center accountable to standards and requirements. As a leader, you take charge of how to make these regulations serve your vision, rather than derail it. Think about these questions:

- In what ways does Roberto inspire you to stronger leadership and self-empowerment?
- Can you imagine adapting any of his innovative practices?
- What are your next steps?

Remember to Nourish Yourself as You Nourish Your Vision

Bringing a vision to life takes time and requires a steady rhythm of breathing in and breathing out. In their own time and ways, Lettie, Michelle, Sarah, and Roberto realized they needed to approach their work as a marathon, not a horse race—pacing, not racing themselves through the to-do list that grew even faster than their vision. They learned to recognize the signs of burnout when their vision blurred or when they became cranky and reactive rather than thoughtful and responsive to concerns teachers or parents brought to them. At these critical junctures, visionary directors know to take a step back, carve out some time, and tease out some renewing perspectives for themselves and the others they are trying to lead.

First in the heart is the dream. Then the mind starts seeking a way.
—Langston Hughes (1943)

Whatever you can do, or dream you can do, begin it.
—William Hutchinson Murray (1951)

Prayer for the Future

May our spring gardens flourish
may love old and new develop
may children blossom

may each of us find a balance
between work and play
may we be fulfilled by our work
and nurtured by our play

may we hold sacred the earth
and our bodies

we will mourn many times
sorrow strengthens us
sharpens our awareness of life

we rise each morning with joy
we stand in this doorway with hope

—Mir Yarfitz

Afterword

Take heart.

Promising initiatives are growing. Around the country an increasing number of early childhood alliances, community collaboration projects, and directors and governing boards with chutzpah are showing promise to move us out of the current crisis in early childhood education. These projects provide support and resources for NAEYC accreditation, supply leadership development and director credentialing programs, train teachers to be reflective practitioners and researchers, lead efforts to ensure developmentally and culturally appropriate practices, and create quality rating systems tied to financing quality child care and improved compensation. Some are small, local efforts with no outside funding, while others have received grant or government funds to launch their projects.

Because you might not be aware of these efforts, we offer here information about and from a sampling of programs to inspire you and whet your appetite for involvement and action. Ours is in no way intended to be a comprehensive list, but rather a variety of snapshots showing where dedicated hard work can lead. For an ongoing review of a wider scope of promising initiatives, visit Web sites such as:

- The Alliance for Early Childhood Finance (www.earlychildhoodfinance.org)
- Child Care Exchange (www.childcareexchange.com)
- World Forum Foundation (www.worldforumfoundation.org)

Three of the programs from our sampling represent forward-thinking arms of large institutions working on overall quality improvement of early childhood programming from different angles—director credentialing efforts; quality rating improvement systems; and research, policy work, and initiatives on early childhood financing. The remainder are homegrown examples—directors and early childhood educators taking bold steps to "color outside the lines," as our late colleague and friend Tom Hunter used to sing. These fall into the categories of restructuring organizations to support ongoing teacher expectations and professional development; new considerations in staff recruitment, stability, and retention; promising approaches to professional and leadership development; and collaborations crossing divides in the wider community to address issues of inequity and disempowerment.

Larger Institutional Quality Improvement Efforts

Director Credentialing Programs

On the following pages you'll find a listing of leadership initiatives or director credential programs provided by Teri Talan and Paula Jorde Bloom (McCormick Tribune Center for Early Childhood Leadership), along with a fuller description of their new online director credential program, AIM4Excellence.

Quality Rating Systems

Quality Rating Systems (QRS) and Quality Rating Improvement Systems (QRIS) are sweeping the country. We worry that these efforts are diverting money into more bureaucratic systems requiring ever more paperwork for directors. Nevertheless, when they are tied to higher reimbursement rates and offer mentoring and financial incentives for self-study and quality improvement, they can both support programs in their efforts to improve quality and offer recognition when they do. Many states are using quality rating systems as a way to integrate state pre-K funds into child care programs.

We have been following the Pennsylvania Keystone STARS Quality Rating System and on occasion have provided consultation and training for the developers. We appreciate how they have moved away from a "report card" approach to one that stresses "continuous quality improvement" and emphasizes that those closest to the work (staff, parents, children) are the real experts and should be the ones actively engaged in assessing the program and making improvements based on those assessments.

Work on Early Childhood Financing

The Alliance for Early Childhood Finance was originally created through a partnership between Anne Mitchell of Early Childhood Policy Research and Louise Stoney of Stoney Associates. With a mission dedicated to seeking more rational financing of early care and education in America through inquiry, analysis, and communication among early care and education policy activists, they actively produce issue briefings on a variety of initiatives with implications for early childhood financing. We find the resources on their Web site (www.earlychildhoodfinance.org) provocative and important.

McCormick Tribune Center for Early Childhood Leadership

Director Credentials

Early Childhood Program Management Specialization Certificate
Central Arizona College
8470 North Overfield Road
Coolidge, AZ 85228
520/494-5477
http://www.centralaz.edu/x642.xml

The Early Childhood Education Program Management Specialization Certificate of Completion consists of 34 credit hours and uses an on-site, one-on-one mentoring model with opportunities for group sessions/interaction. The pace is individualized, open entry/open enrollment exist.

Maryland Child Care Administrator Credential
Maryland State Department of Education
200 West Baltimore Street
Baltimore, MD 21201
410/767-7806
http://www.marylandpublicschools.org/MSDE/divisions/child_care/credentials/

The Maryland Child Care Administrator Credential is a voluntary program that consists of six levels according to training hours, years of experience, and professional activities. Participants complete training in topic areas to develop the knowledge and skills they need to provide the highest quality care. Participation in the credential program at Level Two and higher includes achievement bonuses and training vouchers.

National Association of Child Care Professionals EXECS Credential
National Association of Child Care Professionals
7610 E. Highway 71 West
Austin, TX 78709
512/301-5557
admin@naccp.org
http://www.naccp.org

The EXECS Credential is a national credential for executives and administrators of children's programs available to the early child care, education, and service community that establishes professional standards in management and leadership and is nationally recognized. Applicants must have 120 contact training hours and have been in the field of early care and education for at least three years.

National Administrator Credential
National Child Care Association
2025 M Street, NW, Suite 800
Washington, DC 20036
202/367-1133
http://www.nccanet.org

The National Administrator Credential (NAC) is a 40-hour course designed for directors or aspiring directors to give them training on their administrative responsibilities. Typically, the course is offered over a five-day period from 8 a.m. to 5 p.m. Provided that the participant meets all course requirements, the credential is completed within the week. The NAC is an accepted form of training for director's licensing in many states. Upon successful completion of the NAC, participants are eligible to receive 3 credits in a higher or lower level course through the American College of Education (ACE) or 4.0 continuing education units.

Child Care Director Credential Training Program
Mississippi Forum on Children and Families
615 Barksdale Street
Jackson, MS 39202
601/355-4911

Created in 1995, the Child Care Director Credential Training Program provides job-specific training designed to increase the skills and knowledge of practicing and aspiring directors. The program consists of eight training modules including 120 hours of classroom instruction, plus an additional 15-hour module focused on the integration of knowledge and best practice.

Leadership Training Initiatives for Directors

Buell Early Childhood Leadership Program
University of Denver
2135 East Wesley Avenue #305
Denver, CO 80208
303/871-2379

This program is targeted to meet the needs of experienced and emerging administrators in early care and education settings. This program offers an academic certificate and concentration in educational administration in the field of early care and education.

California Early Childhood Mentor Program
50 Phelan Avenue
San Francisco, CA 94112
415/452-5603
http://www.ecementor.org

The mission of the Director Mentor component of the California Early Childhood Mentor Program is to increase the quality and stability of early childhood program administration. To do this, the Mentor Program identifies experienced directors and offers them professional and financial support for mentoring less-experienced directors or directors facing a new challenge. The program is now supported by the California Department of Education, Child Development Division, with Federal Quality Improvement funds.

CHASE Early Education Emergent Leaders
Governor's Office for Children, Youth, and Families
Division of School Readiness
1700 West Washington Street, Suite 101
Phoenix, AZ 85007
602/542-3199

Initiated in July 2004, Arizona's Early Education Emergent Leaders Program is a leadership program designed for early education practitioners. In 2005, the program became the CHASE Early Education Emergent Leaders Program after receiving a $500,000 grant from Bank One/Chase Bank. Participants in the yearlong program develop projects focused on improving the quality of child care and build leadership, management, and advocacy skills through program activities.

Directors Leadership Academy
Child Care Resources, Inc.
4601 Park Road, Suite 500
Charlotte, NC 28209
704/376-6697

The goal of the Directors Leadership Academy is to inform administrators of best practices in program administration and provide technical assistance in achieving goals, to provide intensive training on the Program Administration Scale (PAS) to guide program improvements, and to support peer mentoring relationships among administrators. Currently, directors residing in Mecklenburg County may take part in Directors Leadership Academy projects.

Early Childhood Administration M.Ed. and C.A.S. Program
National-Louis University
1000 Capitol Drive
Wheeling, IL 60090
800/443-5522
http://www.nl.edu

National-Louis University's Early Childhood Administration (ECA) program is a comprehensive study of the management and leadership skills needed to effectively administer early care and education programs. ECA students attend two or three residencies in Chicago at critical mileposts along the degree sequence. Through online coursework, students stay connected with each other and with early childhood leaders from around the world. The M.Ed. option includes 32 s.h. of graduate credit. The Certificate of Advanced Study (for those who already hold an M.Ed.) includes 30 s.h. of coursework.

Leadership Academy I and II
Center for Early Childhood Professional Development (CECPD)
1801 North Moore Avenue
Moore, OK 73160
888/446-7608
http://www.cecpd.org

Leadership Academy I is designed for child care directors, assistant directors, and administrators. The Academy provides leadership skills training and focuses on ways to become a more effective leader to meet the needs of staff and children in their care. Leadership Academy I provides 40 hours of training and meets the training requirements for Two- and Three-Star Centers. Leadership Academy II is offered in the spring and fall each year in two separate training sessions. Session I content is planned change and collaborative change and is

26 hours in length. Session II content includes philosophy to practice and is 20 hours in length. To be eligible for Leadership Academy II, administrators must have completed the 40-hour training offered in Leadership Academy I.

Leaderhip Institute
Action for Children
78 Jefferson Avenue
Columbus, OH 43215
614/224-0222
http://www.actionforchildren.org

Action for Children has over 16 years of experience serving directors—beginning in 1991 with director training seminars. Then in 1999, with the support of Start Smart/United Way of Central Ohio, Action for Children led the way in director training with director institutes and director reunions over the past several years. Through additional funding from Start Smart, Action for Children instituted two different advanced level experiences for directors: Directors' Leadership Institutes and Directors' Leadership Plus Institutes. Through the institute, directors receive specific skill development focusing on communication, leadership styles, effective staff meetings, staff development, and organizational change.

McCormick Tribune Center for Early Childhood Leadership
National-Louis Univeristy
6310 Capitol Drive
Wheeling, IL 60090
800/443-5522 x5056
http://cecl.nl.edu

The McCormick Tribune Center for Early Childhood Leadership is dedicated to enhancing the management skills, professional orientation, and leadership capacity of early childhood administrators. The activities of the center encompass four areas: training and technical assistance, program evaluation, research, and public awareness. The Center's signature program, Taking Charge of Change (TCC), is now in its 15th year and includes a train-the-trainer component. TCC includes an intensive one-week training followed by two three-day retreats over the course of nine months. The Center also sponsors Leadership Connections, a national conference for early childhood leaders, as well as a number of management institutes and technology training. Most of the initiatives offered by the Center provide participants with the option of receiving college credit. This credit is applicable to the core requirements of the Illinois Director Credential (IDC) and National-Louis University's graduate degree program in Early Childhood Administration (ECA).

National Head Start Fellowship Program
Office of Head Start
1250 Maryland Avenue SW, 8th Floor
Washington, DC 20024
202/205-8572
http://eclkc.ohs.acf.hhs.gov/hslc

The National Head Start Fellowship Program began in 1986. After a competitive selection process, fellows serve as apprentices in the areas of program development, research, child development, health, family development, and policy. The core of the program is an intensive work experience in Washington, DC. Fellows spend a year as full-time, paid special assistants to senior managers in the administrative branch of the U.S. government. In addition to their work assignments, Fellows take part in educational and leadership development programs. They attend seminars as a group and explore national issues with senior government officials, policymakers, researchers, community leaders, and innovative early childhood program practitioners.

Professional Impact New Jersey
56 Dolores Drive
Edison, NJ 08817
732/662-9461
http://www.pinj.org

The Directors' Academy is a 60-hour training in child care administration for directors of early childhood programs. The Directors' Academy, funded by the New Jersey Department of Human Services and administered by Professional Impact New Jersey at Kean University, is mandated for administrators working in Abbott-funded programs and administrators who have not earned a bachelor's degree, but also open to all early childhood professionals.

Aim4Excellence

Aim4Excellence is an online national director credential available to early childhood administrators across the country. The credential includes nine self-paced modules that cover the essentials of early childhood program administration. The credential is approved by NAEYC as an alternative pathway for meeting the director qualifications for NAEYC program accreditation. It is administered by the McCormick Tribune Center for Early Childhood Leadership at National-Louis University. The nine modules can be taken for credit or noncredit. For more information about Aim4Excellence, visit the Center's Web site (http://cecl.nl.edu).

Aim4Excellence Modules

Module	Title
1	Leading the Way
2	Recruiting, Selecting, and Orienting Staff
3	Promoting Peak Performance
4	Managing Program Operations
5	Building a Sound Business Strategy
6	Planning Indoor and Outdoor Environments
7	Supporting Children's Development and Learning
8	Creating Partnerships with Families
9	Evaluating Program Quality

Leading the Way

This module looks at leadership as a way of thinking about your role and the important work you do on behalf of children and families. You'll learn about the importance of self-awareness and understanding your core values as you identify your unique leadership style. You'll be introduced to a model of facilitative leadership as a way to empower staff and support shared decision making at your center. And you'll learn how to apply the principles of effective leadership to create a compelling vision for your program, become an agent of change, walk the talk of ethical behavior, and embrace the paradoxes inherent in your role.

Recruiting, Selecting, and Orienting Staff

Successful employment practices are a critical component of administering high-quality early care and education programs. This module provides a framework for effective recruitment, selection, and orientation practices. You will experience a shift in paradigm from thinking of recruitment as a dreaded event to a continuous process of community outreach. You'll learn about "right fit" criteria and how to use these criteria for finding the right person for the job and for your organization. You'll learn win-win strategies to empower staff and support shared decision making at your center at the same time you increase the likelihood of finding and, even more important, keeping the right person for the job opportunities you have to offer.

Promoting Peak Performance

The heart of effective staff relations is recognizing and appreciating individual differences. This module provides a comprehensive model for supervising staff, promoting their ongoing professional development, and creating a strengths-based team. You'll learn about the importance of tailoring your supervisory style and professional development strategies to the individualized needs of each staff member, how to use performance appraisal as the catalyst for growth and change, and how to nurture a positive work climate that promotes peak performance.

Managing Program Operations

This module introduces you to operations management and looks at the director's critical role in managing the day-to-day operations of the program. You'll learn about the necessary components of effective operations management, including: systems and the importance of systems thinking; stakeholder analysis and management; the strategic planning process; how systems, policies, and procedures are interconnected and how they impact your ability to manage the program effectively and efficiently; and tools for making systems work and for taking charge of program operations instead of being managed by them.

Building a Sound Business Strategy

This module examines the key issues pertinent to managing a fiscally responsible early childhood business. You'll study the legal requirements and tax implications that relate to the operation of programs with differing ownership status. You'll be introduced to the language of accounting and work with budgets, calculations, and financial reports to practice making informed business decisions that are aligned with your program's values and purposes. And you'll learn strategies for promoting and maintaining a positive public image that is specifically targeted to the existing and potential customers of a local child care market.

Planning Indoor and Outdoor Environments

This module considers the importance of the physical environment in early childhood programs. It begins with an overview of the essential elements of environments and how to design and equip indoor and outdoor environments to support children's development and learning. You'll then learn how to ensure that the environment welcomes all children and adults, promotes health and ensures children's safety, and is aesthetically pleasing. Finally you'll learn how to create support spaces for adults, including administrators, teachers, families, and other ancillary staff.

Supporting Children's Development and Learning

Supporting children's development and learning is at the heart of why early childhood programs exist. In this module, you'll learn about the interactive environment, how to ensure continuity of care, and the advantages and disadvantages of different grouping and staffing patterns. You'll then examine the many facets of developmentally appropriate practice (DAP) and the role of play in early childhood programming. Finally you'll learn how to design and implement curriculum and the importance of observation and assessment in achieving program goals.

Creating Partnerships with Families

This module will help you work with families in ways that empower them to partner fully with your program and become skilled, effective first educators of their children. It begins with an overview of the essential components of family-centered early childhood programming. You'll explore the director's role in planning and implementing family involvement programs, learn specific strategies for welcoming and working with diverse families, and consider new approaches to nurture open, two-way communication. Finally, you'll be introduced to tools for evaluating the effectiveness of your family involvement efforts.

Evaluating Program Quality

Program evaluation plays an important role in the administration of high-quality early care and education programs. This module provides a framework for understanding and implementing effective evaluation practices. You'll learn how to select appropriate evaluation tools to achieve your program goals. You'll learn how to implement continuous quality improvement, the leadership practice of assessing program needs, defining desired outcomes, developing an action plan, and evaluating outcomes. Rather than it being threatening, you will discover how evaluation can help you celebrate program strengths, increase staff collaboration, and improve your program's quality.

Reprinted with permission of the McCormick Tribune Center for Early Childhood Leadership at National-Louis University, Wheeling, IL; http://cecl.nl.edu.

Pennsylvania Keystone STARS Quality Rating System

Keystone STARS Quality Rating System is an initiative of the Pennsylvania Office of Child Development and Early Learning (OCDEL), a joint office of the Pennsylvania Department of Public Welfare and the Pennsylvania Department of Education. The goal of the program is to improve, support, and recognize the continuous quality improvement efforts of early learning programs in Pennsylvania. The Keystone STARS Performance Standards provide the foundation for the program. The Performance Standards are grouped into four levels. Each level builds on the previous level and utilizes research-based best practices to promote quality early learning environments and positive child outcomes.

The standards address staff qualifications and professional development, the early learning program, partnerships with family and community, and leadership and management.

Started as a pilot program in 2002, Keystone STARS/Early Learning Keys to Quality began as a continuous quality improvement program and rating system for child care. Through program standards, supports, and assessment, Keystone STARS/Pennsylvania Early Learning Keys to Quality is improving the quality of early learning across Pennsylvania. Pennsylvania Early Learning Keys to Quality is an important support system for early learning programs which consists of the Harrisburg-based Pennsylvania Key and six Regional Keys.

One lesson learned early on in the process was that quality doesn't always look the same for every program. Even though the STARS Standards were set up as indicators of quality, programs could reflect their own character and vision for children and still meet the STARS standards. To help the system understand this concept, the idea of Continuous Quality Improvement (CQI) was promoted. The goal for CQI was to get away from the checklist mentality that forced a program to put something in place to satisfy a STARS quality indicator. It was very disappointing for STARS staff to visit a program a few months after they had achieved a STAR level and see that the quality improvements put in place for STARS had not been maintained. The philosophy of CQI is firmly grounded in the overall mission, vision, and values of the organization. But perhaps most importantly it is dependent on the active inclusion of staff, families, children, and other quality partners (stakeholders) at all levels of the program. CQI becomes the ongoing process by which an organization makes decisions and evaluates its progress. The key to CQI lies in acknowledging and treating those closest to the work (staff, parents, children, and other stakeholders) as the "real experts." Those who are closest to the work should be the ones who are actively engaged in assessing the program and making improvements based on those assessments.

Continuous Quality Improvement Process

Set Vision

Define what you truly want to achieve. A shared picture of the future creates ownership and commitment rather than forced compliance.

Plan

Define and analyze the current process.

Ask:

What is the problem or challenge?
What do we want to change?
What is the current process?
What needs improvement?

Do

Develop a STARS Continuous Quality Improvement Plan.

Ask:

What do we want to have happen?
What changes need to be made?
How will we know if our plan was successful?

Act

Study

Implement the STARS CQI plan and study the results.

Ask:

How is the process working?
Was our plan successful?
What still needs improvement?

Act

Incorporate changes and improvements into the process.

It has been a goal to instill in everyone, at all levels in the system, the idea that it's possible to achieve higher levels of quality by using the continuous quality improvement model and that continuous quality improvement is most effective when it becomes a natural part of the way everyday work is done.

A few of the supports for programs to help them to embrace the CQI philosophy include Director's Institutes around the concepts found in this book and the CQI philosophy; a Director's Credential that includes ongoing work on these ideas; changes in the STARS standards that incorporate the language of CQI; and a required professional development workshop on Continuous Quality Improvement.

From the 2002 pilot that included 100 programs, STARS has grown to 5,034 programs (55% of regulated child care providers in Pennsylvania). This means that over 180,000 children who attend these programs are benefiting from a higher quality early learning experience.

Alliance for Early Childhood Finance

Shared Services: Building Infrastructure for the Early Care and Education Industry

Support for early care and education (ECE) has grown markedly in recent years. Increasingly, policymakers, business leaders, and advocates are talking about taking ECE services "to scale" so that universal access can be assured. If these leaders succeed in obtaining the funding needed to serve many more children, will the ECE industry as a whole be ready to respond? Or will only a small number of providers—such as school districts or large child care chains—quickly dominate the industry?

Market Challenges

Most early care and education services are delivered by the private sector—in nonprofit, faith-based, and for-profit centers as well as thousands of home-based businesses. Most of these providers are very small, and many rely solely on tuition revenue. Fee collection is challenging, and prices frequently fail to cover costs. Third-party funding is scarce and often requires detailed bookkeeping as well as compliance with quality standards beyond the capacity of the bulk of these small providers. And most early childhood program directors aren't accountants or business managers; they are experts in child development, focused on the intimate work of educating and nurturing children. With limited resources and personnel to handle both program and administrative functions, both aspects of the business suffer.

These market challenges and weak business platforms don't just hurt ECE businesses; they hurt children and families as well. Without strong fiscal and program management, quality suffers. Indeed, most of the early care and education services currently available to families do not meet desired quality standards.

The bottom line is that establishing universal ECE isn't just about money. It is about building an industry comprised of strong, stable organizations that are able to tap all available funds and offer children the high-quality early learning opportunities they need to succeed.

Shared Platforms

Most mainstream businesses in the U.S. are supported by a highly developed infrastructure that typically includes: common definitions and standards, rating systems, standardized procedures, industry-wide databases and technology and support services. Financial institutions, for example, share a very complex technology network (e.g., ATMs, credit/debit cards, etc.) and employ a host of industry standards that allow dollars to move easily among institutions. This shared infrastructure enables banks to operate quickly and efficiently. State ECE leaders have begun to craft industry-wide standards (e.g., professional development systems and program requirements) as well as quality rating systems. But the ECE industry has yet to create the infrastructure and supports individual programs and providers need not only to comply with these standards but to operate efficiently. By focusing on shared platforms it is possible to develop business models that enable center- and home-based early care and education programs to offer high-quality services and also succeed as small businesses. Each of the following examples (which are currently being implemented or tested) allows small ECE businesses to retain their autonomy and diversity yet attain critical economies of scale:

Program Alliance—Independent ECE businesses contract with a common administrative agency to handle some or all aspects of program administration and fiscal management. (Chattanooga, TN: http://government.cce.cornell.edu/doc/pdf/CC-GovernanceStructure.pdf)

Consortium—Existing ECE businesses join together as a single nonprofit entity. (Seattle, WA: http://government.cce.cornell.edu/doc/pdf/CC-PugetSound.pdf)

Provider Trust—ECE providers form and join a legal trust (structured as a limited liability corporation), which contracts with a third party to manage fiscal and administrative tasks. (Fairfax, VA: http://government.cce.cornell.edu/doc/pdf/CC-InfantToddler.pdf)

Cooperative—ECE providers create a jointly owned entity that assumes responsibility for administration in multiple, independent sites.

Shared platforms offer many benefits for the early care and education industry. By forging alliances, early care and education programs are more sustainable and better able to offer affordable, high-quality services in a range of settings for children of all ages. Some important benefits include:

- The professional fiscal management and economic strength of a larger organization, making it easier for very small businesses to weather economic ebbs and flows;
- Lower costs from economies of scale in business functions like payroll, benefits management, banking, janitorial, food services, and purchasing;
- Higher quality early childhood education, and the ability to offer a range of comprehensive family support services, due to a more stable financial and organizational structure and a comprehensive approach to professional development;
- Better data and school transitions, via centralized systems, assessments, and technology to support outcomes tracking, reflective practice, and linkages with school districts.

In short, quality businesses can offer quality early learning. Shared services can help the ECE industry attain this goal. For more information on shared services for the ECE industry go to www.earlylearningventures.org.

Reprinted with permission of the Alliance for Early Childhood Finance; www.earlychildhood finance.org.

Examples of Administrative Restructuring

Next are four examples of community-based, not-for-profit early childhood organizations that have undertaken what is almost a regular routine in the corporate world, restructuring their administration or doing a "re-org."

Sound Child Care Solutions (SCCS) is a slowly growing consortium of child care centers in the Puget Sound area of Washington State that was inspired by the shared services model with economies of scale described in Louise Stoney's booklet *Collective Management of Early Childhood Programs*. As centers join the consortium, their directors become part of the leadership team of SCCS, collectivizing some of their administrative functions to allow them to turn more attention to the teachers, children, and families in their centers.

London Bridge Child Care Services in Ontario is the largest of the organizations featured, with fourteen centers across the city. Their journey is quite remarkable in the way they drew upon a wide net of resources and inspiration; the administrators did the soul searching, self-examination work they expected of their teachers.

Chicago Commons Child Development Program is an arm of a larger social service agency in Illinois with multiple sites and a blended funding stream. The administrative work they undertook to develop themselves in order to develop their staff and organization is detailed at length in the book *We Are All Explorers* (Scheinfeld, Haigh, and Scheinfeld 2008). We offer an overview of their professional development structure and efforts as well as an organizational chart for the child development program.

Hilltop Children's Center is the smallest organization we highlight for their continued effort to create an administrative structure to support their vision. Often recognized by name because they are prominently featured in a series of Harvest Resources staff development videos, here you find the behind-the-scenes story of how a core group of teachers continued to advocate for and help create an infrastructure to enhance their work, despite the inconsistent context of their center's leadership.

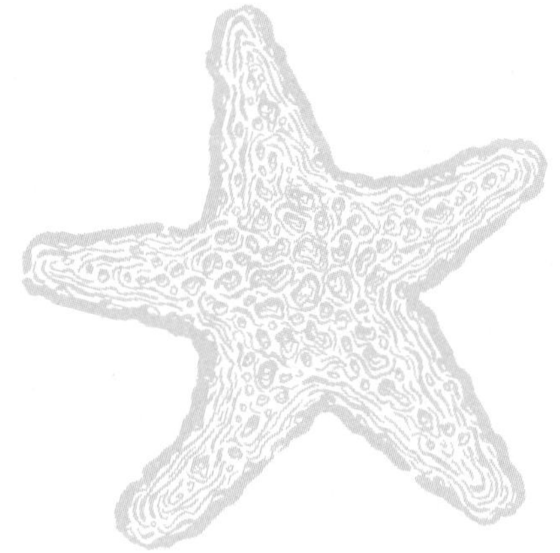

Sound Child Care Solutions

Sound Child Care Solutions: A Consortium of Centers, Better Together

Sound Child Care Solutions is a consortium of nonprofit child care centers in the Seattle Puget Sound area launched through the combined expertise of a bilingual early childhood educator and a public policy and project development specialist, drawing on the collective management and shared services concept promoted by the Alliance for Early Childhood Finance. We are a group of centers joining together to share the business functions of child care while each retaining our own name, community identity, and advisory board. Our consortium has begun with centers that share a common dedication to identified shared principles and values with a commitment to ongoing development and support. Through the power of collaborative operations we gain bulk purchasing discounts, economies of scale in business function, and, in the end, higher quality early childhood education that comes with a more stable financial and organizational structure. By uniting across centers and combining the most cutting-edge business tools and small business practices, we free up resources and lessen the burden on directors to improve the combined practices of teachers and directors and serve more low-income families.

Our incubation year was spent turning our concept into specific governance documents, budgets, and organizational development plans with legal, business, IT, and organizational development consultations; grant writing; and extensive presentations and focus groups across the city. We have intentionally moved slowly and started small, wanting to avoid the pitfalls of rapid expansion and overextension.

The process of joining the consortium involves getting to know each other, sharing information, and thoughtfully exploring how we might strengthen each other by being together. Our process includes an exploration phase, a concrete discussion phase, including negotiation with boards, and then a commitment phase, followed by celebration.

In 2008, with three centers and two others in negotiation with the consortium, we held our first full administrative retreat to further refine our values and vision and set some priorities for the coming year. Indeed, we discovered that the supportive administrative infrastructure we've designed HAS been freeing up the directors' minds and their interconnectedness with us and each other, providing the sense that "all these people have my back." After our unifying vision-building work, we began planning for the coming year, making a list of all the things we COULD do with our time to move toward our vision. Then each person got three sticky dots to vote on their top three choices. Developing a substitute teacher pool was at the top of the list. In our early thinking about the sub pool idea, we decided to flip what other sub pool efforts have experienced as a problem, namely, that subs quickly get hired into permanent positions. We view our sub pool as an intentional recruiting tool, casting it as internship program with intentional mentoring and professional development to qualify people for permanent work.

Another priority for us in the coming year is creating an organizational culture that reflects our vision and values. We want to move past where we are now, just sharing basic financial and insurance services with a little professional development support, to reach the full collaborative consortium model we envision. We will create a model that could be replicated across the country to transform the financing of early education and expand notions of quality for our field with ongoing support for meaningful, transformative professional development.

Current Organizational Chart: A Single, Nonprofit Corporation with Participating Centers as Local Chapters

Building new organizational approaches to administering early care and education programs requires clear values and a vision, and the tools and strategic planning to bring it to life. In the U.S. all of us are schooled in notions of hierarchy and conglomerate control. Our vision is distributed power, an inverted pyramid, designed to bring support to those who are doing the day-to-day work with the children and families. We want every level of our organizational structure to support the relationships between teachers, children, and their families. The bookkeeper, cook, office manager, and IT people all have to be thinking about supporting these relationships.

Recognizing that we are continuing to evolve, our current organizational structure is shown on the following pages, and more detailed documents, such as our governance structure, benefits, and process of joining can be found on the websites provided after the charts.

SCCS Advisors and Supporters

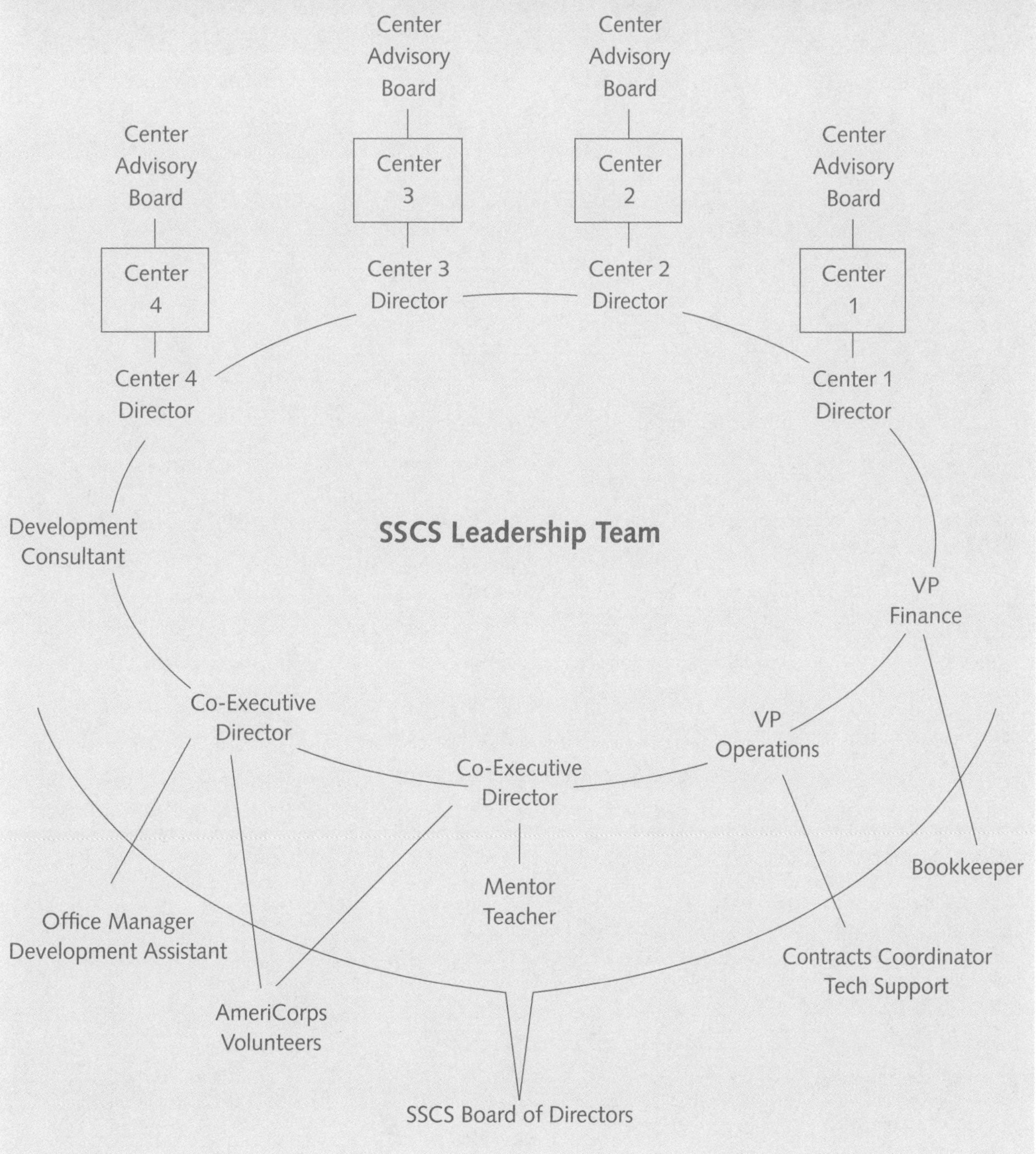

SCCS Leadership Team (Center Directors, VP Operations, Office Manager, Bookkeeper, and Co-Executive Directors) Some of the functions listed below are performed by one center director for all centers in SCCS.			
Education, Professional Development, and Pedagogical Support	**Business and Financing**	**Operations**	**Center Management (responsibilities at center)**
Support center directors with staff recruitment, hiring, and supervision challenges as requested. Provide best practice standards, policies, and procedures.	Budget and accounting systems	Manage contracts for services that operate at more than one center, such as food purchasing, catering, maintenance and janitorial, insurance.	Daily supervision and management of all staff on site, including hiring and firing.
Locate professional resources, higher ed, and pd opportunities to align with NAEYC standards.	Legal support	Manage technology procedures and support, including electronic sign-in sheets, billing, subsidy and licensing reporting, time sheets, and personnel and child records.	Develop annual center budget in conjunction with leadership team.
Set up mentor system.	Secure and administer benefits packages.		Enrollment management.
Design staff trainings and retreats.			Close partnerships with families.
Offer pedagogical support for directors to mentor their staff in building relationships with children and families, curriculum development, and using learning stories to address standards and assessment practices.	Raise funds consortium-wide, and offer consulting support for center-based fundraisers.		Develop, promote, and be accountable to the organizational culture to support values and vision.
Future: Coordinate joint staff recruitment efforts, and manage evolving intern and substitute teacher program.			Mentor and guide teachers in working with an image of competent children, cultural competency, and antibias principles as they plan and respond to children, family, and coworkers.

For more information visit http://soundchildcare.org.

London Bridge Child Care Services Inc.

Program Focus Leadership Model

London Bridge Child Care Services Inc. cares for over 1,200 children daily across fourteen Early Childhood Learning Centres in London, Sarnia, and Exeter, Ontario, Canada. Through the collaboration and dreams of a group of committed individuals, we have embarked on an incredible journey to make an unconventional change in our program structure. In 2000, we began to shift our thinking and the focus of our organization's approach to curriculum planning—from a theme-based approach to an emergent curriculum model. Over the next five years, we discovered a disconnect between what we were trying to do in the classroom and the way our leadership model was structured. We were trying to do something new with an old leadership model.

This prompted us to create an eighteen-month leadership development program with inspiration drawn from business, philosophy, art, and child development theory. In developing this program, we understood that adults, just as children, come with their own unique learning styles and deserve to be engaged fully in order to make meaning of their own work. For this reason, we developed classes that consist of a variety of approaches from hands-on experimentation to group discussion and individual journaling.

We centered our professional development work around three distinct areas: Values, Leadership, and Curriculum. We offer opportunities to work with local artists, study the work of teachers from around the world, and reflect with their colleagues on their own experiences in the classroom.

We are inspired by the teachers in Reggio Emilia and are particularly influenced by their strong image of the child. We consider the work of Lev Vygotsky and John Dewey and their ideas around a constructivist approach to learning. We are also aware of the powerful influences all over North America and are continuously seeking to learn from our colleagues at home. (Margie Carter,

Deb Curtis, Lilian Katz, Sylvia Chard, Ann Pelo, George Forman, Carol Anne Wien, Brenda Fyfe to name but a few, as well as any number of teachers who bravely share their insights with us.)

Along with exploring the resources within our own field, we are also keenly aware of the importance of tapping into the many fields that help us to elevate the work we do. We examine the work of artists such as Jackson Pollock, Andy Goldsworthy, and Vincent van Gogh in an attempt to learn to think creatively. We turned to the business world and have discovered great resources in Marcus Buckingham, Stephen Covey, and Robin Sharma, who teach us about the importance of building strong relationships in leadership. Our leadership team together studied Peter Senge's book *The Dance of Change*. We reflect often on the stories and wisdom of great minds who both went before us and still grace us today, such as Gandhi, Martin Luther King Jr., and Maya Angelou. And we include music and poetry to ensure that we always stay grounded in our own humanity. The leadership development program is grounded in the belief that we all have opportunities to lead in different capacities. We have designed this program to support the growth and development of both our formal leadership and classroom educators.

Another significant change for us was a shift to a Program Focus Leadership Model that redefined the roles and responsibilities for our leaders (centre directors) and resulted in the reshaping of our organizational structure (see charts on the following pages). This change enabled our leaders to spend a significant amount of their time as mentors and co-learners in the classrooms. This evolution in roles, responsibilities, and expectations required a very different set of skills, behaviours, learning dispositions, and level of commitment from our leaders. We understood that it would require a huge investment of time, energy, and resources to allow us to build our capacity for thinking and doing things in a new way. We added new administrator support positions to our centres. This allowed the centre director to focus a significant amount of time on their own growth and development, subsequently shifting the learning culture of their centres. They were able to draw on experiences from the leadership development program while spending time in the classrooms learning along side the educators and children. Our leaders work through projects, meet regularly with teams of educators, participate in regular networking sessions, and spend the majority of their time in the classroom. These changes have improved the relationships between the centre director and the educators, children, and families, allowing for more reflective thinking and collaboration. We have a common set of standards and a performance measurement system across our organization, but it is flexible, with a greater attention in respecting people and treating them well. We are continually thinking about ways to reshape our work.

In building this collaborative infrastructure focused on building the capabilities and success of all our people, from centre director to the new educator, we feel our work has only just begun. The commitment, passion, and care of our people for the work that we do has allowed us to evolve; we continuously evaluate and improve on our thinking as we pursue excellence in our work with children and their families. We continue to believe that the quality of care we provide is measured by the quality of our relationships with children, families, and the community. We understand that we are on a journey that never ends, but through a shared value system and a shift in thinking, we continue to find ways to make our visions a reality. Our Program Focused Leadership Model has formed new collaborative partnerships across all areas of the organization, including program, finance, HR, facilities, and administration, clearly defining our central common focus—the children and families.

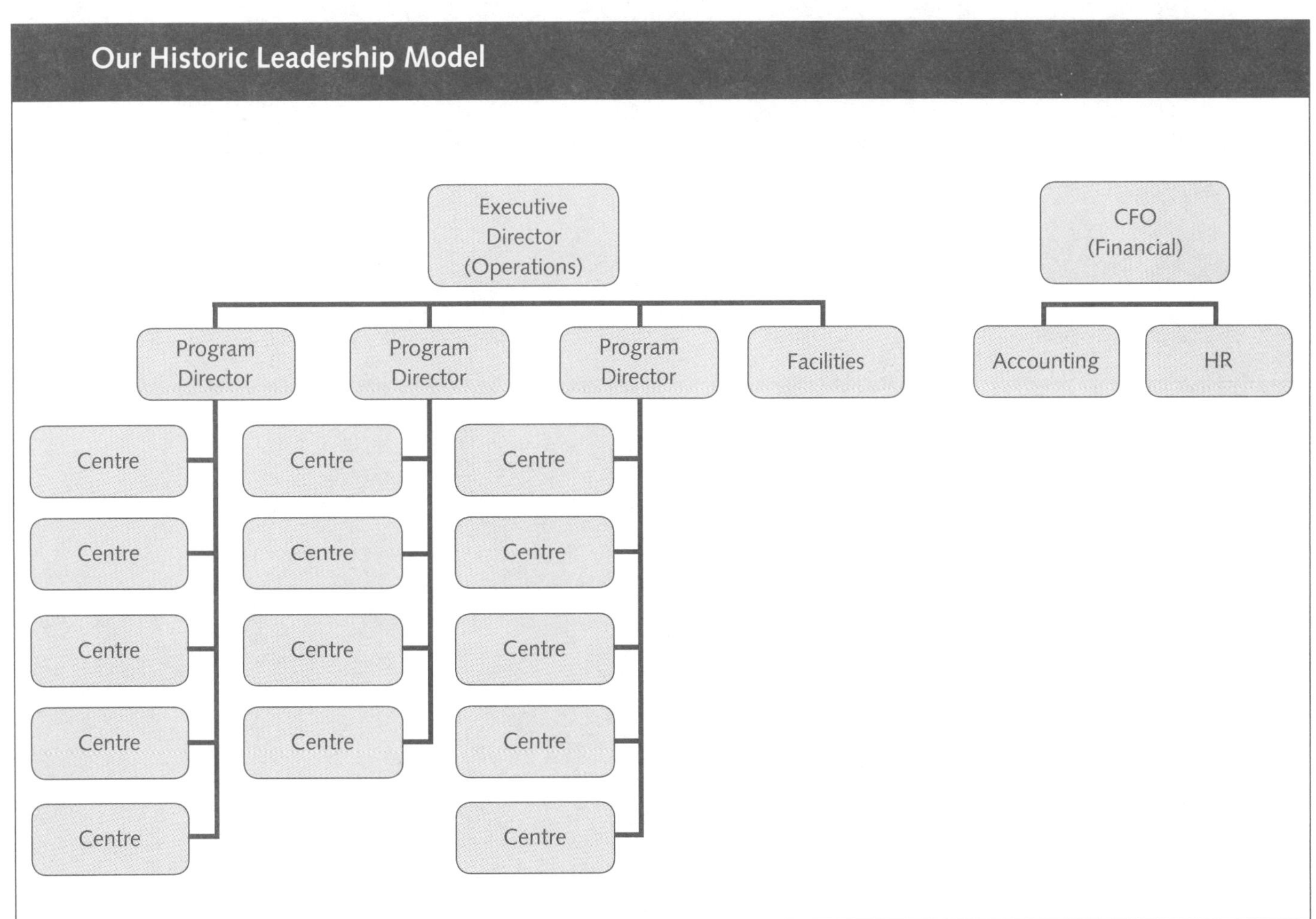

Reprinted with permission of London Bridge Child Care Services, Inc., London, Ontario; www.londonbridge.com.

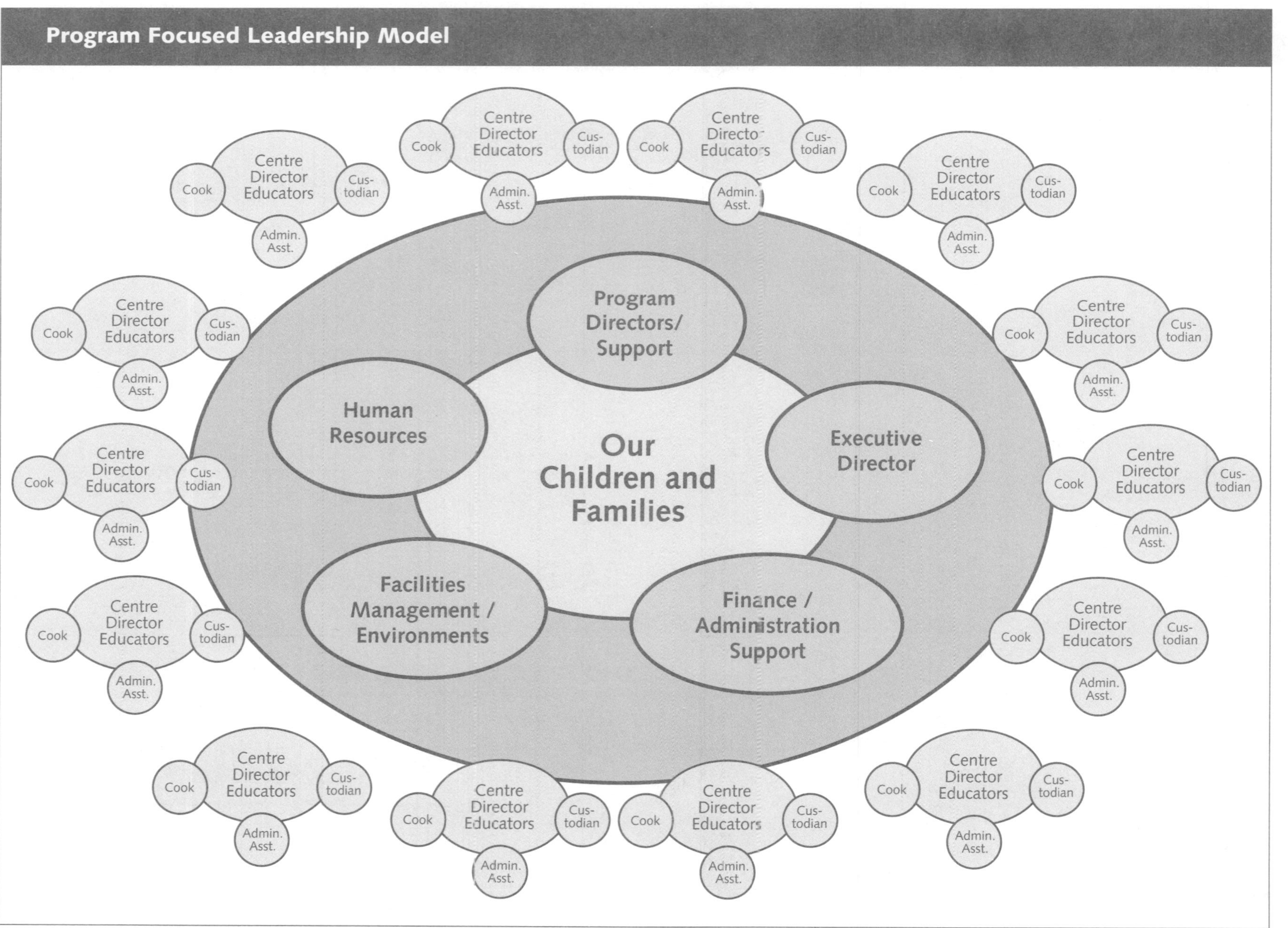

Reprinted with permission of London Bridge Child Care Services, Inc., London, Ontario; www.londonbridge.com.

Chicago Commons Child Development Program

Chicago Commons Child Development Program is a multisite early childhood program primarily serving low-income Latino and African American families with funding from Head Start, state prekindergarden, state-subsidized child care, and occasional private funding. They are part of a larger social service agency with a long history in the Chicago area.

Between 1991 and 2003, with the guidance of Child Development Director Karen Haigh, Commons crafted a remarkable organizational structure to support a growing exploration of Reggio-inspired ideas, starting with a small group of teachers volunteering to participate and ultimately engaging all staff and all sites. To achieve the specific teacher development outcomes they desired, they created a structure to ensure ongoing learning at every level, rather than fall into bureaucratic thinking and practices. The following text is drawn from a detailed book describing their experience, *We Are All Explorers* (Scheinfeld, Haigh, and Scheinfeld 2008).

Seven Teacher Development Goals

1. Learning to engage in moment-to-moment dialogues with children that build on their interests and involve the co-construction of understandings.
2. Learning the skills and understandings involved in carrying out emergent curriculum cycles, involving listening/observing, documenting, interpreting, projecting/deciding, planning, hypothesizing, and implementing.
3. Learning to design and construct classroom environments that promote small-group learning, communicate the children's identities, invite children to take multiple perspectives, promote a sense of

well-being, and encourage parents to engage with the life of the classroom community.

4. Learning to participate in collaborative dialogues with other staff to co-construct understandings and teaching strategies.
5. Learning to engage in dialogues with parents that connect the perspectives of parents and teachers to support the development of the child.
6. Learning to be a researcher. . . . Infusing a research perspective into all that one does as a teacher: experiencing curiosity and engaging the object of one's curiosity, formulating questions, hypothesizing, gathering and analyzing pertinent data with one's questions in mind, coming to conclusions, reflecting on the application of the conclusions, and pondering next steps in the research.
7. Developing a sense of agency. . . . Experiencing oneself as an active, self-directed agent who can, individually and in collaboration with others, formulate personally meaningful learning goals, figure out strategies to achieve them, engage the world to pursue them, construct understandings, and communicate the newly developed understandings to others (130).

Administrative Responsibilities and Systems to Accomplish These Goals

Commons developed an organizational structure with roles, responsibilities, and communication systems to engage with each other and in the learning process together. Their system includes:

> Weekly meetings with each teaching team, their site director, a coordinator from the central office, and sometimes the center's family worker. These often include two classroom teams together. Meetings are used to enhance one or more of the goals above through dialogue, listening to different perspectives, study of observations and documentation, practicing the emergent curriculum cycle, etc.
>
> Weekly education and/or studio coordinator meetings with the director and biweekly site director meetings to deepen exploration of the guiding values and concepts and develop the pedagogical leadership skills to guide the staff in their learning process. Specific examples of progress toward goals are shared, along with a critiquing of weekly teaching team meetings.
>
> Weekly administrator meetings with all administrators except site directors to share goals and activities, coordinate activities, deal with

issues of accountability and reporting, sharing future plans, promoting the overall integration of the program.

Staff development efforts also include teacher research projects, a two-day annual retreat in August to explore materials and a particular focus of their philosophy and its application; an annual "close-down" day for gathering of all staff, including kitchen staff, maintenance, clerks, etc., to reflect on the past and future, introduce a new focus for the year, and hear everyone's voice; application process to attend conferences and study tours to Reggio and Reggio-inspired programs; preparing and giving presentations at learning tours hosted by Commons.

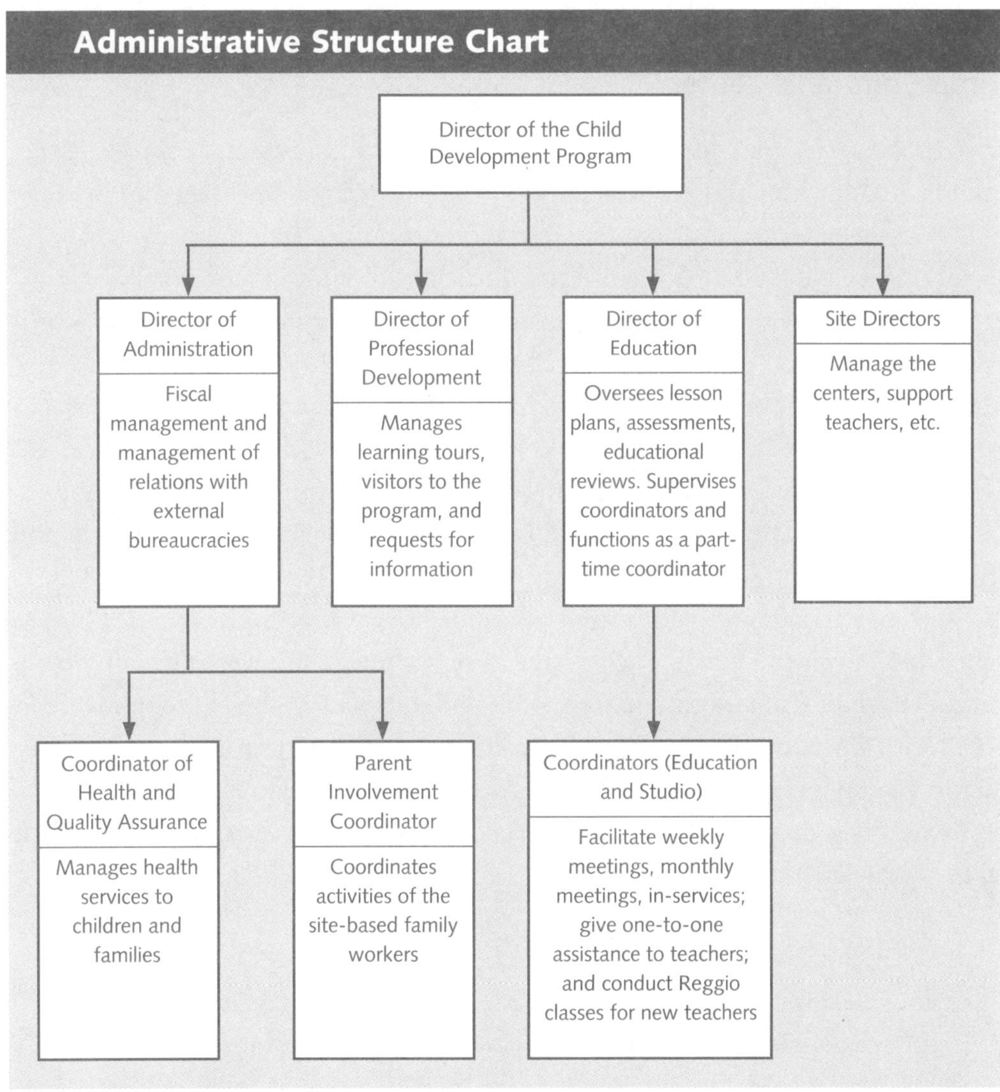

(Scheinfeld, Haigh, and Scheinfeld 2008, 160)

Hilltop Children's Center

Child care work is often dismissed as not particularly intellectual, as the feel-good work of playing with children overlaid with the daily chores of caregiving, none of it especially engaging and certainly not a long-term professional path. With exposure to the practices of Reggio Emilia, teachers at Hilltop Children's Center began to craft a different understanding of our work at a full-time nonprofit child care center serving 65 children ages 3-10 years old. We began to see ourselves as thinkers, as researchers engaged in the study of children and of the process of learning—children's and our own—and as collaborators with the children's families. We became determined to work in a child care program that honored our intellectual and emotional engagement, both in its compensation of our work and in the program culture.

With two decades of inconsistent administrative leadership, a handful of teachers have been the thread of consistency at Hilltop. Empowered by conviction in the value of our work and in children's right to a top-flight program, we worked with the administration and board to build an organizational culture and structure to support our work. Our changes unfolded in tiny steps, over many years, slowly weaving professional development and improved working conditions into the everyday life of Hilltop.

- We inched away from catch-as-catch-can staff meetings on the hallway floor during naptime, gradually adding weekly paid prep and planning time, early closures on the first Friday of each month for staff meetings, full-day closures four times a year for in-service and classroom work, and an annual staff retreat weekend in a beautiful place.
- New teachers now have a series of orientation classes, videos, and a self-study booklet.
- After years of involvement in the Worthy Wage Movement, we have a union contract.

- We've been featured in a series of videos used widely for teacher education across North America and beyond.
- In recent years, we sacrificed other professional development benefits to fund a 20-hour/week mentor teacher position to create an in-depth professional development system with individual and teaching team support for pedagogical documentation, collaborative conferences with families, and an annual research study focus for our work.
- To strengthen our administrative team, we've reorganized our structure several times, with the most recent version outlined below. It is an evolving process to keep our business and pedagogical practices true to our vision.

This story is energizing to tell, but it is humbling as well. During stretches when the administrative leadership has changed or been absorbed by major challenges, new teachers have floundered in the absence of clear expectations and accountability, and, unaware of our history of struggle, have pushed at established standards and the discipline of the pedagogical work. A blurred line between empowerment and entitlement at Hilltop has grown from the staff's class and race privilege. There is significant work to be done at Hilltop on this front: unpacking our social and cultural privilege through consistent self-study and community reflection; partnering with teachers at a range of programs to learn from them about their collective efforts for the common good. This is the next chapter to Hilltop's story. May it be as energizing and full of hope as the first chapter. For more information about Hilltop's professional development study tours visit www.hilltopcc.org.

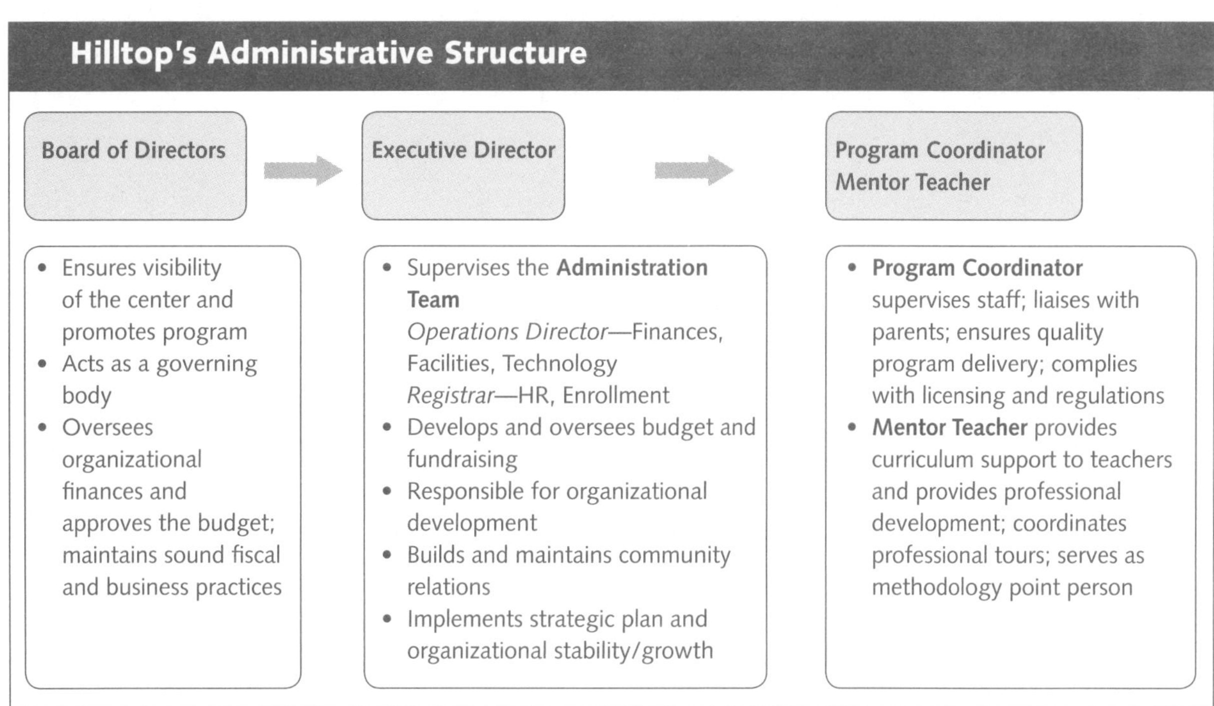

Reprinted with permission of Hilltop Children's Center, Seattle, WA; www.hilltopcc.org.

Staff Recruitment, Stability, and Retention

Now you'll find an overview of the efforts of the Men in Early Childhood Education World Forum, with specific ideas on how to recruit, retain, and expect male involvement, from a Canadian colleague. Also following is the unique Staff Stability Plan of the Old Firehouse School in the San Francisco Bay Area, with unusual financial rewards for teachers who stay through a cycle of continuity of care with the children in their group.

Men in Early Childhood Education

From Ron Blatz, Executive Director of Discovery Children's Centre, Inc.

At the World Forum in Montreal, Canada (2005), Don Piburn of Hawaii approached me and placed a promotional pin on my shirt that read: "Expect Male Involvement—Gender balance is good for young children." Don further explained the phrase on the pin by saying that all change starts with the expectation of change. When we as ECE directors hire our staff, do we really expect there to be men in our classrooms? Do we believe something important for children is missing if every staff in the room is female? I do, and I believe you should too!

Some lessons I've learned from my friends around the world are:

- To recruit men you must target your advertising. A first step is to realize that there is an invisible message (but not invisible to men) that is attached to every job advertisement you put in the paper, and that the same message is posted above your center's entrance doors, and this is how it reads, "Only women need apply." To counter this powerful message we must invite men in, not just wait for them to come. This should be done through personal invitation and through job ads like this one placed in a Winnipeg, Canada, newspaper for one day. It resulted in 30 male applicants for the job.

> "Looking for a few good men and women with the courage to work in Child Care. Discovery Centre believes gender balance is good for young children. Interested? Call . . . "

- To retain men we must find ways to support men and encourage directors. This is why I have started a Men in Early Childhood Education

(MECE) support group in my city. We meet every two months, with the men sharing a meal together prior to the evening meeting time. For the meeting we also invite our female colleagues to join us and look for ways to support the recruitment and retention of men in our field. We also have initiated a "Club 2-10" which is a way to recruit directors to our movement. Joining the club requires a director to make a commitment to work toward employing at least two male staff, and build towards 10% male staff. Without a vision, nothing will change.

- When working toward a diverse staff, remember that gender diversity is a part of the equation. It has been overlooked for too long. If half our children are boys (who will grow up to be men), we better find a way to provide the range of experiences and the role models necessary for this transition to happen successfully.

My hope and prayer is that more men will find open doors in the ECE world. When they do, I hope they will find their career to be as personally satisfying and fulfilling as I have. Remember: "Expect male involvement—gender balance is good for young children."

For more information contact rblatz@discoverycc.com, or go to www.menteach.org, www.mencare2.com, www.meninchildcare.com, or www.ecmenz.org.

Reprinted with permission of Ron Blatz, executive director of Discover Children's Center, Inc., Winnipeg, Canada.

Old Firehouse School Staff Stability Plan

In 1996 Dorothy Stewart founded the Old Firehouse School with the goal of keeping children and caregivers together anywhere from two to four years using a primary caregiver model. Stewart's vision was influenced by the work of John Bowlby on the importance of human attachment relationships. In her second year of operation, her toddler teacher left to take a job with the phone company for a salary $18,000 more than she was making at the school. This experience left Stewart pondering the issues of staff retention, salaries, and program quality. She gathered the staff together to devise a plan, and they created a two-pronged financial package to address issues of stable relationships, compensation, and quality programming. Parents were to add $1,000 to their fees each year, with that money set aside for their child's teacher to receive *if* the teacher stayed through the child's graduation from preschool. To sell the plan to the school families, each teacher wrote an essay on why they are in this field and why they worked at the Old Firehouse School. They included examples of what their friends with similar education were making in other fields. Then they made a video of the teachers working with the children and had the teachers read the essays in a voice-over. They gave each family a video and asked them to watch it over the weekend. By the next Monday, most of the families returned with comments like "This will be hard for us, but we are proud to be part of a community that would do this." They had close to 100% buy-in. Over the last 10 years the plan has been updated and is still keeping turnover uncharacteristically low for the early childhood field. A copy of the original plan is included on the following pages.

Currently, with three school locations and thirty teachers, the plan works as follows, with specific governance issues described below. On October 15th each year, families pay a "Staff Stability Fee" (currently $1,050 for full-time children). This money is intentionally designated as separate from tuition to call attention to the value of continuity of care *and* quality-of-life issues for teachers who make very little money compared to the parents at the schools. Each teacher receives half of that year's accumulation at the end of each academic year. This can be anywhere from $2,000 to $4,500 per teacher, depending on the number of children and the mix of part-time and full-time children in each caregiver's group. The rest accumulates and is distributed when the children in that primary caregiving group graduate—this can be as much as $18,000 per teacher. This new version of the plan is not yet available to the public.

A second program to promote continuity of care at OFS was developed in 2005. This plan uses money from an annual auction and a portion of each child's one-time registration fee for a Housing Assistance Fund. One teacher a year at each school can apply for these funds. It is a loan, but one that includes a 1/3 forgiveness sum for each year a teacher works for the school. (Again, the motive is to promote the stability of staff at OFS; home ownership is a major quality-of-life issue for teachers.) It is generally from $7,000 to $20,000.

Stewart's advice to others: (1) If your family population is less able to afford $1,000 annually, consider some smaller amount. (2) Remember to work with an accountant to consider the tax implications for everyone.

A Simple but Profound Plan

Purpose: To reward staff for their long-term loyalty to the children and to the program

Section 1: The Plan

1) Each child's parents pay $1,000 each year. Monies go into an account called the Staff Stability Trust Fund.
2) This money will go to the primary caregiver of their child if the caregiver:
    i) stays the entire time the child's cohort stays in the school
    ii) meets standards of professional growth
    iii) receives a favorable annual evaluation
3) The money does not belong to the staff member unless they meet the above criteria. It is not an entitlement and should never be thought of as such.
4) The money will be due on October 15th of each year.
5) If a teacher starts out in the infant room, their personal account will accumulate the following amounts each year, culminating in the 5th year for a total of $31,000, minus any associated taxes and costs to administer the fund.

6) A teacher may elect to take up to 33.3% (1/3) or $3,500, whichever is least, at the time her children move from the Dragon Room (under threes). The rationale for this is that while caregiver loss is always hurtful to the children, it is particularly damaging to children under 3 years of age.
7) In the event a new teacher is hired, then her/his share of the $1,000 per child will be prorated from hire date, with September as the beginning month of the year.
8) New families who begin on a date other than September shall have their fee prorated.
9) In the event a teacher or teachers leave their position here, either willingly or unwillingly, the money in her/his account shall be divided with the following priorities in place—wait and tenure.

   First Priority: Wait time
   50% to the Infant Teachers' Fund until it reaches $10,000 (since the Infant teacher has to wait longest to receive her/his money).
   20% to the Toddler Teachers' Fund until it reaches $7,900.
   10% percent to the Two-Year-Old Teachers' Fund until it reaches $7,300.

   Second Priority: Tenure
   Any remaining monies shall be divided equally among those with three years or longer of service until each is compensated up to $3,000.
   The rest of the monies shall be divided among staff with 1 year of service up to $1,000.
   Additional monies shall be divided among staff with 1 year of service up to $1,000.
   If, after all of the above priorities are met, there is additional monies, it shall be distributed equally among all the staff.
10) Administration and adjustment to this plan is the right of the Executive Director and Board of Directors of the Old Firehouse School.

Section II. Exceptions

1) If a family has two children enrolled at OFS, then the second Stability fee shall be reduced by 50%, unless the second student is in the infant toddler room. In that case the fee remains $1,000.
2) In cases of true financial hardship, some adjustments to the fee schedule can be made at the Executive Director's discretion.
3) If a family withdraws from the program, then the $1,000 stays in the Caregiver's account. If a new child is enrolled and takes the first

child's slot, then 50% of the second child's fee goes to the primary caregiver, and 50% goes to the general fund to be distributed as stated above under Section I, #9.

4) If a teacher leaves for any reason prior to their group's graduation, then she/he forfeits the monies in her account.
5) If the school closes, then the distribution formula shall be what is in each account. Any additional monies will be distributed by Section I, #9, Tenure Priority.
6) Only full-time primary caregivers are eligible for this plan.
7) Part-time children's share shall be prorated with an additional 10% added on to the total due.
8) A teacher with a child at the school (who pays no tuition) shall pay the full Staff Stability fee.

For more information visit www.oldfirehouseschool.com.

Reprinted with permission of the Old Firehouse School, Lafayette, CA, www.oldfirehouseschool.com.

Promising Approaches to Professional and Leadership Development

The leadership circles and cohort model for professional development in Houston's United Way Bright Beginnings program are not only leading to outcomes of improvements on the ITERS and ECRES, but are bringing a new voice and sense of agency to historically disempowered directors and teachers.

This is also one of the goals for the work of our own organization, Harvest Resources Associates: we have been developing new formats for professional development that lead to reflective practices and new leadership development in a variety of training settings.

The Hildebrandt Learning Centers have developed "Napinars" to provide professional development across their forty centers. Their example should provoke our field to take advantage of technology to engage teachers in learning together across multisite organizations.

United Way Bright Beginnings (UWBB): Cohort Model for Professional Development

Founded by ExxonMobil and United Way in 2002, the United Way Bright Beginnings initiative is a model early education program designed so that children achieve developmental milestones (social, emotional, physical, and cognitive) through better quality child care. The program aims to improve child care quality for centers serving and staffed by some of the low-income communities in the Houston area through intensive staff training and professional development, comprehensive curriculum approaches, appropriate indoor and outdoor equipment, leadership development, and parental involvement.

Over the past seven years, 25 child care centers have received extensive teacher training, consultations twice a month, leadership training in cohorts of directors and teachers, wage supplementation for teachers and directors meeting experience and education requirements, and indoor and outdoor equipment. The comprehensive approach has created a landscape in which young children with few means are entitled to a higher quality of life by providing positive and emotional environments priming them for learning. Central to these outcomes is a pedagogy for empowering practices for the children and adults. We have supported learning opportunities for teachers in a field traditionally economically depressed and opportunities for administrators who are overwhelmed by the demands of their jobs to improve the leadership skills required to perform their duties.

Our program has created leadership support circles with time in a place of refuge for directors to reflect on the nature and demands of their job. In the words of one of our facilitative consultants, "This act is much like attempting to extract the head engineer from a moving train." At these retreats, our directors were introduced to a leadership capacities framework based on the work of Linda Lambert and Debra Ren-Etta Sullivan, augmented by other leadership development theories and nurtured to develop the kind of skills necessary for effective leadership. This created the platform with trusting relationships and self-awareness to benefit from participating in wider professional development conferences to enhance their knowledge and skills. By the end of the sixth year, our directors are reaching out to the wider Houston community to provide leadership in forming more support circles for directors.

Simultaneously, we formed cohort circles with promising Bright Beginnings teachers based on the ages of the children they work with. Paralleling the pedagogy used with the directors, this opportunity for professional development sprang from our belief that early childhood teachers deserve extended time for reflection and study, individual support and opportunities for collaboration, and participation in a learning community that challenges them to take intellectual and emotional risks in order to deepen their own learning and improve their daily practice with young children and their families.

In keeping with the research of Fleet and Patterson (2001) we recognize staff as empowered learners who build their working knowledge through spirals of engagement with many aspects of early childhood philosophy and practice over time.

Our goals with the teacher cohort project are:

- to enliven the spirits of teachers and strengthen their identities as professionals with an important contribution to make to children, families, and the early care and education field;
- to deepen teachers' work with children, emphasizing a protocol for reflection and critical thinking as the foundations for high-quality teaching and care giving;
- to enhance teacher observation and communication skills so that their documentation of children's conversations and activities becomes a resource for attending to the details of children's thinking, not only their behavior; also using documentation to develop curriculum and deeper relationships with the children's families;
- to engage teacher confidence and competence in collaborative study of early childhood professional literature;
- to strengthen and expand the leadership that teachers bring to their early childhood programs and to UWBB;
- to develop early childhood classrooms that will serve as models for the larger early care and learning professional community.

The University of Houston Institute for Urban Education has evaluated the results of our program for six years, documenting change in classroom quality, teacher retention, and teacher and director views of their centers. Scores on our assessment with the ITERS and ECERS tool have made substantial improvements. Not only have the children benefited greatly from our efforts at quality improvement, but we have seen positive outcomes and leadership development with the teachers, directors, and UWBB consultants who have been engaged with our cohort work and wider professional development efforts.

We are convinced that the foundation for the academic, social-emotional, and career development we are seeking for the children and families in our program can be summarized as follows:

Love yourself.
Develop a confident identity as a member of a community and as a learner.
Love your work.
Have a curious mind, notice details, build relationships, plan and respond with intention and joy.
Love life.
Become open to possibilities, emotionally and intellectually engaged, eager to communicate and live fully.

For more information contact United Way of Greater Houston—713-685-2300, www.unitedwayhouston.org.

Reprinted with permission of United Way Bright Beginnings, Houston, TX; www.unitedwayhouston.org.

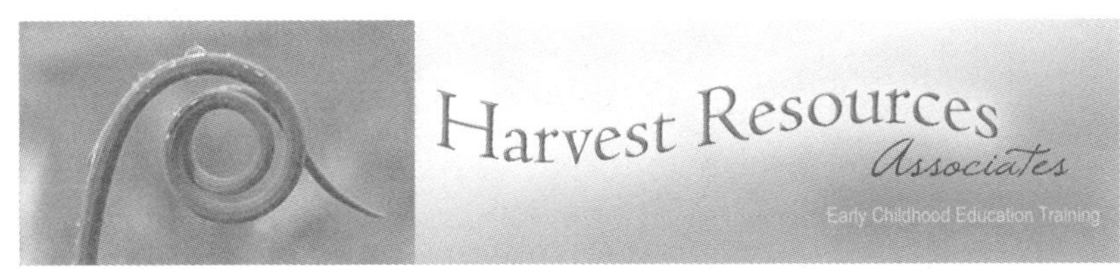

Harvest Resources Associates: Resources for Early Childhood Professional Development

Typical approaches to early childhood professional development emphasize techniques, adopting commercial curriculum, and focusing on limited views of outcomes through checklists and assessments. To counter this, Margie Carter and Deb Curtis have founded Harvest Resources Associates to inspire early childhood educators to engage fully in their own learning. In this era of standardization and prescription, we stand for creative and critical thinking. We strongly believe that high quality care and education for young children and their families requires leaders and practitioners who are able to think through the dynamics of their work with a larger purpose and vision than a checklist or quick fix. We believe our profession must expand definitions of quality and stop accepting mediocrity as the best we can offer children, families, and teachers. Despite the many barriers and current resource limitations, we encourage early educators to think big, be visionary, and take responsibility for transforming current limitations.

- We believe directors and teachers and children should be emotionally and intellectually engaged with each other in learning.
- We believe directors and teachers deserve the time and resources to nourish their hearts and challenge their thinking.
- We believe seeking diverse perspectives is central to education for democracy. When directors and teachers become thoughtful, competent decision makers, they take leadership to transform and advance the profession.
- We design trainings and resources to actively engage professionals in ideas and reflective practices, which bring theory to life and real life to theory.

Whatever the specific content focus, our approach to professional development emphasizes reflection, collaboration, transformation, and leadership development. We offer a Thinking Lens to guide this process. We work with program directors to identify the values, vision, and goals they have for their program and then help to design an approach to professional development that will express their vision, referencing a view of quality that includes but goes beyond compliance issues, standards, and scores associated with quality rating systems.

Online Resources

Our website regularly features discussion questions, activities, and examples of innovative programs that encourage critical thinking and self-reflection to provoke ongoing professional development in a variety of settings. A selection of resources that are compatible with our philosophical and pedagogical approach are also available for purchase on our website.

Leadership Development

Because we envision a cadre of diverse leaders informing, promoting, and supporting reflective practices, we actively recruit and mentor new leaders to work with us. They serve as facilitators in our Institutes and join us in gatherings for ongoing professional development. We refer requests for training to these associates to add to their leadership opportunities.

Consultations

Guided by a program's vision, consultations focus on examining administrative systems and the physical and social emotional environment to align with values, as well as documenting children's work to plan curriculum, and using documentation to assess the effectiveness of program practices and meet requirements. We follow up our consultations with collaborative meetings or workshops to debrief and share ideas and discoveries.

Workshops and Seminars

Short workshops are effective only if they are a part of a larger, ongoing focus for professional development. Our workshops promote visionary thinking and a view of quality that transcends current practices. They include a mixture of presentations with visual elements, case studies, and hands-on experiences to practice applying the concepts introduced. Our workshops usually include some kind of music, poetry, storytelling, or improvisational theater. We provide participants multiple opportunities to reflect on their current thinking and experiences and ask them to engage with group discussions, stories, and props to think through ideas and understandings. They conclude by defining their next steps.

Two- and Three-day Institutes with Facilitators

Institutes offer an opportunity to explore a particular focus of ideas over the course of two or three days. During this time we create a learning environment and pedagogy that parallel what we hope participants will take back and create in their work settings.

We help the sponsoring organization identify facilitators for the Institute. Facilitators support a small group working as a mini-learning community during all sessions of the Institute.

Institutes typically result in significant transformation for the participants. Ongoing projects are launched from the Institute as program staff make commitments and design structures for follow-through in their classrooms, workplaces, and communities.

Cohort Projects

Cohort projects provide expanded opportunities for Institute participants to continue to reflect, study, and collaborate together. Small groups work together to challenge and support each other to take intellectual and emotional risks in order to deepen their own learning and develop as leaders. Cohorts meet regularly (virtually or in person) over a year or longer to engage in critical reflection, to study and apply professional readings, and to implement a Thinking Lens for their everyday work and their ongoing professional development. Through work with their cohort, professionals are challenged to apply what they are learning to their actual work settings; they regularly return to their cohort to discuss and evaluate their outcomes.

For more information, support, and resources visit www.ecetrainers.com.

Hildebrandt Learning Centers: Reinventing Our Organization and Our Approaches to Professional Development

Hildebrandt Learning Centers, LLC (HLC), is a regional family-owned child care management company that provides high-quality child care for employers and other sponsors who strive to offer a "family friendly" atmosphere at their workplace. In our nineteenth year, we recognized that with our growth to over forty early learning centers in several states, we needed to revisit our vision, management sytems, and approaches to providing ongoing professional development for our administrators and teachers. Meeting around the "kitchen table," our expanded management team asked, "How do we maintain the highest quality care as measured by NAEYC and state QRS systems and expand our organization's mission to a vision that includes our particular passions and views of how children and teachers learn best?" We struggled with ideas about how to maintain the intimacy of a small company that needs to respond to our midsize realities. We agreed that our growth had to be thoughtful and intentional if we were to maintain quality and provide the support that our centers deserve. As we talked, our management team experienced the discomfort of re-examining job responsibilities. To reinvent ourselves we needed to relinquish control over existing systems and develop new communication and trust. We decided that our company motto, "Touching Minds, Shaping Futures," should be accompanied by the question, "Is it good for children and families?" to guide our every decision. This "dance of attunement" between our values, mission, and management systems continues today.

Leadership Development for Directors

A central challenge for us has been designing a system to engage everyone in our organization in reflective practices, from our home administrative office to our multisites currently consisting of 40 directors and 750 employees partnering with families in the shared care of 3,500 children. For us this has meant rethinking director support and training so that directors can better lead their centers with a vision. We began with a director self-reflection process to analyze needs. Our directors made it clear they needed training that was meaningful and applicable. We took the step of eliminating long travel days for training and set up regional director groups to provide smaller group instruction, networking, and reflection. We decided to scaffold the directors' leadership role as trainers who would lead their centers in a yearlong professional development focus on authentic partnerships with families. Toward this end we held a series of interactive trainings with directors centered on Brazelton's Touchpoints Model (2000) so that our directors could make the Touchpoints principles central to their conversations, observations, feedback, and meetings with their staff. These principles now guide us in answering the question, "Is it good for children and families?" The Touchpoints Practitioner Assumptions provide the framework for our approach to professional development:

- each practitioner is the expert in the field;
- practitioners want to be confident and competent;
- practitioners need the kind of support and respect we are asking them to give to families;
- practitioners need time to reflect on their work.

Professional Development for Practitioners

Ultimately, we acknowledge the quality of care in our centers rests in the hands of the practitioner that "walks the talk" of our mission each day. We had to take a careful look at what we were doing in our staff training and ask ourselves some challenging questions. How do we assure the content and quality of ongoing professional development that offers the necessary tools, strategies, and dispositions that are characteristic of exemplary early childhood educators? How do we affect the greatest number of staff in a fiscally responsible manner across hundreds of miles? We recognized that sending someone to do on-site training at any given center supported only a few employees at a time; likewise, regional trainings were typically underattended due to staffing issues on any given day. Our Program and Curriculum management team brainstormed the "what ifs" and "how coulds." What if we use the reduced ratios of naptime? How could training be provided during the day rather than the evening in order to be respectful to our practitioners' time and commitment? How could technology provide a "hands on" training experience that is meaningful, thought provoking, and engaging? What would this look like? What do we know our staff responds well to? How could our staff be held accountable for professional development and not just "do the hours"? Exploring a range of answers to these questions led us to the creation of a new format for providing professional development for all our staff.

We've invented the NAPINAR™ as a thirty-minute image-rich PowerPoint presentation with content related to our mission, NAEYC, and early learning standards. The Napinar is broadcast live with voiceover between 1:00 and 2:00 p.m. via Live Meeting software. A poem or quote provides inspiration for the theme. Each presentation is focused on one BIG idea illustrated with photographs of best practices from our own centers to serve as provocations. The BIG idea is spelled out using words and pictures. One week prior to the Napinar, we give directors a guidesheet with ideas for supporting their staff to put the content into practice; we also send staff a choice of journal articles to read as preparation for the content in our thirty-minute presentation. In order to receive "official" training credit for participating in a Napinar, practitioners must submit a "Project of Understanding" that documents in words or pictures their implementation of three strategies related to the BIG idea of the Napinar.

A Sample Napinar

Our yearlong professional development focus on Family Partnerships was divided into succinct BIG ideas. Thus, the BIG idea of one Napinar was family-friendly environments and this was themed as a quilt, piecing together ways to authentically partner with families. Our agenda followed along these lines:

Our goals for family partnerships
Reflective questions:
  What do you know about yourself in relating to families?
  What do you know about families?
Poem about quilts and how they represent families
Overview of NAEYC Standards on working with families
Slides with examples from our centers that illustrate each of the letters in the word FAMILIES:
  F – first impressions; creating a center identity;
  A – acquire family information and actively use to adapt program;
  M – meet in comfortable spaces;
  I – interest families with intriguing objects;
  L – learn about children's learning together as partners;
  I – involve families in meaningful ways, not just chores;
  E – every day seek conversations to build relationships;
  S – show families they can be safe and secure with us.

Review Project of Understanding assignments:

Draw a floor plan of your classroom indicating where you have existing family friendly elements

Implement three new strategies and send in documentation of what you have done

Final slide of available resources to utilize

Discoveries, Lessons Learned, and Challenges

For us, the Napinar holds significant potential for staff development in a multisite organization. Directors report that Napinars generate a "buzz" and excitement that are immediate, palpable, measureable, and evident. For instance, within minutes of viewing the Family Friendly Environments Napinar, directors reported that staff were busy in their classrooms rearranging and creating welcoming areas. The number of Projects of Understanding submitted caught us by surprise and they were as diverse as our staff, ranging from photo essays, handwritten dialogue, use of construction paper, scrapbooking, and their own PowerPoint presentations. Examples of strategies implemented included revamping sign in areas, getting adult-sized seating, including more family photographs in the environment, rethinking drop-off and pickup time conversations.

A thirty-minute Napinar has the potential to inspire staff, but we must continue to find ways to sustain their engagement. With the goal of continuous quality improvement, our Professional Development Director works with an overall professional development plan with Napinars as a central feature. Each component balances our core values with research, standards, and hands-on strategies to nurture teacher dispositions that sustain high-quality environments and interactions. Most important, we've seen that with the implementation of our structure to develop directors as leaders and offer regular Napinars, our staff is now engaging in reflective practice, gaining confidence, and utilizing strategies to revitalize not only classroom spaces, but also themselves as practitioners.

Reprinted with permission of Hildebrandt Learning Centers, Dallas, PA; www.hildebrandtlearningcenters.com.

Community Collaborations to Address Inequity and Disempowerment

Across the United States, lab schools are shutting their doors because their colleges can no longer subsidize them. The Francis Institute at Metropolitan Community College–Penn Valley in Kansas City, Missouri, took a different approach and handed their building over to Plaza de Niños, which has added new life, laughter, and diversity to the halls of Francis Institute.

In Arizona, a community collaboration called the Tucson Children's Project came together to encourage early educators and families to join forces in advocating for their children. Their Hopes and Dreams Project was so successful it launched an offspring, the Wall Project.

Francis Institute: Plaza de Niños una Asociación de la Comunidad

La comunidad de la educación temprana en Kansas City tiene una nueva y emocionante comunidad de colaboración que esperamos pueda inspirar a otros. Desde 1990 Francis Institute por el Desarrollo del Niño y la Juventud en el Metropolitan Community College (MCC)-Penn valley ha subsidiado un laboratorio en la escuela para complementar su programa en el crecimiento y desarrollo del niño y un Centro de Recursos en educación temprana y edad escolar. En una difícil situación económica en el 2008, el colegio decidió que ya no podía ofrecer este subsidio para el laboratorio de la escuela.

Plaza de Niños (PDN) un programa bilingüe en educación temprana acreditado nacionalmente, estaba pasando por significantes necesidades en sus instalaciones en el verano 2008. La Directora de PDN Alexis Delaney describe su situación de esta manera. "Como un programa sin fines de lucro, organismo con recursos financieros limitados, Plaza de Niños ha demostrado a la comunidad que puede ofrecer calidad en la educación temprana a pesar de los desafíos físicos de nuestro edificio. Nuestro ingenio fué una constante prueba. Cualquier logro pequeño nos unió y fortaleció nuestras relaciones. En agosto del 2008, mientras que todavía permaneciamos en la antigua ubicación, fuimos reacreditados por NAEYC. No está mal para un programa ubicado en un edificio con múltiples filtraciones con techos viejos, las unidades del aire acondicionado funcionaban esporádicamente y aún mantener el 80% de niños inscritos de familias humildes y trabajadoras".

Las preocupaciones inmediatas de MCC, con su falta de recursos para el laboratorio de la escuela, y las necesidades de las instalaciones de PDN, esto fué una pequeña parte de un problema mucho más grande para las dos instituciones. A pesar que el Instituto Francis y MCC-Penn Valley se encuentra dentro de los límites del barrio del Westside, la casa cultural de la comunidad latina, la comunidad latina fué lamentablemente insuficientemente representada en la inscripción y la dotación del personal en el Colegio. El Instituto reconoció la gravedad de esta cuestión durante una sesión de planificación que mostró la comunidad latina como el más rápido crecimiento de la población en Kansas City, pero tambien la más alta tasa de deserción escolar en las escuelas públicas.

Para abordar estas cuestiones Francis Institute y MCC-Penn Valley entró en una asociación con Plaza de Niños y su empresa matriz, Guadalupe Centers, para dar un techo a Plaza de Niños en el Francis Institute. Porque Plaza de Niños no podría solventar los costos de ocupación, el colegio renunció a los costos de la propuesta del valor en el cuál PDN ofreciera a los estudiantes del colegio el desarrollo del crecimiento del niño, y el cuidado de los niños para los estudiantes de la universidad, hacer de ésto un gran-gran logro para ambos. Como Directora de PDN Delaney lo describe, "Está colaboración con MCC y Francis Institute ha infundido nueva vida a nuestro programa. Tenemos la ventaja de una instalación maravillosa que nos permite concentrarnos en los niños y en sus familias. El personal exuda un sentido de orgullo en sus aulas para sustituir a la frustración de trabajar en torno a las cuestiones de nuestro antiguo edificio. Nuestras inscripciones han aumentado en unos pocos meses. Diariamente nos encontramos con más oportunidades para la asociación de diferentes formas con el colegio y la comunidad. Para las familias de nuestra comunidad que trabajan en múltiples trabajos y sueñan con un título universitario para sus hijos, esta asociación es una puerta abierta. La asociación tiene mucho que ofrecernos. Es como explorar en el espacio ultraterrestre. No sabemos todo lo que hay afuera, pero estamos apasionados por la oportunidad de investigar!"

Plaza de Niños ha infundido nueva vida y risa en los pasillos de Francis Istitute. Se han sumergido los pasillos y los salones de clase en su rica tradición, y han aumentado considerablemente a la deliciosa diversidad del Instituto. La asociación ha sido positiva para todos los involucrados y representa una gran promesa para el futuro del Colegio y para la comunidad latina.

Francis Institute: Plaza de Niños Community Partnership

Kansas City's early childhood community has an exciting new community partnership that we hope can inspire others. Since 1990 Francis Institute for Child and Youth Development at Metropolitan Community College (MCC)–Penn Valley has subsidized a lab school to complement its child growth and development program, and early childhood and school age Resource Center. With difficult economic conditions in 2008, the College decided it could no longer offer this subsidy for the lab school.

Meanwhile, Plaza de Niños (PDN), a nationally accredited bilingual early childhood program, was experiencing significant facility needs approaching the summer of 2008. PDN Director Alexis Delaney describes their situation this way: "As a program of a not-for-profit agency with limited financial resources, Plaza de Niños proved that it could offer quality early education to the community in spite of the physical challenges of our aging building. Our resourcefulness was constantly tested. Any small accomplishment united us and strengthened our relationships. In August 2008, while still at the former location, we were reaccredited by the NAEYC. Not bad for a program housed in a building with multiple leaks from an old roof, air-conditioning units that functioned sporadically, and a client base of more than 80% of children enrolled from working poor families."

The immediate concerns for MCC with their lack of resources for the lab school, and the facility needs for PDN, were but a small part of a much larger issue for the two institutions. Even though the Francis Institute and MCC–Penn Valley were located within the boundaries of the Westside neighborhood, the cultural home of the Latino community, the Latino community was woefully underrepresented in enrollment and staffing figures at the College. The Institute recognized the seriousness of that issue during a planning session that showed the Latino community as the fastest growing population in Kansas City, but also with the highest dropout rate in the public schools.

To address these issues Francis Institute and MCC–Penn Valley entered into a partnership with Plaza de Niños and their parent company, Guadalupe Centers, to house Plaza de Niños in the Francis Institute. Because PDN couldn't afford occupancy costs, the college waived those costs for the value proposition in which PDN would offer student internships for the child growth and development division, and drop-in child care for College students, making this a win-win proposition for both. As PDN Director Delaney describes it, "This partnership with MCC and Francis Institute has breathed new life into our program. We have the advantage of a wonderful facility that allows us to concentrate on children and their families. The staff exudes a sense of pride in their classrooms, replacing the frustration of working around the issues of our former aging building. Our enrollment has almost doubled in a few short months. Daily we find more opportunities for partnering in different ways with the college and the community. For the families of our community who work multiple jobs and dream of a college degree for their children, this partnership is an open door. The partnership has so much to offer us. It's like exploring outer space. We don't know everything that's out there, but we're passionate about the opportunity to investigate!" Plaza de Niños has infused new life and laughter into the halls of Francis Institute. They have immersed the hallways and classrooms in their rich tradition, and have added significantly to the delightful diversity of the Institute. The partnership has been positive for everyone involved and holds great promise for the future of the College and the Latino community.

Tucson Children's Project

Celebrating The Potential Of All Children

Tucson Children's Project: The Hopes & Dreams Project and the Wall Project

The Hopes & Dreams Project is an initiative of the Tucson Children's Project, which is an action advocacy initiative of the Southern Arizona Association for the Education of Young Children (SAzAEYC). The intention of this project is to provide opportunities for families and teachers to share the hopes and dreams they have for the young children in their lives and to create documentation (both in early childhood classrooms and for a proposed traveling exhibit) of these hopes and dreams.

We hope the documentation of these hopes and dreams for children will:

- give greater visibility to children, families, and teachers in early childhood programs and schools in our Southern Arizona communities;
- communicate with strength and clarity the vital role of high-quality early childhood education for the future learning of all children;
- improve the educational possibilities for young children in a state that is ranked 37th in the nation for the care and well-being of its young children and last in support of education;
- deepen relationships between families, schools, communities, and state and local organizations, agencies, and institutions;
- increase the development of other advocacy efforts that will improve the educational possibilities for young children and their families in Southern Arizona;
- encourage educators and families to join forces in advocating for their children in order to realize the hopes and dreams they have for them.

As we conducted interviews and reflected on this project, we posed the following questions for reflection:

- Is collecting and communicating the hopes and dreams of parents and teachers for their young children a worthwhile and appropriate effort?
- What do the children think about the hopes and dreams their parents and their teachers have for them? Do these hopes and dreams put personal, social, cultural, or educational pressure on them?
- How do we build relationships of trust? What particular efforts, knowledge, abilities, and skills are necessary in collecting the hopes and dreams of families for their children?
- How can teachers share their own hopes and dreams for children?
- Does this collection imply that there are right and wrong hopes and dreams to have for children?
- What is the impact of having hopes and dreams on the living of life?
- How does the Hopes & Dreams Project collaboration represent our collective voices?

As an outgrowth of the perceived value of the Hopes and Dreams, we have begun a new endeavor, The Wall Project. We are seeking a way for the serious barriers to child well-being in our community to become more visible and hope that through studying walls we will be able to identify, confront, and ultimately break through some of the many "walls" that keep children in our world from realizing what we—their families, teachers, and friends—hope and dream for them. The human rights issues connected with walls are huge, and these issues will likely be a big part of what could bring us together as Border States.

For more information please contact: Pauline Baker at paulinembaker@yahoo.com or Paula McPheeters at mcpheeters4@cox.net.

Reprinted with permission of the Tucson Children's Project, Southern Arizona Association for the Education of Young Children, Tucson, AZ; http://sazaeyc.org.

Appendixes

Assessment and Evaluation Tools

Appendix 1 Assessing Systems
Appendix 2 Ten Dimensions of Organizational Climate Assessment Tool
Appendix 3 Model Work Standards Assessment Tool
Appendix 4 Program Administration Scale (PAS)
Appendix 5 Teacher and Director Evaluation Materials
Appendix 6 Sample Licenser Self-Evaluation Tool

Planning Tools

Appendix 7 Strategic Planning Form
Appendix 8 Calculating the Full Cost of Quality Care
Appendix 9 Continuity of Care: Barriers and Solutions

Staff Development Tools

Appendix 10 Conference Attendance Planning Form
Appendix 11 Observation Form for Visiting Other Programs
Appendix 12 Conflict Resolution Samples
Appendix 13 Writing Learning Stories
Appendix 14 A Thinking Lens for Reflection and Inquiry
Appendix 15 Use the Thinking Lens to Analyze and Write Learning Stories

Appendix 1 Assessing Systems

Assessing Your Systems, Policies, and Allocation of Resources

Value we want reflected:______________________________
(e.g., Relationships at the center of all we do)

	What we do now	What we should reconsider	Barriers to overcome	Goals and next steps
Systems and policies with families • Enrollment policies; systems for communicating and working with families • Tours for prospective families • Enrollment and "move-ups" • Paperwork systems • Orientation of new families • Communication systems • Meetings with families • Conferences about children • Resources for families • Other?				

Assessing Your Systems, Policies, and Allocation of Resources

Value we want reflected:________________________________
(e.g., Relationships at the center of all we do)

	What we do now	What we should reconsider	Barriers to overcome	Goals and next steps
Systems and policies with staff • Interviewing, hiring, orientation, probation • Paperwork systems • Mentoring and support • Team, staff meetings (scheduling and focus) • Planning time and requirements • Professional development • Working with families • Accountability, evaluation • Other?				

Assessing Your Allocation of Resources

Value we want reflected:______________________________

(e.g., Relationships at the center of all we do)

	What we do now	What we should reconsider	Barriers to overcome	Goals and next steps
Space resources and appearance • Cross-age opportunities for children • Adult work room • Adult lounge • Meeting area • Supply storage areas • Maintenance and tools • Technology area • Food area • Outdoor areas • Other?				

Assessing Your Allocation of Resources

Value we want reflected:________________________________

(e.g., Relationships at the center of all we do)

	What we do now	What we should reconsider	Barriers to overcome	Goals and next steps
Use of time as a resource • Staffing patterns • Agendas for team meetings • Agendas for staff meetings • Agendas for family meetings • Agendas for conferences with families • Retreats, renewals, and celebrations • Release time for special projects • Advocacy • Other?				

Assessing Your Allocation of Resources

Value we want reflected:______________________________
(e.g., Relationships at the center of all we do)

	What we do now	What we should reconsider	Barriers to overcome	Goals and next steps
Use of money • Nontraditional renovations • Nontraditional vendors • Budget for meetings • Budget for planning time • Budget for conferences with families • Nontraditional staff development opportunities • Budget for staff excursions • Budget for advocacy work • Budget for special projects • Other?				

Appendix 2 Ten Dimensions of Organizational Climate Assessment Tool

For a number of years we have adapted the work of Paula Jorde Bloom to create an assessment tool programs can use to get a "weather report" on their program (see description of this strategy at the end of chapter 5).

Ten Dimensions of Organizational Climate	
Dimension	**Definition**
Collegiality	Extent to which staff are friendly and supportive and trust one another; peer cohesion and esprit de corps of the group.
Professional Growth	The degree of emphasis placed on personal and professional growth.
Supervisor Support	Measures the presence of facilitative leadership that provides encouragement, support, and clear expectations.
Clarity	The extent to which policies, procedures, and responsibilities are clearly defined and communicated.
Reward System	The degree of fairness and equity in the distribution of pay, benefits, and opportunities for advancement.
Decision Making	The degree of autonomy given to the staff and the extent to which they are involved in center-wide decisions.
Goal Consensus	The degree to which the staff agree on the philosophy, goals, and objectives of the center.
Task Orientation	The emphasis placed on good planning, efficiency, and getting the job done.
Physical Setting	The extent to which the spatial arrangement of the center helps or hinders staff in carrying out their responsibilities.
Innovativeness	The extent to which the center adapts to change and encourages staff to find creative ways to solve problems.

Adapted from *Blueprint for Action: Achieving Center-Based Change through Staff Development* (p. 190) by Paula Jorde Bloom. Lake Forest, IL: New Horizons. Copyright © 2005 by Paula Jorde Bloom. Reprinted with permission.

Appendix 3 Model Work Standards Assessment Tool

With the input of hundreds of teachers, directors, and providers from around the country, the Model Work Standards have been developed to complete the picture of a high-quality early care and education program by articulating the components of an adult work environment that enables teachers to do their jobs well. The Standards are divided into thirteen categories, ranging from Wages and Benefits to Professional Development, Diversity, and the Physical Setting. You can use the Standards as an assessment tool, rating each item as Consistently Met, Partially Met or Unmet/High Priority, or Partially Met or Unmet/Low Priority. A fuller description of the complete Model Work Standards assessment tool along with guidelines for its use can be found in the publication *Creating Better Child Care Jobs: Model Work Standards for Teaching Staff in Center-Based Child Care*, available for $10 from the Center for the Child Care Workforce (www.ccw.org).

The following pages offer a few extracts from the Model Work Standards to give you a flavor of only the first few of the Standards in four of the thirteen categories. Guidelines for their use include these ideas:

1. Look at each Standard area and determine if all staff agree that your program adequately addresses this issue. Identify what you currently have that satisfies staff and what you want to work for right now. If not everyone agrees, it will be important to work toward understanding why the staff have varying perspectives on this subject.
2. Ask each staff person to identify one or more of the Standards that they want to achieve. Rank the top one to three priorities that are agreed upon by all staff members. Taking your top priority, use the worksheet provided to develop your plan of action. You may want to start with a Standard that will be fairly easy to achieve but important to you. For example, increasing your number of paid sick days. For those child care teachers who are represented by a union, this process can be used to improve the current union contract.
3. Determine the cost for each of your top priorities. It is important to place a dollar amount on the various goals you have set. Some programs decide how much money they can allocate or will raise to make changes (for example, $5,000 for the coming year) and then select their top priority.

4. Develop a plan and a timeline. This will include whose support and what resources you will need to accomplish your goal.
5. Document progress. This will help you evaluate, learn from, and adapt strategies to sustain continued efforts.
6. Celebrate and broadcast your accomplishments. Every victory, no matter how large or small, moves us closer to our goal of achieving good child care jobs.

Consistently Met	Partially Met or Unmet/ High Priority	Partially Met or Unmet/ Low Priority	Category: Communication, Team Building, and Staff Meetings	Essential
			Proposed changes in policies and procedures are circulated in writing to all staff, and a sufficient period is allowed for meaningful staff input and response before changes are adopted or implemented. Paid staff meetings engaging all staff are held at least once a month. Staff meetings are primarily for improving program quality, enhancing staff communication, and promoting professional development of staff. Staff have input into the agenda of staff meetings, the agenda is distributed in advance of meetings, and a written record of the meeting is kept and posted. Opportunities exist for teachers to work collaboratively on projects, share resources, and solve problems together.	

Consistently Met	Partially Met or Unmet/ High Priority	Partially Met or Unmet/ Low Priority	Category: Decision Making and Problem Solving	Essential
			Teaching staff make decisions regarding daily activities, room arrangements, and other matters that affect their day-to-day practice. Teaching staff share decision making with the administration in situations where decisions impact their work life. These decisions include but are not limited to staffing for paid leave time, scheduling, rotation of responsibilities, ordering materials for the classroom, screening and interviewing new staff, and managing staff turnover with consideration for the needs of children and staff. Staff are engaged in setting program goals, identifying priorities to meet the goals, and measuring progress.	

Consistently Met	Partially Met or Unmet/ High Priority	Partially Met or Unmet/ Low Priority	Category: Professional Support	Essential
			Staff have access to petty cash funds for immediate consumable supplies, and a system is in place for requesting funds when needs are apparent.	
			Staff have input in determining the program's operating budget for supplies and equipment.	
			Professional development plans, as well as recruitment and promotion practices, ensure that peer support is available to all staff, from entry level to those with the greatest education and experience.	

Consistently Met	Partially Met or Unmet/ High Priority	Partially Met or Unmet/ Low Priority	Category: Physical Setting	Essential
			There is adequate classroom space that is designed with the developmental needs of children in mind. Staff have input into room arrangements and are provided resources, training, and support to improve classroom space.	
			Classrooms have comfortable places for adults to sit and be with children.	
			Staff are encouraged to add artifacts, photographs, and other objects that reflect their lives as well as the lives of the children.	
			A staff room or designated area is available which allows for staff interaction and a relatively quiet place for reflection and breaks.	
			Staff have a safe place to put personal belongings and a work area for preparation and planning.	

Appendix 4 Program Administration Scale (PAS)

Overview of the Program Administration Scale

Rationale

The genesis of the *Program Administration Scale* (PAS) was the growing professional consensus that early childhood program quality should be viewed through a broader lens than only that of the classroom learning environment, and that it should incorporate multi-sources data collection methods including interview, document review, and observation. While there are several instruments available to measure the quality of teacher-child interactions and the quality of the classroom instructional practices, there does not currently exist a valid and reliable instrument that solely measures the administrative practices of an early childhood program. The Program Administration Scale was designed to fill that void.

Research has consistently found that overall administrative practices are crucial for ensuring high-quality outcomes for children and families (Bloom, 1989, 1996a, 1996b; Cost, Quality, and Child Outcomes Study Team, 1995; Kagan and Bowman, 1997; Phillips, Mekos, Scarr, McCartney, and Abbott-Shim, 2000; Whitebook, Howes, and Phillips, 1990). Without quality systems in place at the organizational level, high-quality interactions and learning environments at the classroom level cannot be sustained.

The *Program Administrative Scale* (PAS) was designed to serve as a reliable and easy-to-administer tool for measuring the overall quality of administrative practices of early care and education programs and as a useful guide to improve programs. The development of the PAS began with a review of the literature on best practices that foster collaboration, diversity, cultural sensitivity, and social justice.

The instrument includes 25 items clustered in 10 subscales that measure both leadership and management functions of center-based early childhood programs. Leadership functions relate to the broad view of helping an organization clarify and affirm values, set goals, articulate a vision, and chart a course of action to achieve that vision. Management functions relate to the actual orchestration of tasks and the setting up of systems to carry out the organizational mission (Bloom 2003).

Designed for early childhood program administrators, researchers, monitoring personnel, and quality enhancement facilitators, the PAS was constructed to complement the widely used observation-based classroom environment rating scales designed by Harms, Clifford, and Cryer (1998, 2003). Both the PAS and the environment rating scale (ECERS-R, ITERS-R) measure quality on a 7-point scale, and both generate a profile to guide program improvement efforts. If used together, these instruments provide a focused look at best practices at the classroom level and the broad view of program quality from an organizational perspective.

The Program Administration Scale (PAS) Profile

Program name: ______________________ Date: ____________

Subscales	Items	1	2	3	4	5	6	7
Human Resources Development	1. Staff Orientation							
	2. Supervision and Performance Appraisal							
	3. Staff Development							
Personnel Cost and Allocation	4. Compensation							
	5. Benefits							
	6. Staffing Patterns and Scheduling							
Center Operations	7. Facilities Management							
	8. Risk Management							
	9. Internal Communications							
Child Assessment	10. Screening and Identification of Special Needs							
	11. Assessment in Support of Learning							
Fiscal Management	12. Budget Planning							
	13. Accounting Practices							
Program Planning and Evaluation	14. Program Evaluation							
	15. Strategic Planning							
Family Partnerships	16. Family Communications							
	17. Family Support and Involvement							
Marketing and Public Relations	18. External Communications							
	19. Community Outreach							
Technology	20. Technological Resources							
	21. Use of Technology							
Staff Qualifications	22. Administrator							
	23. Lead Teacher							
	24. Teacher							
	25. Apprentice Teacher/Aide							

Total PAS Score ________ ÷ **Number of items** ________ = **Average PAS Item Score** ________

Appendix 5 Teacher and Director Evaluation Materials

These pages include examples of evaluation tools that can be used both as self-assessments and to assess a director or staff member's job performance.

Possible Teacher Behaviors

Which is most typical for you?

1. When children are engaged in self-directed play, I am
   - ☐ doing assessment checklists
   - ☐ doing housekeeping chores
   - ☐ taking children aside to teach them skills
   - ☐ keeping an eye on children who tend to get into trouble
   - ☐ joining in so I can help them focus on skills
   - ☐ closely observing and analyzing the flow of individual and group play
   - ☐ interacting by describing what I see them doing
   - ☐ gathering documentation with notes, quotes, work samples, sketches, photos

2. My approach to parent communications is
   - ☐ reminding them of our policies
   - ☐ posting a daily schedule, curriculum plans, and written daily report on activities
   - ☐ making sure children have a theme project to take home each day
   - ☐ writing in the monthly newsletter
   - ☐ holding conferences once or twice a year
   - ☐ conducting home visits once or twice a year
   - ☐ having general conversations at the beginning or end of the day
   - ☐ regularly telling stories of specific conversations, ideas, and activities of a child
   - ☐ sending home a periodic checklist, progress report, or "happy gram"
   - ☐ regularly sending home anecdotal notes
   - ☐ making individual photo-book stories of a child's thinking, skills, or activities
   - ☐ creating visual documentation displays that analyze the significance of the ongoing activities within the classroom

3. To fulfill school requirements for curriculum plans, assessments, and documentation, I usually
   - ☐ fill out all the required forms (sometimes without much meaning for me)
   - ☐ post my schedule and weekly lesson plans
   - ☐ have a box of miscellaneous notes, work samples, forms, and checklists
   - ☐ have well-organized files for each child and program component requirements
   - ☐ write regular anecdotal observation notes and collect photos and work samples in a portfolio for each child
   - ☐ involve children in choosing work samples for their portfolios
   - ☐ collaborate with my coworkers in regular analysis of children's development and emergent curriculum
   - ☐ make books and visual displays of children's evolving ideas as well as curriculum projects
   - ☐ see myself as an engaged collector and broadcaster of the unfolding stories in the life of our program
   - ☐ analyze and translate the stories of our classroom into required documentation

4. My approach to keeping children aware of their learning is
   - ☐ using praise and stickers as a reward for good behavior and learning new skills
   - ☐ telling children what they need to be learning
   - ☐ letting the children know I will be having conferences with their parents
   - ☐ involving children in portfolio development and parent conferences
   - ☐ telling the children stories about what I see them doing and thinking
   - ☐ writing down and reading stories of what I see the children doing and thinking
   - ☐ making audio or video recordings of their activities and playing them back
   - ☐ sketching and taking photos with descriptive details and quotes to show in book or documentation display formats

5. My approach to developing myself as a professional is
   - ☐ attending trainings required by my agency or school
   - ☐ trying to sample a wide variety of seminars and workshops
   - ☐ setting priorities and focusing on particular goals
   - ☐ looking for useful ideas and resources outside the ECE profession
   - ☐ continually cultivating an ability to describe what I understand about such things as the natural world, art, science, and human interactions

- ☐ regularly reading stories by observers of children
- ☐ spending time enhancing my writing skills through such things as keeping a journal and writing letters, stories, or articles

6. Overall my primary role with children is like a
   - ☐ census taker
   - ☐ paper pusher
   - ☐ court reporter
   - ☐ bird-watcher
   - ☐ storyteller
   - ☐ news broadcaster
   - ☐ archivist
   - ☐ curator
   - ☐ archaeologist
   - ☐ astronomer
   - ☐ improvisational artist
   - ☐ circus ringleader

Appendix 6 Sample Licenser Self-Evaluation Tool

Wherever we go, directors tell us that working with licensers and monitors is an issue for them. The experience and responsibilities of a director and a licenser usually differ greatly, which can lead to an adversarial rather than a supportive relationship. On the other hand, when licensers come to their work with an early childhood background, we have seen wonderful partnerships formed with directors and creative problem solving with an attitude of mutual support.

In our seminars with licensers we often offer this assessment tool to alert them to the knowledge they need in forming partnerships with directors. We reprint it here as a resource for you to use with your licenser and as a set of considerations should you consider becoming a licenser in your career path.

Self-Assessment and Goal Setting for Licensers

Check what is true for you:

- ☐ I have a clear vision of the elements of childhood I want to preserve.
- ☐ I continually clarify the role I can play in advocating for child care policies and services that support this vision.
- ☐ I am satisfied with my level of knowledge about early childhood education, developmentally appropriate practices, and culturally relevant programming.
- ☐ I am competent in identifying the community and professional resources available for child care providers.
- ☐ I am familiar with the following child care and early childhood education terms, concepts, and organizations:

ORGANIZATIONS

- ☐ CDA
- ☐ CDF
- ☐ Child Care Coordinating Committee (4Cs)
- ☐ Council for Professional Recognition
- ☐ Creative Curriculum
- ☐ DAP

- ☐ Even Start
- ☐ Family Day Care Association
- ☐ High/Scope
- ☐ Montessori
- ☐ NABE
- ☐ NAEYC
- ☐ NAEYC Accreditation
- ☐ NCBDI
- ☐ NCCIC
- ☐ NCCR & R's
- ☐ PITC/WestEd
- ☐ QRS/QRIS
- ☐ RIE
- ☐ Smart Start
- ☐ STARS
- ☐ TEACH
- ☐ Zero to Three

PUBLICATIONS

- ☐ *Child Care Information Exchange*
- ☐ *School-Age Notes*
- ☐ *Teaching Young Children*
- ☐ *Young Children*
- ☐ Other ______________________

CONCEPTS

- ☐ antibias curriculum
- ☐ cultural relevancy
- ☐ emergent curriculum
- ☐ making learning visible
- ☐ portfolio assessment
- ☐ project approach
- ☐ Reggio Emilia approach
- ☐ scaffolding learning
- ☐ social constructivism
- ☐ teacher research

- ☐ I am familiar with adult learning theory and effective methods of staff training.
- ☐ I have effective communication skills in the following areas:
    - ☐ active listening
    - ☐ speaking
    - ☐ writing
    - ☐ problem solving
    - ☐ conflict mediation
    - ☐ making learning visible
- ☐ I can do objective observations and give constructive feedback.
- ☐ I can guide providers to information and resources on small business practices and IT assistance.
- ☐ I can effectively field questions and complaints from concerned parents and the community at large.
- ☐ I have adequate time management skills to meet deadlines and follow through in a timely fashion.

After reviewing this assessment, use another sheet of paper to identify a learning goal for yourself and three action steps toward meeting it.

Appendix 7 Strategic Planning Form

Vision			
Goals	**Barriers and Issues**	**Specific Objectives**	**Action Steps (Who and When)**

Appendix 8 Calculating the Full Cost of Quality Care

To supplement the worksheets in *Reaching the Full Cost of Quality in Early Childhood Programs* (Willer 1990), the Worthy Wage Campaign developed the guidelines on the following pages. They are useful to alert you to what it really costs to provide quality, rather than limiting your budgeting to the money you think you have available. These worksheets can lead to strategic planning as well as parent and public education. At the end of this appendix is an invoice for parents based on these worksheets.

One of the biggest obstacles to raising teacher and provider salaries is the inability of most parents to pay the full cost of high-quality child care. When wages are primarily dependent on parent fees in the current system, they necessarily remain low. Most programs are reluctant to raise fees, especially if parents are already paying as much as they can. Calculating the subsidy provided by teachers is not meant to scare parents. Rather, it is a way for business leaders, policymakers, and parents to learn how expensive quality care actually is—or would be—if teachers and providers were paid a living wage.

Minnesota Method

There are two ways to calculate the subsidy. We call the first the Minnesota Method because the Minnesota Worthy Wage Coalition used it to prepare an invoice for the 1992 Worthy Wage Day. The Minnesota Method is very simple: you subtract what parents are currently paying from the estimated cost per child for a year for high-quality care. This number is then multiplied by the number of children using child care statewide (or countywide, citywide) to reach the subsidy—the amount not covered by parent fees and is instead "donated" by staff through low wages.

To calculate the subsidy using the Minnesota Method, you need the following numbers:

- the cost of high-quality care per year per child (estimated by some to be $8,000.00)
- the average cost of child care in your city, county, or state
- the number of children using child care in your city, county, or state

Once you have these numbers, the equation looks like this:

the cost of high-quality care
– the average fee for child care

= amount each child is subsidized
× the number of children in child care

= amount the system is subsidized

EXAMPLE

$8,000
– 4,000

$4,000
× 5,000

$20 million

This method is not precise because it is based on a general estimate about the full cost of care and thus the amount of salary enhancement required. It is generally agreed that in most communities current salary levels need to be doubled to attract and retain high-quality professionals. If you would like to use this method but are unsure of what high-quality care really costs, complete the full-cost-of-care invoice prepared by NAEYC. This will tell you how much a high-quality program in your area costs annually per child.

Michigan Method

The second method is called the Michigan Method because it was developed by Steve Sternberg, former director of the Children's Centers at the University of Michigan. This method is adapted from a computer program he developed that calculates parent fees based on variables like ratios, reimbursement rates, and teacher salaries. It is a more precise system than the Minnesota Method because the subsidy is calculated from specific salary figures rather than an estimate of the full cost of quality care.

The process begins with a search for the total number of paid hours of teachers and family child care providers in your city, county, or state. This number is then multiplied by the current and average wage per hour. This gives you the total amount spent on wages in the current child care system. From there you can manipulate the subsidy figure based on what you think teachers should be earning. In some cases, you may want to double the current average wage. Others may want to compare the cost of care if salaries equaled those of elementary or even kindergarten teachers in their county or state.

Step 1

The difficult number to find is the first number, or the total number of paid teacher hours. To determine it, you'll need to find the total number of hours of children in care. Contact your state or county resource and referral agency (or licensing agency) to find out how many children are served in licensed center-based and family child care programs. (You may want to calculate center-based and family child care separately because of different ratio requirements.) Also ask for the percentage of children in the various age groups, such as infant/toddler, preschool, and so on. Then estimate the average number of hours each child spends in care.

For example, the agency may state that there are a hundred centers in your community, serving approximately 2,500 children. There are 50 percent under two years old, and 50 percent are over two.

Since the ratio of teachers to children under two years old is 1:6, and the ratio for children over two is 1:12, the average ratio is 1:9. If all 2,500 children attend care for approximately 7 hours per day (and this may be even higher), and there are 260 working days in each year, then the equation looks like this:

2,500 children × 7 hours per day × 260 days per year
= 4,550,000 total child hours per year

Using the ratio of 1 teacher/provider for every 9 children, divide 4,550,000 by 9 and the answer is 505,555.55 total teacher hours per year.

Add 15 percent to account for planning, meetings, in-service, sick pay, vacation pay, and substitutes, which comes to 581,388 total paid teacher hours per year.

Step 2

For the second number, you need the current average wage per hour. If there is recent data available for your community, you're in luck. If you're not sure, contact the Center for the Child Care Workforce (www.ccw.org).

Once you have an average teacher/provider wage, your equation continues:

581,388 total paid teacher hours × $10.00 average wage per hour
= $5,813,880 spent per year on teacher and provider salaries

Step 3

If you want the current wages to double, your equation would look like this:

581,388 total paid teacher hours × \$20.00 average wage per hour
= \$11,627,760 spent per year on teacher and provider salaries

Step 4

Then subtract the amount currently being spent to find the current subsidy:

\$11,627,760 (cost of wages at \$20.00 per hour) – \$5,813,880 (current cost of wages) = \$5,813,880 (the amount of subsidy provided by the work force)

Submit this number on the "invoice" to community leaders to let them know how much teachers and providers are currently subsidizing the child care system through their low wages.

If you want to go a step further, calculate how much each child (that is, each parent) is being subsidized by dividing the subsidy by the total number of children. In this case, the equation continues:

\$5,813,880 subsidy ÷ 2,500 children = \$2,325.55 subsidy per child per year

This figure represents how much it would cost each family to raise the current wage to \$20.00 per hour.

Compare the current average wage to that of a kindergarten teacher. To find out how much kindergarten teachers are earning, ask the state Department of Education or a reference librarian. When you divide a teacher's salary to find out the average wage per hour, divide by 1,500 hours per year (because of summer break) and not the standard work year of 2,080.

Final Notes

Whichever method you use to determine the subsidy teachers and providers supply to the system, be sure to keep careful records of all your calculations. If someone asks how you arrived at your estimate, you should be prepared to answer.

If you are planning to use the subsidy number primarily to raise awareness, the Minnesota Method may be easier. However, if your state or local officials are seriously considering a salary enhancement project, the Michigan Method may be more useful.

Mock Invoice Reflecting Full Cost of Care

<table>
<tr><th colspan="2">Full Cost of Child Care</th></tr>
<tr><td>
____
Center Name

____
Child's Name

____
Month

____
Service Provided
</td><td>
Dear Parents,

If we were paying our staff a livable wage (about _______ per hour), here is what your monthly cost would be. We can no longer ask our staff to subsidize the cost of care. How can we work together to solve this problem?

Sincerely,

Full cost of care if teachers earned a living wage:
$_______________

Current amount you pay for care:
$_______________

Amount your child's teacher subsidizes your fee:
$_______________

Total subsidy by your child's teacher for class:
$_______________
</td></tr>
</table>

Appendix 9 Continuity of Care: Barriers and Solutions

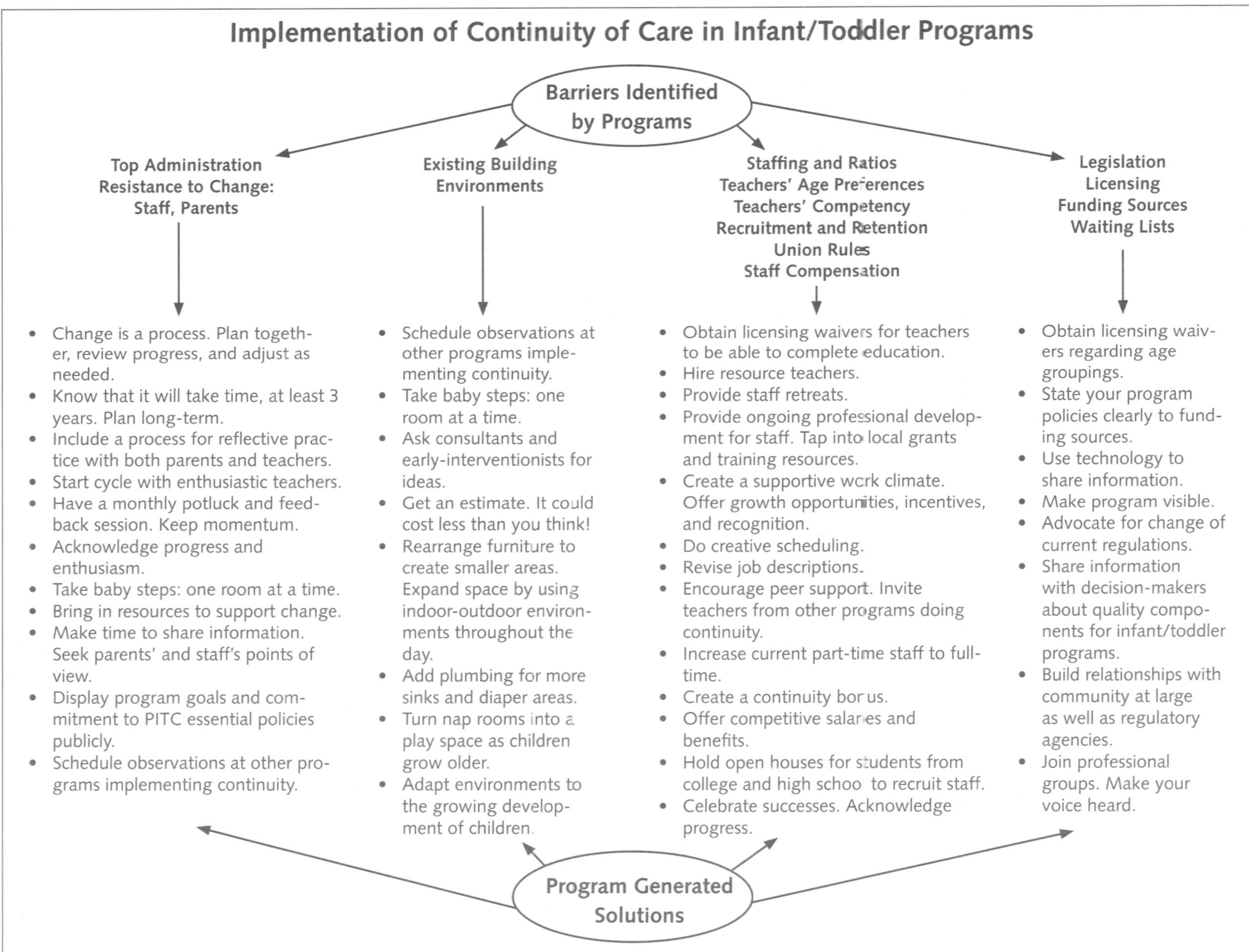

Appendix 10 Conference Attendance Planning Form

Here's an example of how you can prepare your staff to get the most out of a conference. Consider adapting it for your own use and adding a section on how this fits into the goals and focus of your individual or in-service training. Include a question on how to share and integrate what is learned into your program.

Professional Development Conference Planning Form

Developed by Deb Curtis and adopted by the Washington Association for the Education of Young Children (WAEYC)

Making the Most of the Conference	
1. **Begin with a self-assessment.** You can do this alone, with a friend, or with a group of co-workers. It can be an informal assessment, or you can use the CDA Competency Areas, NAEYC Accreditation Criteria, or a recent job performance evaluation or goal setting meeting.	**Self-Assessment:**
2. **Choose one or two goals.** Narrow your focus to just one or two goals that you will be able to accomplish. Choosing goals for yourself and working cooperatively with others toward a goal are two important aspects of effective training.	**Focus area goals:** 1) 2)
3. **Select workshops.** Plan a track of workshops for yourself that relate to your focus or goals. Consider choosing workshops from one of the Coordinated, In-Depth Tracks. Effective learning happens if the content is integrated and cumulative and the theoretical framework is consistent. Select workshops that offer hands-on practice and group discussion as well as content and resources. Adult learning research substantiates the need for interaction and active participation.	**Workshop sessions that relate to goal:** A) B) C) D) E)

4. Attend workshops. Use the following questions to reflect on workshop content alone or with colleagues: What do I already know about this topic? What knowledge or skills do I still need to acquire? Does the framework seem consistent with my own ideas? If I feel discomfort, what is this discomfort related to? How inclusive, flexible, and respectful of diverse ethnic and cultural backgrounds is the content being presented?	**Reflections on workshops:**
5. Document training. You can obtain college credit, clock hours, or CDA training hours for the workshops you attend (see conference booklet for information). Determine which method will be best for you. At the very least, have the certificate of completion put in your personnel files, and keep a copy for yourself.	**Method of documentation:** College credit Clock hours CDA training hours
6. Implement new ideas. Effective training provides opportunities to practice in an actual work setting, receive feedback, and explore issues and ideas individually and with peers. Make a commitment to yourself to try out the new strategies and techniques that you have learned.	**Summary of workshop ideas to implement:**

Reprinted with permission of the Washington Association for the Education of Young Children, Kent, WA; www.waeyc.org.

Appendix 11 Observation Form for Visiting Other Programs

Sending staff members to visit other rooms within and outside your program is a valuable professional development activity. To get the most out of this, it is useful to meet with those going to observe to plan how they will focus their attention for learning. From this you can develop an informal observation form to use for data collection and reflection. What you include as questions can alert the observer to the various components of the topic or focus. Here are some simple examples.

Observation Focus: Self-esteem and identity development

Teacher/Program Observed: ______________________ **Observer:** __________________

Date/Time: ____

1. What did you see that demonstrated a child was being valued, acknowledged, or encouraged by the teacher?
2. What opportunities for self-help and independence did you see?
3. Did you see the teacher encouraging a sense of cultural or group identity for the child? If so, how?
4. How were children's lives and families reflected in the program?
5. Did you see a teacher referring one child to another for collaboration, help, or problem solving? If so, briefly describe these situations.
6. Write down specific examples you saw of how self-esteem and a child's sense of identity were promoted.
7. How did you see the teacher scaffolding a child's learning?
8. Did you see evidence that the teacher uses documentation as a planning tool?

Observation Focus: How adults talk with children

Teacher/Program Observed: ______________________ **Observer:** ____________________

Date/Time: ____

Write down specific examples you saw of teachers in the room doing the following:

1. Ignoring child-initiated talk

   Acknowledging child-initiated talk

2. Correcting a child

   Acknowledging with interest something a child said or did

3. Using questions to test for knowledge

   Using questions that indicate teacher curiosity or genuine interest

   Using problem-posing questions

4. Having a conversation about mutual interests or something the teacher wanted to share about her/his life or interests

5. Using documentation to engage a child in conversation

Observation Focus: Communication and collaboration

Teacher/Program Observed: ____________________ **Observer:** ____________________

Date/Time: ____

Write down specific examples you saw of the following:

1. Meaningful communication between the program staff and families

2. Teachers working together as a team, using direct or indirect communication

3. Systems in place that promote collaboration among the staff

4. Documentation of the life and history of the program

Appendix 12 Conflict Resolution Samples

Here are examples of statements developed by two programs in their efforts to work with conflict. Written statements of assumptions and processes about conflict can serve as a reference point for learning to work through disagreements.

Cambridgeport Children's Center

At Cambridgeport Children's Center, we assume that . . .

1. Conflict can be healthy and can foster growth, learning, responsibility, and trust.
2. Helping children resolve conflict gives children control of their environment and their relationships with others. It also fosters their social and personal growth and maintains self-respect and respect for other children.
3. Children's ability to resolve conflict is influenced by multiple factors, including developmental stages, cultural expectations, models from family and significant others, experience, and the media.
4. Teachers' approaches to conflict are influenced by their knowledge of their students through observations, parental input, previous experiences, and the understanding that each child learns in a different way over time.
5. Children are capable of taking responsibility for their actions, and they are able to come up with creative, positive solutions. They can be empathetic to peers and are able to understand the consequences of their actions.

These are the implications of these assumptions:

1. Classroom curriculum must include multifaceted approaches to meaningfully address and readdress conflicts over time for each child. Children can revisit a painful conflict through books, drama, drawing, songs, writing, and empathetic dialogue with peers and teachers.
2. Our classroom will be a safe place where everyday conflict is used as a "teachable moment" to build children's self-reliance, self-esteem, problem-solving skills, trust in peers, empathy, and compassion. Teachers participate as facilitators, allowing children to practice their evolving conflict-resolution skills in varied ways.

Reprinted with permission of Cambridgeport Children's Center, Cambridge, MA; www.totlot.org.

Multnomah Playschool

The Background of Our Conflict Resolution Procedure

It is essential that confidentiality is maintained at a high level throughout conflict resolution.

This process is based on a proven, innovative, and cooperative procedure developed by a cooperative preschool association.

It is also based on a proactive, positive, problem-solving model developed by Resolutions Northwest.

This process incorporates a method to document the evolution of a conflict and the attempts made at resolution.

Follow-up communication is an integral part of the procedure to ensure that the issue is being satisfactorily resolved and that all parties' needs are being met.

Conflict Resolution Model

1. Listen actively to each person.
   Paraphrase what was said and clarify your understanding.
   Acknowledge the person's feelings.
2. Ask each person in turn what his or her needs are in the situation.
3. Jointly brainstorm many possible solutions to meet the needs.
   Accept all suggestions as possibilities.
   Do not evaluate at this point.
4. Evaluate possible solutions, and select one.
5. Make an action plan together.
   Distribute copies of the action plan to those involved.
6. Implement the action plan.
7. Check back.
   Phone the conflicting parties in one week to see how they are doing.
   Phone back one week after that.
   Modify the action plan and/or call additional meetings as necessary.

From Multnomah Playschool, Portland OR; www.multnomahplayschool.com.

Conflict Resolution Agreement

If I have a concern, complaint, conflict, issue, or problem with any member of the Multnomah Playschool community, I agree to follow the steps of conflict resolution outlined below.

1. I will contact the person with whom I have a conflict or concern directly, respectfully, and in a timely manner. We will attempt to use the "Conflict Resolution Model" as a guide to help resolve the problem. Discussing the conflict with anyone other than those directly involved or the class representative is not appropriate.
2. If the issue is not resolved, I will contact the class representative, who will mediate for us using the Conflict Resolution Model.
3. If the issue remains unresolved or if the class representative or I feel it would be beneficial, Multnomah Playschool's Resolution Team will meet with the parties involved to help resolve the issue to our mutual satisfaction.
4. If concerns remain after meeting with the Resolution Team, a professionally trained mediator will be called in to mediate.

Signed_________________________ Date_______________________

Signed_________________________ Date_______________________

From Multnomah Playschool, Portland, OR; www.multnomahplayschool.com.

Appendix 13 Writing Learning Stories

A Learning Story is first and foremost a story. It tells a tale to the child, to the family, to guests, and to ourselves as teachers of children. It builds upon the very human tradition of oral storytelling. There is not one right way to do it. A story may emerge from a child's initiative or an adult's provocation. Stories are always about things we value—nothing negative at all. The tale progresses through the subsequent stages of engagement (becoming involved) and intentionality (causing something), if it gets that far. This is what to look for to include in a Learning Story:

- Initiative
- Engagement
- Intentionality
- Relationships
- Dispositions and approaches to learning

Learning Story Conventions (A Way to Start Finding and Writing Them)

It is essential to have at least one picture of the child, or group of children if it is a group Learning Story. Of course, the more photographs you have, the more your story can convey. Then you write the text to accompany the photographs or video captures. The text should be a story with descriptive details, not just a caption for the photos.

1. Begin with your own interest in what the child has taken the initiative to do. When you talk about yourself in the first person using "I . . . " you give a "voice" to the storyteller. The observer brings a perspective that is essential to the tale.
2. Describe what the child does and says from your perspective as someone who cares and is listening closely to discover what is happening. It is not totally objective: you are present with your heart and your mind. You are curious. You have a strong image of the child. You pay close attention. This is the heart of the story.
3. Title a paragraph "What It Means" and write about the significance of what you saw. This meaning making is best done in a dialogue with other teachers and the children's families. Many perspectives can be

included here. If this is voiced directly to the child, the child can hear you speak your words. When voiced to teachers, families, and monitors, you can also include reference here to standards, outcomes, theoretical perspectives, and goals for children's development. "You . . . "

4. Title a second paragraph "Opportunities and Possibilities" and describe what we (adults, teachers, parents, etc.) can provide next and imagine what the future may hold. This gives insight to the participants in the school about how teachers think about what they do for children and what it could lead to over time. "We . . . "
5. Offer a blank page for the family to respond with their view. Many members of the family may have things to say to the child and to the teachers. Make two copies, one for the child and one for the school. Some teachers like to get the family's perspective as part of the exploration of opportunities and possibilities.
6. Give the story a title. Like every good story, your Learning Story has a title.

Learning Stories are the way we can all do research and create communities of practice that help us grow as teachers and as human beings.
—Tom Drummond (2008)

With thanks to Margaret Carr and Wendy Lee, our New Zealand colleagues, who created these gems. Adapted by Tom Drummond, tdrummon@sccd.ctc.edu, and Margie Carter and Deb Curtis; http://earlylearningstories.info.

Appendix 14 A Thinking Lens for Reflection and Inquiry

Knowing Yourself

How am I reacting to this situation and why?
What in my background and values is influencing my response to this situation and why?
What adult perspectives—e.g., standards, health and safety, time, goals—are on my mind?

Examining the Physical/Social/Emotional Environment

How is the organization and use of the physical space and materials impacting this situation?
In what ways are the routines, adult behaviors, and language undermining or strengthening the child's ability to demonstrate their competence?
How could we strengthen relationships here?

Seeking the Child's Point of View

How do I understand the child's point of view in this situation?
What might the child be trying to accomplish?
What developmental themes, ideas, or theories might the child be exploring?

Finding the Details that Engage Your Heart and Mind

What details can I make visible to heighten the value of this experience?
Where do I see examples of the child's strengths and competencies?
What is touching my heart and engaging my mind here?

Expanding Perspectives through Collaboration and Research

What other perspectives could enhance my understanding of the meaning of this situation, e.g., perspectives of families, coworkers, colleagues?
How might issues of culture, family background, or popular media be influencing this situation?
What theoretical perspectives and child development principles could inform my understandings and actions?

Considering Opportunities and Possibilities for Next Steps

What values, philosophy, and goals do I want to influence my response?
How can I build on previous experiences of individuals and the group?
Which learning goals could be focused on here?
What new or existing relationships could be strengthened?
What should we do next and think about for the future?

Appendix 15 Use the Thinking Lens to Analyze and Write Learning Stories

Title of this story: ______________________________

What specifically happened?
(Use first person "I" to tell the details of the story considering these questions to guide your reflection and writing.)

Know yourself

What captures my attention as the child explores and follow his pursuits?

What delights me as I watch and listen to the child's ideas?

How am I reacting to this situation and why?

What in my background and values is influencing my response to this situation and why?

Details that touch my heart and engage my mind as I watch and listen

What do I notice in the child's face and the quality of her voice as the child works and communicates?

What details do I want to make visible that heighten the value of this experience?

Where do I see examples of children's strengths and competencies?

What it means.
(Use these questions to guide your analysis and interpretation of the significance of the details of the story. Write directly to the child.)

Take the child's point of view

As I notice the child's work, what is he drawn to and excited about?

What might the child be trying to accomplish?

As she plays, what is the child experiencing?

Why is he moving his hands in that particular way?

Why is she turning her head at that specific angle?

Why is he standing up instead of sitting in a chair?

Why might she be interacting with others this way?

Consider multiple perspectives

What ideas or theories might the child be exploring or communicating?

What might the child be learning from this play and exploration?

How might issues of culture and family background be influencing this situation?

What theoretical perspectives, standards, and child development principles could inform our understandings?

Examine the physical/social/emotional environment

How is the organization and use of the physical space and materials impacting this situation?

How are relationships being strengthened here?

What opportunities and possibilities are available from this moment? (Consider these questions to help you describe what you can provide next and imagine what the future may hold for the children and you. Write directly to the children.)

Reflect on opportunities and possibilities for action

What values, philosophy, and goals do I want to influence my response?

How can I build on previous experiences of individuals and the group?

Which learning goals could be focused on here?

What new or existing relationships could be strengthened?

What should we do next and think about for the future?

References

Ashton-Warner, Sylvia. 1972. *Spearpoint: Teacher in America.* New York: Knopf.

Ayers, William. 1989. *The good preschool teacher: Six teachers reflect on their lives.* New York: Teachers College Press.

Bateson, Mary Catherine. 1989. *Composing a life.* New York: Plume.

Block, Peter. 1987. *The empowered manager: Positive political skills at work.* San Francisco: Jossey-Bass.

———. 2008. *Community: The structure of belonging.* San Francisco: Berrett-Koehler.

Bloom, Paula Jorde. 1989. *The 1989 Illinois directors' study.* Springfield: Illinois Department of Children and Family Services.

———. 1996a. *Improving the quality of work life in the early childhood setting: Resource guide and technical manual for the early childhood work environment survey.* Wheeling, IL: McCormick Tribune Center for Early Childhood Leadership, National-Louis University.

———. 1996b. The quality of work life in NAEYC accredited and non-accredited early childhood programs. *Early Education and Development* 7 (4): 301–1.

———. 1997. *A great place to work: Improving conditions for staff in young children's programs.* Rev. ed. Washington, DC: National Association for the Education of Young Children.

———. 2003. *Leadership in action: How effective directors get things done.* Lake Forest, IL: New Horizons.

———. 2005. *Blueprint for action: Achieving center-based change through staff development.* 2nd ed. Lake Forest, IL: New Horizons.

Bowlby, John. 1973. *Separation: Anxiety and anger.* Vol. 2 of *Attachment and loss.* New York: Basic Books.

Brazelton, T. Berry, and Stanley I. Greenspan. 2000. *The irreducible needs of children: What every child must have to grow, learn, and flourish.* Cambridge, MA: Perseus.

Brown, Margaret Wise. 1972. *The runaway bunny.* New York: Harper & Row.

Carter, Margie, and Deb Curtis. 1994. *Training teachers: A harvest of theory and practice.* St. Paul: Redleaf Press.

———. 1996. *Spreading the news: Sharing the stories of early childhood education.* St. Paul: Redleaf Press.

Carter, Margie, and Jan Reed, producers. 1991. *Time with toddlers: Training for caregivers.* Mechanicsburg, PA: Harvest Resources. Video.

Center for the Child Care Workforce. 1999. *Creating better childcare jobs: Model work standards for teaching staff in center-based child care.* Washington, DC: Center for the Child Care Workforce.

Chocolate, Debbi. 1995. *On the day I was born.* Illustrated by Melodye Rosales. New York: Scholastic.

Clarke, Jean Illsley, and Connie Dawson. 1998. *Growing up again: Parenting ourselves, parenting our children.* 2nd ed. Center City, MN: Hazelden.

Copple, Carol, and Sue Bredekamp, eds. 2009. *Developmentally appropriate practice in early childhood programs serving children from birth through age 8.* 3rd ed. Washington, DC: National Association for the Education of Young Children.

Cost, Quality, and Child Outcomes Study Team. 1995. Denver: Department of Economics, University of Colorado.

Curtis, Deb, and Margie Carter. 1996. *Reflecting children's lives: A handbook for planning child-centered curriculum.* St. Paul: Redleaf Press.

———. 2000. *The art of awareness: How observation can transform your teaching.* St. Paul: Redleaf Press.

———. 2003. *Designs for living and learning: Transforming early childhood environments.* St. Paul: Redleaf Press.

———. 2008. *Learning together with young children: A curriculum framework for reflective teachers.* St. Paul: Redleaf Press.

Davis, Donald. 1993. *Telling your own stories: For family and classroom storytelling, public speaking, and personal journaling.* Little Rock, AR: August House.

Day, Carol Brunson, ed. 2004. *Essentials for child development associates working with young children.* 2nd ed. Washington, DC: Council for Professional Recognition.

Epstein, Ann S. 1993. *Training for quality: Improving early childhood programs through systematic inservice training.* Ypsilanti, MI: High/Scope Press.

Espinosa, Linda. 1997. Personal dimensions of leadership. In *Leadership in early care and education,* ed. Sharon L. Kagan and Barbara T. Bowman, 97–102. Washington, DC: National Association for the Education of Young Children.

Fisher, Anne. 1997. Tom Peters, professional loudmouth, the famed author of business books, has very rude things to say about Al Dunlap. *Fortune*, December 29.

Fleet, Alma, and Catherine Patterson. 2001. Professional growth reconceptualised: Early childhood staff searching for meaning. *Early Childhood Research and Practice* 3(2).

Fox, John. 1995. *Finding what you didn't lose: Expressing your truth and creativity through poem-making.* New York: Putnam.

Gardner, Howard. 1993. *Multiple intelligences: The theory in practice.* New York: Basic Books.

———. 1995. *Leading minds: An anatomy of leadership.* New York: Basic Books.

Goffin, Stacie, and Valora Washington. 2007. *Ready or not: Leadership choices in early care and education.* New York: Teachers College Press.

Gonzalez-Mena, Janet. 2000. *Multicultural issues in child care.* Mountain View, CA: Mayfield.

Gray, Libba Moore. 1993. *Miss Tizzy.* New York: Simon and Schuster.

Greenman, Jim. 1992. Living in the real world: Places for childhoods. *Child Care Information Exchange* 86 (July/August): 21–23.

———. 2007. *Caring spaces, learning places: Children's environments that work*. Redmond, WA: Exchange Press.

Greenman, Jim, Anne Stonehouse, and Gigi Schweikert. 2008. *Prime times: A handbook for excellence in infant and toddler programs.* 2nd ed. St. Paul: Redleaf Press.

Gross, Susan. 1987. The power of purpose. *Child Care Information Exchange* 56 (July): 25–29.

Harms, Thelma, Richard M. Clifford, and Debbie Cryer. 1998. *Early childhood environment rating scale.* Rev. ed. New York: Teachers College Press.

———. 2003. *Infant/toddler environment rating scale.* Rev. ed. New York: Teachers College Press.

Hughes, Langston. 1994. *The collected poems of Langston Hughes*. New York: Random House.

Hunter, James C. 1998. *The servant: A simple story about the true essence of leadership.* Rocklin, CA: Prima.

Joosse, Barbara M. 1991. *Mama, do you love me?* Illustrated by Barbara Lavallee. San Francisco: Chronicle Books.

Kagan, Sharon L., and Barbara T. Bowman, eds. 1997. *Leadership in early care and education.* Washington, DC: National Association for the Education of Young Children.

Kagan, Sharon L., and Michelle J. Neuman. 1997. Conceptual leadership. In *Leadership in early care and education,* ed. Sharon L. Kagan and Barbara T. Bowman, 59–64. Washington, DC: National Association for the Education of Young Children.

Katz, Lilian G. 1995. *Talks with teachers: A collection.* Greenwhich, CT: Ablex.

Keeler, Rusty. 2008. *Natural playscapes: Creating outdoor play environments for the soul.* Redmond, WA: Exchange Press.

Kozol, Jonathan. 2000. *Ordinary resurrections: Children in the years of hope*. New York: Crown Publishers.

Lally, J. R. 2007. Why continuity of care? Paper presented at the National Association for the Education of Young Children's Annual Conference and Expo, Chicago.

Lobel, Arnold. 1975. *Owl at home.* New York: Harper and Row.

Long, Sylvia. 2000. *Hush little baby.* San Francisco: Chronicle Books.

Mardell, Ben, and Mara Krechevsky. 2003. *Making teaching visible: Documenting individual and group learning as professional development.* Cambridge, MA: Project Zero, Harvard University Graduate School of Education.

McDonald, Joseph P., Nancy Mohr, Alan Dichter, and Elizabeth C. McDonald. 2003. *The power of protocols: An educator's guide to better practice*. New York: Teachers College Press.

McLerran, Alice. 1991. *Roxaboxen.* Illustrated by Barbara Cooney. New York: Lothrop, Lee, and Shepard.

Moore, Gary. 1997. The common core of a child care center. *Child Care Information Exchange* 114:82–86.

Neugebauer, Roger. 2007. Dear reader. *Child Care Information Exchange* 178:4.

Olds, Anita Rui. 1999. *The child care design guide: Day care centers that honor the spirit of place.* New York: McGraw-Hill.

Palmer, Parker. 2007. *The courage to teach: Exploring the inner landscape of a teacher's life.* San Francisco: Jossey-Bass.

Phillips, Carol, and Sue Bredekamp. 1998. Reconsidering early childhood education in the United States: Reflections from our encounters with Reggio Emilia. In *The hundred languages of children: The Reggio Emilia approach—advanced reflections*, 2nd ed., ed. Carolyn Edwards, Lella Gandini, and George Forman, 439–54. Greenwich, CT: Ablex.

Phillips, Deborah A., Debra Mekos, Sandra Scarr, Kathleen McCartney, and Martha Abbott-Shim. 2000. Within and beyond the classroom door: Assessing quality in child care centers. *Early Childhood Research Quarterly* 15 (4): 475–96.

Rinaldi, Carlina. 2005. *In dialogue with Reggio Emilia: Researching and learning.* New York: Routledge.

Scheinfeld, Daniel R., Karen M. Haigh, and Sandra J. P. Scheinfeld. 2008. *We are all explorers: Learning and teaching with Reggio principles in urban settings.* New York: Teachers College Press.

Senge, Peter M. 1990. *The fifth discipline: The art and practice of the learning organization.* New York: Doubleday.

———. 2006. *The fifth discipline.*

Siegel, Daniel J. 1999. *The developing mind: How relationships and the brain interact to shape who we are.* New York: Guilford Press.

Sussman, Carl. 1998. Out of the basement: Discovering the value of child care facilities. *Young Children* 53 (1): 10–17.

Talan, Teri N., and Paula Jorde Bloom. 2004. *Program administration scale: Measuring early childhood leadership and management.* New York: Teachers College Press.

Whitebook, Marcy, Carol Howes, and Deborah Phillips. 1990. Who cares? Child care teachers and the quality of care in America. Final report of the National Child Care Staffing Study. Oakland, CA: Child Care Employee Project.

Wien, Carol Anne. 1995. *Developmentally appropriate practice in "real life": Stories of teacher practical knowledge.* New York: Teachers College Press.

———. 2004. *Negotiating standards in the primary classroom: The teacher's dilemma.* New York: Teachers College Press.

Wien, Carol, and Susan Kirby-Smith. 1998. Untiming the curriculum: A case study of removing clocks from the program. *Young Children* 53 (September): 8–13.

Willer, Barbara A. 1990. *Reaching the full cost of quality in early childhood programs.* Washington, DC: National Association for the Education of Young Children.

W.K. Kellogg Foundation. 1996. *Families for kids: Building the dream.* Battle Creek, MI: W.K. Kellogg Foundation. Quoted in V. Washington. 1997. Commentary. In *Leadership in early care and education,* ed. Sharon L. Kagan and Barbara T. Bowman, 65–66. Washington, DC: National Association for the Education of Young Children.

Resources

The following resources are among our favorites and have been recommended by directors and other administrators we admire. Although some of the resources here are out of print, we left them on the list because we believe they are valuable resources and you can still get them from online book distributors or libraries.

Print Resources for Growing a Vision

Bateson, Mary Catherine. 1989. *Composing a life.* New York: Plume.

Brazelton, T. Berry, and Stanley I. Greenspan. 2000. *The irreducible needs of children: What every child must have to grow, learn, and flourish.* Cambridge, MA: Perseus.

Center for the Child Care Workforce. 1999. *Creating better child care jobs: Model work standards for teaching staff in center-based child care.* Washington, DC: Center for the Child Care Workforce.

Gardner, Howard. 1993. *Frames of mind: The theory of multiple intelligences.* 10th anniversary ed. New York. Basic Books.

———. 2006. *Multiple intelligences: New horizons.* Completely rev. and updated. New York: Basic Books.

Goffin, Stacie G., and Valora Washington. 2007. *Ready or not: Leadership choices in early care and education.* New York: Teachers College Press.

Greenman, Jim, Anne Stonehouse, and Gigi Schweikert. 2008. *Prime times: A handbook for excellence in infant and toddler programs.* 2nd ed. St. Paul: Redleaf Press.

Greenspan, Stanley, with Nancy Breslau Lewis. 1999. *Building healthy minds: The six experiences that create intelligence and emotional growth in babies and young children.* Cambridge, MA: Perseus.

Hendrick, Joanne, ed. 2004. *Next steps toward teaching the Reggio way: Accepting the challenge to change.* 2nd ed. Upper Saddle River, NJ: Pearson/Merrill/Prentice Hall.

Katz, Lilian G. 1998. What can we learn from Reggio Emilia? In *The hundred languages of children: The Reggio Emilia approach—advanced reflections,* 2nd ed., ed. Carolyn Edwards, Lella Gandini, and George Forman, 27–46. Westport, CT: Ablex.

Lally, J. Ronald. 2007. Why continuity of care? Paper presented at the National Association for the Education of Young Children's Annual Conference and Expo, Chicago.
Lehn, Barbara. 1999. *What is a scientist?* Minneapolis: Millbrook Press.
Peters, Tom. 1997. *The circle of innovation: You can't shrink your way to greatness.* New York: Knopf.
Phillips, Carol, and Sue Bredekamp. 1998. Reconsidering early childhood education in the United States: Reflections from our encounters with Reggio Emilia. In *The hundred languages of children: The Reggio Emilia approach—advanced reflections*, 2nd ed., ed. Carolyn Edwards, Lella Gandini, and George Forman, 439–54. Greenwich, CT: Ablex.
Shonkoff, Jack, and Deborah Phillips, eds. 2000. *From neurons to neighborhoods: The science of early childhood development.* Washington, DC: National Academy Press.
Siegel, Daniel J. 1999. *The developing mind: How relationships and the brain interact to shape who we are.* New York: Guilford Press.
Sussman, Carl. 1998. Out of the basement: Discovering the value of child care facilities. *Young Children* 53 (1): 10–17.
Willer, Barbara, ed. 1990. *Reaching the full cost of quality in early childhood programs.* Washington, DC: National Association for the Education of Young Children.

Print Resources for Building and Supporting Community

Alexander, Christopher, Sara Ishikawa, and Murray Silverstein. 1977. *A pattern language: Towns, buildings, construction.* New York: Oxford University Press.
Boal, Augusto. 2002. *Games for actors and non-actors.* 2nd ed. New York: Routledge.
Boise, Phil. 2009. *Go green rating scale for early childhood settings.* St. Paul: Redleaf Press.
Bruchac, Joseph. 1997. *Tell me a tale: A book about storytelling.* San Diego: Harcourt Brace.
Carter, Margie. 1992. Honoring diversity: Problems and possibilities for staff and organization. In *Alike and different: Exploring our humanity with young children*, rev. ed., ed. Bonnie Neugebauer, 43–47. Washington, DC: National Association for the Education of Young Children.
Carter, Margie, and Deb Curtis. 1996. *Spreading the news: Sharing the stories of early childhood education.* St. Paul: Redleaf Press.
Covey, Stephen M., with Rebecca R. Merrill. 2006. *The speed of trust: The one thing that changes everything.* New York: Free Press.
Curtis, Deb, and Margie Carter. 2003. *Designs for living and learning: Transforming early childhood environments.* St. Paul. Redleaf Press.
Day, Christopher. 2003. *Places of the soul: Architecture and environmental design as a healing art.* 2nd ed. Boston: Architectural Press.
Diffily, Deborah, and Kathy Morrison, eds. 1996. *Family friendly communication for early childhood programs.* Washington, DC: National Association for the Education of Young Children.
Greenman, Jim. 2007. *Caring spaces, learning places: Children's environments that work.* Redmond, WA: Exchange Press.
LaChapelle, Carol. 2008. *Finding your voice, telling your stories: 167 ways to tell your life stories.* Oak Park, IL: Marion Street Press.
Ludin, Stephen C., John Christensen, and Harry Paul, with Philip Strand. 2002. *Fish! tales: Real-life stories to help you transform your workplace and your life.* New York: Hyperion.
Nair, Prakash, and Randall Fielding. 2005. *The language of school design: Design patterns for twenty-first century schools.* Minneapolis: DesignShare.com.

Olds, Anita Rui. 1999. *The child care design guide: Day care centers that honor the spirit of place.* New York: McGraw-Hill.
Senge, Peter, C. Otto Scharmer, Joseph Jaworski, and Betty Sue Flowers. 2005. *Presence: Exploring profound change in people, organizations, and society.* New York: Doubleday.
Tatum, D. 2003. *"Why are all the black kids sitting together in the cafeteria?" And other conversations about race.* New York: Basic Books.
Williams, Leslie R., and Yvonne De Gaetano. 1985. *ALERTA: A multicultural, bilingual approach to teaching young children.* Menlo Park, CA: Addison-Wesley.

Print Resources for Coaching and Mentoring

Bellm, Dan, Marcy Whitebook, and Patty Hnatiuk. 1997. *Trainer's guide.* Vol. 1 of *The early childhood mentoring curriculum and trainers guide.* Washington, DC: Center for the Child Care Workforce.
Bloom, Paula Jorde. 1997. *A great place to work: Improving conditions for staff in young children's programs.* Rev. ed. Washington, DC. National Association for the Education of Young Children.
———. 2000. *Workshop essentials: Planning and presenting dynamic workshops.* Lake Forest, IL: New Horizons.
———. 2002. *The right fit: Recruiting, selecting, and orienting staff.* Lake Forest, IL: New Horizons.
———. 2007. *From the inside out: The power of reflection and self-awareness.* Lake Forest, IL: New Horizons.
Carter, Margie, and Deb Curtis. 1994. *Training teachers: A harvest of theory and practice.* St. Paul: Redleaf Press.
Curtis, Deb, and Margie Carter. 1996. *Reflecting children's lives: A handbook for child-centered curriculum.* St. Paul: Redleaf Press.
———. 2000. *The art of awareness: How observation can transform your teaching.* St. Paul: Redleaf Press.
———. 2008. *Learning together with young children: A curriculum framework for reflective teachers.* St. Paul: Redleaf Press.
Howard, Gary R., and Sonia Nieto. 2006. *We can't teach what we don't know: White teachers, multiracial schools.* New York: Teachers College Press.
Jones, Elizabeth. 1993. *Growing teachers: Partnerships in staff development.* Washington, DC: National Association for the Education of Young Children.
———. 2007. *Teaching adults.* Washington, DC: National Association for the Education of Young Children.
Lipman, Doug. 2006. *The storytelling coach: How to listen, praise, and bring out people's best.* Little Rock, AR: August House.
McDonald, Joseph P., Nancy Mohr, Alan Dichter, and Elizabeth C. McDonald. 2003. *The power of protocols: An educator's guide to better practice.* New York: Teachers College Press.
Pelo, Ann, ed. 2008. *Rethinking early childhood education.* Milwaukee: Rethinking Schools.
Ruef, Kerry. 2003. *The private eye: Looking/thinking by analogy.* 2nd ed. Seattle: Private Eye Project.
Stremmel, Andrew. 2002. Research in Review. Teacher research: Nurturing professional and personal growth through inquiry. *Young Children* 57 (5): 62–70.
Sullivan, Debra Ren-Etta. 2003. *Learning to lead: Effective leadership skills for teachers of young children.* St. Paul: Redleaf Press.

Vella, Jane. 2003. *Learning to listen, learning to teach: The power of dialogue in educating adults.* San Francisco: Jossey-Bass.

———. 2007. *On teaching and learning: Putting the principles and practices of dialogue education into action.* San Francisco: Jossey-Bass.

Wasserman, Thelma. 2000. *Serious players in the primary classroom.* New York: Teachers College Press.

Wien, Carol Anne. 1995. *Developmentally appropriate practices in real "life": Stories of teacher practical knowledge.* New York: Teachers College Press.

———. 2004. *Negotiating standards in the primary classroom: The teacher's dilemma.* New York: Teachers College Press.

Wien, Carol, and Susan Kirby-Smith. 1998. Untiming the curriculum: A case study of removing clocks from the program. *Young Children* 53 (September): 8–13.

Print Resources for Managing and Overseeing

Berry, T. H. 1991. *Managing the total quality transformation.* New York: McGraw-Hill.

Bloom, Paula Jorde. 1985. *Early childhood work environment survey.* Wheeling, IL: National-Louis University.

———. 2000. *Circle of influence: Implementing shared decision making and participative management.* Lake Forest, IL: New Horizons.

———. 2002. *Making the most of meetings: A practical guide.* Lake Forest, IL: New Horizons.

———. 2003. *Leadership in action: How effective directors get things done.* Lake Forest, IL: New Horizons.

———. 2005. *Blueprint for action: Achieving center-based change through staff development.* 2nd ed. Lake Forest, IL: New Horizons.

Bolman, Lee G., and Terrence E. Deal. 2008. *Reframing organizations: Artistry, choice, and leadership.* 4th ed. San Francisco: Jossey-Bass.

Doyle, Michael, and David Straus. 1993. *How to make meetings work! The new interaction method.* New York: Berkley Books.

Eiselen, Sherry Storm. 1992. *The human side of child care administration: A how-to manual.* Rev. ed. Washington, DC: National Association for the Education of Young Children.

Haigh, Karen M. 2007. Exploring learning with teachers and children: An administrator's perspective. *Theory into Practice* 46 (1): 57–64.

Harms, Thelma, Debby Cryer, and Richard M. Clifford. 2005. *Early childhood environment rating scale.* Rev. ed. New York: Teachers College Press.

———. 2006. *Infant/toddler rating scale.* Rev. ed. New York: Teachers College Press.

Web Resources

The Alliance for Early Childhood Finance: http://www.earlychildhoodfinance.org/organizations.htm

The Alliance for Early Childhood Finance is dedicated to seeking more rational financing of early care and education in America through inquiry, analysis, and communication among early care and education policy activists. The Alliance was originally created through a partnership between Anne Mitchell of Early Childhood Policy Research and Louise

Stoney of Stoney Associates. The Web site will serve to link you with new resources, ideas, meetings and online discussions on a variety of topics related to early care and education finance.

Blogger: http://www.blogger.com

Blogger is a free and easy-to-use blogging site powered by Google. Blogger includes an HTML editor, a spell-check feature, free templates, photo- and video-posting capabilities, and third-party applications. Blogger is for beginners and nonprofessional bloggers.

Child Care Exchange: http://www.childcareexchange.com

For over thirty years, Child Care Exchange has promoted the exchange of ideas among leaders in early childhood programs worldwide through its magazine, books, training products, training seminars, and international conferences. *Exchange Every Day* is its official electronic newsletter, mailed five days a week, and includes news stories, success stories, solutions, and trend reports.

Early Education Advocates: http://www.earlyeducationadvocates.org

This group's mission is to define and promote democratic, participatory, and diverse early education provisions for children from birth to school-age.

Edublogs: http://www.edublogs.org

Edublogs is powered by WordPress and is a free blogging site for anyone involved in education, including teachers, students, librarians, and administrators.

The Education Resources Information Center: http://eric.ed.gov

ERIC—the Education Resources Information Center—is an online digital library of education research and information. ERIC is sponsored by the Institute of Education Sciences of the U.S. Department of Education. ERIC provides ready access to education literature to support the use of educational research and information to improve practice in learning, teaching, educational decision making, and research.

Good360: http://about.good360.org

Good360 is the twelfth largest charity in America, generating nearly $750 million in donations in 2008. Good360 receives donations from large and small companies and distributes them to charities around the world.

LiveJournal: http://www.livejournal.com

LiveJournal is one of the largest personal blogging sites in the world. The basic accounts are free, but users can upgrade to a premium account for a yearly or monthly fee. LiveJournal is for intermediate to advanced bloggers.

The McCormick Tribune Center for Early Childhood Leadership: http://cecl.nl.edu

The Center is dedicated to enhancing the management skills, professional orientation, and leadership capacity of early childhood administrators. Its activities focus on four areas: training, program evaluation, research, and public awareness.

National Association for the Education of Young Children: www.naeyc.org

This is the world's largest organization working on behalf of young children with a national network of state and local affiliates as well as global alliances. The organization sponsors conferences and publishes two journals, *Young Children* and *Teaching Young Children,* as well as a variety of books and position statements.

National Wildlife Federation: http://nwf.org/gardenforwildlife

This site provides information to help your child care play yard become certified as a wildlife sanctuary.

Nature Explore: http://www.arborday.org/explore

Nature Explore is a collaborative project of Arbor Day Foundation and Dimensions Educational Research Foundation. The site provides ideas and resources for connecting young children with nature.

The Program for Infant/Toddler Care: http://www.pitc.org

The program's mission is to

1. increase the availability and quality of child care for all children under age three;
2. disseminate information that increases the practice of responsive, respectful, and relationship-based infant/toddler care;
3. influence national, regional, and local policies and practices so that the needs and interests of individual infants, toddlers, and their families are the foundation for all curriculum development and program activity.

Smart Start's National Technical Assistance Center: http://www.ncsmartstart.org/ntac

The center "provides assistance to states and localities that are working to assure that every child arrives at school healthy and ready to succeed."

My Vision

My Vision

My Vision

About the Authors

Deb Curtis holds a master's degree in human development from Pacific Oaks College and has been an infant/toddler caregiver, preschool and school-age child care teacher, CDA trainer, Head Start education coordinator, college instructor, and assistant director of a child care program.

Margie Carter also holds a master's degree from Pacific Oaks College and has worked as a preschool, kindergarten, and primary school teacher, curriculum developer, High/Scope trainer, child care director, and college instructor.

Margie and Deb first met in 1989, when Deb was working as an education coordinator for Head Start and Margie was the training coordinator for a local resource and referral agency in Seattle. They immediately discovered shared passions for promoting adventurous childhood experiences, voracious quests for new learning, and raising sons with a feminist consciousness. Influenced by the work of Elizabeth Jones, they attended graduate school together at Pacific Oaks College, where their twenty-year collaborative partnership began.

Together they have designed and taught college-level classes, worked side by side with classroom teachers, produced professional development videos, and coauthored seven Redleaf Press books. In the last decade, Margie has focused her attention on working with directors to develop strong administrative systems that support reflective teaching. Deb has returned to working directly with children, putting into practice the philosophy and vision she and Margie promote in their extensive travels across North America, Australia, and New Zealand, where they give presentations and consult with early childhood programs. Both are regular writers for *Child Care Information Exchange* and contributors to other publications.

In this era of standardization and prescription in education, Deb and Margie stand for the creative and critical thinking that lead to education for democracy. They strongly believe that high-quality care and education for young children and their families require leaders and practitioners who are able to think through the dynamics of their work with a larger purpose and vision. Margie and Deb encourage early educators and administrators to think big, be visionary, and take responsibility for transforming the current limitations and mediocrity in early childhood.